Spirituous Journey

Spirituous Journey

A HISTORY OF DRINK

BOOK TWO:
FROM PUBLICANS TO MASTER MIXOLOGISTS

ANISTATIA MILLER & JARED BROWN

FOREWORD BY
GARY REGAN

MIXELLANY LIMITED

Mixellany books may be purchased for educational, business, or sales promotional use. For information, please write to Mixellany Limited, 13 Bonchurch Road, West Ealing, London W13 9JE United Kingdom or email jared@mixellany.com

First edition

ISBN 13: 978-1-907434-06-8

British Library Cataloguing in Publication Data.
A catalogue record for this book is available from the British Library.

Dedication

This book is dedicated to the memories of two passionate and devoted adherents to the cocktail and to the art of bartending who passed away while we were writing this manuscript.

Gregor DeGruyther made everyone feel honoured to be served by a bartender who each and every person a VIP. In his short 30 years, he dispensed his special talents around the world. We will never forget the few precious moments that we were blessed with his smile, his guitar, and his friendship.

The great and gentle Jose Luis Maruenda, husband of Maria Dolores Boadas and disciple of her father Miguel Boadas of the remarkable Bar Boadas in Barcelona also stepped beyond the reach of us poor mortals. Only his large hands could manage the custom silver shaker he used to make frosty specialities. Only his love for the bartender's art compelled him to amass a huge collection of cocktail tomes and vintage spirits. We only met a handful of times, shared a meal, and a few nightcaps. Those magical moments will always remind us that if the world ended tomorrow, at least we know we encountered true greatness.

Contents

Foreword

WHAT'S THE CONNECTION between famed nineteenth-century bartender Harry Johnson, and Irving Berlin's "Alexander's Ragtime Band"? What are tipiculars when they're at home? Who the heck was Bloody Mary anyway? These questions, and approximately 17 million more are answered in this book. Okay, okay, I'm given to exaggeration, but wait till you see what lies ahead of you. You're gonna be astounded. And in case you think that you know about the first printed mention of the word "cock-tail", let me tell you now—I doubt that you do. You will soon, though . . .

I nearly missed my five o'clock Manhattan because I got so engrossed in this damned book, and anyone who knows the least bit about me knows that I'm never late for my five o'clock Manhattan. I was in a state of shock when I realized I had less than two minutes to get to the kitchen and mix it. I pulled it off, though, cursing Brown and Miller all the way.

In *A Spirituous Journey: A History of Drink, Book Two*, we see deeper into the mindset of Brown and Miller than in any of their previous works, and this proves interesting in of itself. They reveal themselves pretty well within the first paragraph of the preface, no less, when Brown notes that "a successful miner doesn't pass by a vein of silver in search of gold," and explains himself quite neatly by pointing out that drinks historians are well advised to "chase after the information [they] are finding rather than what [they] are not finding." Rather, then, than starting with conclusions and looking for corroborating evidence, this pair of researchers do their jobs the way nature intended. The hard way.

Did I mention that Brown and Miller are name droppers, too? You're going to come across tidbits about F Scott Fitzgerald, Émile Zola, Alec Waugh, Duke Ellington, Noël Coward, Ernest Hemingway, and a slew of presidents and assorted politicians from all over the place, not to mention every famous bartender who has ever graced the planet with his or her presence. Oh yes, these authors certainly know how to drop names.

If I had a nickel for every time I've been proved wrong about this thing and that, it would take approximately 1,478 pick-up trucks to get them to the bank, but that bothers me not a whit. When someone proves me wrong I learn something. Miller and Brown are similar souls. "We cross our fingers that someone will confront us with a letter, a newspaper article, a diary that we have not uncovered and prove us incorrect in our conclusions," they write, concluding that "that, dear reader, is how history gets written. That's how it gets righted." God bless their little cotton socks.

I don't seem to be able to get much further with this foreword without pointing out that darling Anistatia and dear Jared are a somewhat peculiar couple. I keep wanting to describe them as whacky, but that doesn't quite fit, and pixilated doesn't fill the bill, either, since both of them live quite soundly in the moment. Off the wall? Nope. That's not it. Eccentric might work, though.

Dictionary.com defines "eccentric" as "deviating from the recognized or customary character, practice, etc.," and that describes Brown and Miller quite well, I think. They are prone to dressing in outrageous costumes, they throw the very finest of parties, they crop up in the most unusual of places, and they enjoy staying home and doing absolutely nothing, too. Most of the group with which we cocktail geeks tend to hang can do the costumes, throw the parties, and know how to travel, but few of us learn how to fade into the background well. It's something that Brown and Miller have perfected.

I bring their oddness to light here because it becomes apparent, as you read this tome, that they attack the history of drinks and drinking from a slightly different angle than anyone else in the business, and it's their peculiar (as in *unique*) way of looking at things that makes this book so damned good. Once you read what's coming, you'll grasp exactly what I'm saying.

That's about all from me, then. I've managed to write this foreword without giving away too very much about the words that lie before you, and I've also seemingly managed to get away with calling my hosts eccentric and peculiar name droppers. Hope they still have a spare room for me in England . . .

You've heard enough from me, now. Go see what the authors have to say.

With Lotsa Love from gaz regan

PS: If you don't read the preface you'll be kicking yourself for years.

Preface

WHEN WE LAST saw our friends Rocky and Bullwinkle . . . Wait a minute. Wrong script. When we last visited our intrepid drinks explorers Jared and Anistatia, they made it from infused rice wine in ancient China to the birth of the cocktail in *Spirituous Journey: A History of Drink, Book One*. But as Jared recently said in an interview when asked to provide a few tips for aspiring drinks historians: "A successful miner doesn't pass by a vein of silver in search of gold. When you research a bartender or a drink, you will stumble on unrelated information. Allow yourself to be distracted. Chase after the information you are finding rather than what you are not finding and you will go a lot further. Don't let your beliefs misguide your research. The facts you uncover will not always confirm your pre-conceived notions. Let the facts sway you and report them as you find them."

Sorry, dear readers of the first volume, it's time for a revision. And to those of you who are just joining us, we say: "HEY YOU! STEP RIGHT UP AND READ THIS!"

THERE ARE MOMENTS for humility. And there are moments for PT Barnum-style showmanship. This falls into the latter category. Many people skip a book's preface, eager to plunge into the meat of the text. So, without the slightest trace of modesty we'd like to say there's a big, juicy, rare slab straight off the bone in the following paragraphs. (Apologies to all you vegetarians...a garden-fresh carrot?)

Research doesn't stop when a book is done. It should, but the obsession that drove us here didn't come with a reliable set of brakes. Yes, the following discovery should have appeared in the first volume of *Spirituous Journey: A History of Drink*. And it would have if we'd found it before it was time to go to press. It will appear in its proper place in any future edition. But we were not going to leave it on the shelf until then. It has been hard enough keeping our mouths shut to save the surprise. Thank goodness, the wait is over. Here goes.

WE HAVE DISCOVERED that the earliest published use in the English language of the word "cocktail" was in a 1798 London newspaper. But this cocktail did not just appear in London. It sprouted up in the heart of London politics: Downing Street, in a pub on the corner of Downing and King Streets. Yes, politics (or at least politicians) have been soaked in cocktails since the birth of the word.

On 16 March 1798, the *Morning Post and Gazetteer* reported that a pub owner won a lottery and erased all his customers' debts:

> *A publican, in Downing-street, who had a share of the 20,000 l. prize, rubbed out all his scores, in a trans-*

port of joy: This was an humble imitation of his neigh-
bour, who, when he drew the highest prize in the State
Lottery, not only rubbed out, but actually broke scores
with his old customers, and entirely forgot them.

The next week, on 20 March 1798, the *Morning Post and Gazetteer* satirically listed details of 17 politicians' pub debts, including the following:

> *Mr Pitt,*
>   *two petit vers of "L'huile de Venus"*   *0 1 0*
> *Ditto, one of "perfeit amour"*   *0 0 7*
> *Ditto, "cock-tail"*
>   *(vulgarly called ginger)*   *0 0 3/4*

The fact that the "cock-tail" was one of Mr Pitt's drinks—listed after two obviously French beverages—suggests that the word "cock-tail" might have had French origins. After all, Mr Pitt's tenure as Premier (as the Prime Minister was called back then) was marked by the French Revolution and the Napoleonic Wars.

The *Morning Post and Gazetteer* did not have any love for Mr Pitt. Earlier that year, he had raised the tax on their publication to 50 percent of the newsstand price. In retaliation, they listed the price on the front page as follows:

> *Price in 1783, - - - -*   *3d.*
> *Taxed by Mr PITT,*   *3d*
> *Price*   *6d.*

Downing Street only had one corner, its intersection with King Street. While King Street once boasted up to 50 taverns, only one was situated on the corner of Downing: the Axe and Gate.

The name of the lucky lottery-winning publican is lost in time. Perhaps this is because he was not in residence nearly as long or as formidable a presence as his predecessor, John Wild. Standing six feet three inches at a time when the average man was five foot five. Wild had been a Yeoman of the Guard before retiring to the Axe and Gate on the corner of Downing Street where he tended bar for 40 years. His obituary, in the December 1793 edition of *The Gentleman's Magazine*, reported that he was found drowned in a ditch near a pub called The Bell in Bushey, Hertfordshire. Apparently, he had died without making a will despite accumulating considerable wealth. The magazine speculated he had feared that penning his last wishes would hasten his demise.

The pub was reported, in 1794, as being "Mrs Gough's". However, in 1797, solicitors advertised for creditors of "Ann Gough, late of the Axe and Gate, Downing Street" to receive dividends from her estate. No doubt, this is the point at which the lucky mystery landlord arrived for his short stint behind the bar.

In the early nineteenth century, the Axe and Gate's lease was purchased back: Of all the pubs in London, only 29 were leasehold properties, unlike those of today. The pub was torn down, by 1824, to make room for the expansion of the prime minister's Whitehall abode.

If the word "cocktail" originated as a bastardization of a French word, what would that word have been? Mixologist and drinks historian Charles Vexenat suggests it was derived from the term "*coquetel*". He also points out that around that time there was a drink by that name. Another possible origin is the term "*coqueter*", which would sounds similar and means to tease: one of those activities a coquette—or a cocktail, for that matter—engages in.

The argument against the theory that *coqueter* became cocktail is that we have not yet found the word used in France before H L Mencken wrote about this in his book, *American Language*. Mencken never let a lack of facts stand in the way of making a provocative statement.

S O MUCH for our latest revelation. Back to our prologue. When we first thought about sitting down with the veritable lorry-load of scribbled index cards, dog-eared notebooks, well-thumbed books, newspapers and periodicals, plus more than a few external hard drives of images and hastily keyboarded notes, we knew that as we put them in some form of order we would find ourselves digging for more.

You'd think we get it out of our system fairly quickly and go on to something else. On the contrary. We delayed the publication of this second book to give ourselves a chance to catch our breath, go into shock, have a giggle, and present you with even more heretofore unknown data and refreshed conclusions about the origins of the Bloody Mary, the French 75, the Martini, the Manhattan, Ramos Gin Fizz, blue drinks, and Jelly Shots.

The most amazing find led us to the final resting place of a man with whom we became acquainted as we thumbed through a fragile copy of his 1882 *Bartenders' Manual* back when we wrote our 1996 book *Shaken Not Stirred: A Celebration of the Martini*[x]. Harry Johnson has been our hero since those early days, when we couldn't find a Martini recipe in Jerry Thomas's early editions. We did find it in Harry's. Yet, no one ventured to write his biography in all this time. In this book, we disclose as thorough a biography as we could excavate.

We also add to the body of information on other mixological masters such as Willy Schmidt (AKA: "The Only William"), Henry C Ramos, and Tom Bullock.

What can we say? In truth, history is not as conclusive as one would wish. Now that we are taking this book to press, we are certain that both volumes of *Spirituous Journey: A History of Drink* will incite our historian colleagues and aspiring "cocktail authorities" to shamelessly quote our findings without citation or due credit. With any luck, it will provoke more than a few heated debates on the Internet and in print about our current findings. We cross our fingers that someone will confront us with a letter, a newspaper article, a diary that we have not uncovered and prove us incorrect in our conclusions. We did that with a number of facts that were penned during the 1800s and 1900s. So bring 'em on!

That, dear reader, is how history gets written. That's how it gets righted.

T HERE ARE MORE PEOPLE to thank at this next crossroads. Thanks and hugs to the European tribe of cocktail and spirits geeks who include but are in no means limited to Nick Strangeway, Jake Burger (thanks for finding Jared's pen, a tool as essential to a writer as a shaker is to a bartender), Peter Dorelli, Chris Edwardes, Joërg Meyer, Stephan Berg, Jeff Masson, Dick Bradsell, Tony Conigliaro, Spike Marchant, Sean Harrison, Desmond

Payne, Geraldine Coates, Mauro Mahjoub, Charles Vexenat, Ludovic Miazga, Giuseppe Gallo, Domenico Constanzo, and Simon Ford.

Now for the Americans. First and foremost a huge thanks and our eternal gratitude goes to Nacht Waxman of Kitchen Arts & Letters in Manhattan, who first suggested that we should write a comprehensive drinks history. Big love goes to our "sister" Audrey Saunders and her man Robert Hess. Hugs and kisses to our cohorts in historical research crime Dave Wondrich and—that Northerner who used to be called Gary Regan—Gaz Regan. Slaps on the back and the next round go to our Museum of the American Cocktail and Tales of the Cocktail compatriots Dale DeGroff, Phil Greene, plus Chris and Laura McMillian.

Then a toast and a round to our friends and co-conspirators who have encouraged us to dig harder, dig deeper into history, including Nick Blacknell of Jameson, Sue Leckie of Beefeater and Plymouth, Yves Schladenhaufen and François Renie of Havana Club, Helmut Adam and Tanja Bempreiksz of *Mixology Magazine*, Alice Lascelles of *Imbibe* UK, Simon Difford of *Class Magazine*, Andy Bishop of the London Bar Show, plus Illy Jaffar, Claire West, and Tim Cunningham of Pernod-Ricard.

As we said at the end of the preface to the first book: Make yourself a drink, sit back, and enjoy the next pit stop along the road to perdition. We'll see again soon.

Cheers,
Anistatia Miller and Jared Brown

CHAPTER EIGHT

A Brilliant Idea or Two

HOW THE AGE OF ENLIGHTENMENT ILLUMINATED THE ROUTE TOWARD LIGHTER SPIRITS

I T WAS A NEW DAWN in many ways. The Age of Enlightenment that rose with the eighteenth century transported thinking out of the cloistered realms of academia into the public sphere. It was a time when news sources proliferated, and the general public openly gathered to discuss mutual concerns in public spaces, in town halls, in taverns. As they openly debated government, religion, and economics, and questioned established concepts about nature and the physical universe as set down by academics and the clergy, they savoured a new range of libations that were directly improved because of this new climate of open thinking.

As we mentioned in book one of *Spirituous Journey: A History of Drink*, the invention of the Newcomen engine, in 1712, literally put the wheels in motion for the cocktail's true evolution. Ironmonger Thomas Newcomen (1664-1729) was not alone in transforming the world by designing an atmospheric steam pumping engine. Thinkers from all walks of life changed the way people worked, travelled, and lived. How was the world of drinks and drinking involved in this social revolution?

Lunaticks Change the World

I T ALL STARTED with a group of British intellectuals who met for dinner and to discuss "natural philosophy." These men were wrapped up in the study of nature and physical science, precursors to modern science. Because they argued late into the night, they chose to meet on the Sunday nearest to a full moon so they could see their way home. (Street lights were rare in those days.). This dinner club called itself the Lunar Society of Birmingham and its members nicknamed themselves the Lunaticks.

Physician Erasmus Darwin and potter Josiah Wedgwood (Charles Darwin's paternal and maternal grandfathers), metal manufacturer Matthew Boulton, natural philosopher William Small, chemist and inventor James Keir, mechanical engineer James Watt (whose namesake measure of power appears on light bulbs), polymath and founding father of the United States Benjamin Franklin, as well as natural philosopher Joseph Priestley were all Lunaticks at one time or another between 1755 and 1791. It was a beehive of scientific enquiry. (We told you earlier about Priestley's contribution to the development of carbonated water.)

The Lunaticks would never become legendary for their drinking exploits or for inventing new mixes as Darwin had sworn off drink in an effort to cure his gout and, once cured, pressed others to become "water drinkers". However, their contributions to modern drink cannot be overstated.

By this time, Newcomen engines had been pumping water out of coal mines throughout Britain and Europe for half a century. But the monstrous machine was slow to condense steam, and thus provided limited power.

It wasn't the first device of its kind. Hero of Alexandria made a steam engine around 120 BC; Taqi Al'Din, an Egyptian or Syrian Muslim scientist made one in 1551; Solomon de Caus did the same in 1615, shortly before an Italian, Giovanni Branca sketched out a plan for one in his 1629 book *Le Machine*. Hero used his to demonstrate a mechanical principle. Taqi Al'Din used his to make dinner: it was the world's first steam-powered rotisserie. Branca thought it would be good for powering pestles and mortars, grinding machines, raising water, and sawing wood.

Lunatick James Watt (1736-1819) first became interested in this steam-powered engine concept late in 1764, when someone brought him a broken model and asked if he could fix it. Watt realized that the engine was hopelessly inefficient. It took tons of coal to generate enough steam to make the pistons drive a couple of strokes.

He talked to his friend, mentor, and fellow Lunatick Joseph Black (1728-1799), a physicist who was born in Bordeaux, France to Northern Irish and Scottish parents whose families were in the wine trade. After studying at

Aside from regular Lunaticks Matthew Boulton, Erasmus Darwin, Thomas Day, Richard Lovell Edgeworth, Samuel Galton, Jr., James Keir, Joseph Priestley, William Small, Jonathan Stokes, James Watt, Josiah Wedgwood, John Whitehurst and William Withering, there were part-time attendees such as Richard Kirwan, John Smeaton, Henry Moyes, John Michell, Pieter Camper, RE Raspe, John Baskerville, Thomas Beddoes, John Wyatt, William Thomson, Cyril Jackson, Jean-André Deluc, John Wilkinson, John Ash, Samuel More, Robert Bage, James Brindley, Ralph Griffiths, John Roebuck, Thomas Percival, Joseph Black, James Hutton, Benjamin Franklin, Joseph Banks, William Herschel, Daniel Solander, John Warltire, George Fordyce, Alexander Blair, Samuel Parr, Louis Joseph d'Albert d'Ailly, Barthélemy Faujas de Saint-Fond, Grossart de Virly, and Johann Gottling.

Joseph Black's discovery of the principle of latent heat not only made whisky production more profitable, it improved the efficiency of the steam engine.

the University of Glasgow, Black taught at Edinburgh University and then returned to Glasgow, where he first met Watt. Black was one of three professors who, in 1758, helped Watt set up a mathematical instrument workshop within the university.

At the time, many of Black's students were the sons of whisky distillers. He was frequently asked for advice on improving the pot still's output. In 1761, Black found the answer. He discovered that when water reaches the boiling point the temperature plateaus at 100 degrees Celsius, no matter how high you turn up the heat under it. He realized that heat only provides enough kinetic energy to turn liquid into vapour. Because additional heat appears to be lost, Black called it "latent heat" or "hidden heat". This lost energy cost the distillers quite a bit of money; and its discovery gave birth to modern thermal science.

The fruit of the discussions between Watt and Black was a simple solution: Keep the cylinder hot and condense the steam somewhere else. By May of 1765, while walking on Glasgow Green, Watt thought of using a separate condenser.

According to some stories, Watt built his first prototype in a tiny cottage behind the Bo'ness home of his financial backer Lunatick John Roebuck. But he could not get a steam-tight fit between the piston and the cylinder. Sometime during the 1760s, nonconformist minister and inventive engineer Humphrey Gainsborough (the brother of artist Thomas Gainsborough) showed Watt the improvements he divined on a condensing steam engine. Some of those concepts appeared in Watt's final design.

Mechanical engineer James Watt was inspired to improve the design of a steam engine that was based on a principle that changed the way whisky was produced.

Watt took out a patent, in 1769, for his steam engine. On his way to London, he attended a Lunaticks dinner, where Small, Darwin, and Boulton did their best to persuade him to move to Birmingham. When his wife Margaret Miller died in childbirth, in 1772, and his financier went bankrupt, Watt made the move and formed a partnership with Boulton, who owned the Soho Manufactory.

A new boring machine, invented by iron-master John "Iron-mad" Wilkinson, provided the last element Watt needed to perfect his design. In 1775, Wilkinson built a new boring machine to make better cannons. By casting the barrel solid, and boring a smooth cylindrical hole, Wilkinson hoped to make a more powerful and accurate cannon. Watt heard about this, and then asked Wilkinson to make a cylinder for a steam engine. Within weeks of getting his new cylinder, Watt got his first steam engine to work.

In return, Watt built a steam engine to drive the blowers for Wilkinson's furnace. The relationship lasted 20 years, with Wilkinson making the cylinders for Boulton & Watt's steam engines.

Thanks to the collaborative efforts of the Lunaticks a powerful, practical steam engine was born and so was the Industrial Revolution. Technological advancement spread throughout Britain, changing the social, cultural, and economic fabric of the nation. That, in turn, transformed life in the American colonies and in just about any country that Britain traded with or engaged in war.

Manual labour had been the backbone of the British agriculturally-based economy until practical inventions such as textile machines lured country folk into cities, where they made more money than they ever had by growing food and raising livestock. Improved roads, transport canals, and eventually steam-powered ships and railways kept goods and people on the move.

With all that extra money in pocket, the concepts of leisure and adventure finally trickled down to the masses. Industrialism overtook mercantilism as the economic model. And drinks filled with exotic yet affordable ingredients were one of the small luxuries that the public craved.

More Bitters Truths

AN EXTRACT from the bark of the South American cinchona tree, quinine was isolated and named in 1820 by the French researchers Pierre Joseph Pelletier (1788-1842) and Joseph Caventou (1795-1887). Prior to their discovery, cinchona (or *quina-quina*) was dried, powdered, and mixed in a fermented beverage by indigenous peoples as a remedy for the chills: a common symptom of malaria. As early as 1631, non-extracted quinine was used by Italian physicians to treat the same thing. But Pelletier's and Caventou's published research sparked broader interest and application when it took on a very practical and palatable form.

Although Jean-Jacob Schweppe had retired in 1798, the soda water manufacturer enjoyed overwhelming success in the hands of its third set of owners, John Kemp and William Evill. The partners developed and patented, in 1858, a commercial "Indian tonic water" that combined its successful soda water with quinine and sweetening. Paired with gin, and touted as healthy, this drink had already been adopted as a daily quencher for British subjects living in tropical areas. The commercial distribution of tonic water, in the 1870s, simply vaulted the Gin & Tonic to the top of the drinks menu, standing shoulder to shoulder with the John Collins and the Tom Collins.

Scurvy had plagued exploration and naval fleets for centuries until the British Royal Navy adopted a daily ration of fresh lemons for its crews during the Napoleonic Wars (1803-1815). Equally a scourge on land, citrus was harder to come by unless you could afford to procure a private shipment from Spain. At the time, citrus was a seasonal ingredient, not a perennial as it is today. If a shipment of lemons did arrive, they were quickly gobbled up in lemonade or made into sherbet, shrub, or syrup to preserve their goodness and flavour.

GIN & TONIC

1 part London dry gin
2 parts Indian tonic water
Build ingredients in a rocks glass
and add 2 to 4 ice cubes. Garnish
with a lime wedge.

To answer this demand, the new partners launched Schweppes Aerated Lemonade, in 1834, which blended the soda water with fresh lemon juice. The drink became a staple that was later marketed, in 1957, as Original Bitter Lemon.

Another cure-slash-cocktail ingredient that arose during the same decade also capitalised on the high demand for quinine. While serving as surgeon general for revolutionary leader Simón Bolívar in Angostura, Venezuela, around 1824, Dr Johann Gottlieb Benjamin Siegert developed his

SAZERAC

1 sugar cube or 1 tsp sugar
1 tsp cold water
2 dashes Peychaud's bitters
90 ml rye whiskey
1 tsp absinthe

Fill a small rocks glass with ice and allow it to chill. Empty the ice into a second small rocks glass. In the first glass, add the sugar, water, and bitters. Using a small muddler, or spoon, crush the sugar cube until it dissolves in the water and bitters. Add rye whiskey and stir. Pour the contents of the first glass into the ice filled second glass. Pour the absinthe into the first glass, and twirl the glass to coat it well. Discard any remaining absinthe. Strain the contents of the second glass into the absinthe-coated first glass. Garnish with a lemon peel that is first twisted over the top of the glass.

medicinal bitters to aid the appetite and digestion in the tropical climate. Focusing on cinchona as a primary herb combined with other exotic tropical botanicals that were infused in a rum base, he initially named his formula Amargo Aromatico. Its efficacy and popularity quickly spread. By 1830, Siegert began exportation of his product to Britain and Trinidad. It was not his only product. For decades he also produced Dr Siegert's Angostura Elixir and Dr Siegert's Bouquet.

A LESSER-KNOWN BITTERS introduced a couple of years later, in 1832, was the basis of a cocktail-origin controversy that lasted until the twenty-first century. After leaving Haiti for New Orleans as a child at the height of the Haitian Revolution (1791-1804), Antoine Amedée Peychaud became a pharmacist and opened an apothecary at 437 Rue Royale (formerly 123 Rue Royale). He developed a restorative and tonic bitters that prevented indigestion, an ailment that was "prevalent in hot and humid climates."

As was custom in those days, Peychaud promoted his formula by serving customers a drink made with brandy, sugar, and dashes of his bitters, which he served in a *coquetier* [egg cup]. Response was overwhelming to both his product and to his libation. His signature recipe was adopted, in 1850, as the house offering at the Sazerac Coffee House in the French Quarter, where owner John Schiller replaced the expensive imported brandy that Peychaud employed with readily available domestic rye whiskey.

Before the decade was out, Peychaud went into commercial production, marketing his "American Aromatic Bitter Cordial", which is still produced today by the Sazerac Company.

Of course, Peychaud had competition. There were dozens of aggressive rivals in the national market including Dr J Hostetter's Celebrated Stomach Bitters (made in Pittsburgh, Pennsylvania) and Boker's Stomach Bitters (made in New York). Boker's did not survive Prohibition in the United States. Jacob Hostetter left his heirs and partners fighting over an estate worth millions when he passed away, before his bitters faded out after the Second World War, at about the same time Abbott's Bitters, from Baltimore, went out of business.

Another rare survivor from the heyday of bitters was Fee Brothers Bitters from Rochester, New York. Fee's has been owned and operated by the same family since 1863, when they initiated production in the family's grocery and liquor store.

A notice in the 1903 *Atichison Globe* newspaper of Atchison, Kansas, remarked: "More trouble: The Sazerac cocktail, a particularly seductive cocktail, has struck town."

Sometime after John Schiller sold the Sazerac Coffee House to his secretary John Handy, absinthe was added to Peychaud's drink. Thus, the Sazerac was born. (Schiller is also remembered for making money—literally. During the Civil War, he stamped pennies with his name "JB Schiller" on one side and an "X" on the other, indicating the value was ten cents. These are now highly collectable, selling for as much as $4,000 USD.)

The French Touch

LESS THAN 20 YEARS after Antonio Carpano first produced his formulation of vermouth, the craze swept westward, by 1813, from the Piemonte in Italy to the Rhône-Alpes region of France. A Lyonnaise absinthe and liqueur maker named Joseph Noilly created a vermouth formula that macerated 20 herbs and spices with two styles of barrel-aged white wine, Picpoul and Clairette. Noilly liked the distinctive effect that the intense Languedoc sun and Mediterranean salt spray had on the base wines that he shipped down the Canal du Midi to Marseillan, Hérault, the small fishing village where he set up production.

Fortified with a distilled grape spirit called *miste* and flavoured with a considerable amount of chamomile (along with lavender, orris, cinchona, orange peel, wormwood, thistle—between 20 and 30 botanicals in total) he achieved a light, amber-toned vermouth with a dry finish, which gained steady acceptance as an apéritif.

Noilly's son Louis took over the business, in 1829, renaming it Louis Noilly & Sons. Exportation of its absinthe, liqueurs, and vermouth outside of France commenced the following year. When Louis' brother-in-law Claudius Prat joined the firm, in 1843, it was renamed Noilly-Prat. The next year, the company shipped its products across the Atlantic to the United States. Business grew to such a point that the vermouth and absinthe bottling operations as well as the firm's management offices were moved to the city of Marseilles while its liqueur production was moved to Lyon.

The only vermouth to be granted an Appellation d'Origine Controllée (AOC), in 1932, was born shortly after Noilly began to market his product. Joseph Chavasse developed Dolin Vermouth de Chambéry, in 1821, which focuses on the local alpine botanicals that are found in the Rhône-Alpes region of southeastern France. Besides producing dry and sweet varieties, the company created the world's first clear vermouth, Vermouth Blanc, as well as one that was flavoured with alpine strawberries, Chambéryzette.

But let's get back to spirits for a while.

The production of Noilly-Prat's dry vermouth requires vast quantities of botanicals. It is estimated that the Noilly-Prat company currently uses half of the annual chamomile harvest that is grown in France.

Prove Up

SO HOW DID YOU KNOW how strong your potable spirit was before legislation insisted that the alcohol by volume (ABV) be labelled on the bottle? From the 1700s until New Year's Day 1980, the British measured their spirit on the proof scale.

Remember we said that rum rations were a common form of compensation and that as a guarantee that regular seamen were given undiluted rum, the spirit was "proved" by dousing a small mound of gunpowder with the liquid in question? If the mound ignited, the spirit was at least "at proof" or "100 degrees proof"; if the powder failed to ignite, it was "under proof."

Eventually, a bright chemist determined that 100 degrees proof occurred at 57.15 percent ABV: close to a ratio of four parts alcohol to seven parts liquid. This was a simple equation: percentage of ABV multiplied by 1.75 equals total degrees of proof.

Although hydrometers had been around since physicist Archimedes (circa 287-212 BC) developed one in ancient Greece, no one had designed an instrument that could measure alcoholic density in a liquid. When the British government decided that the best way to control the manufacture of spirits and brewed beverages was to tax the products based on their alcohol strength, they adopted British physicist Robert Boyle's hydrometer, invented in 1675, as the legal standard of measure. Designed to detect counterfeit guinea and half-guinea coins, the instrument was relatively inaccurate in measuring alcohol, but it was the only device

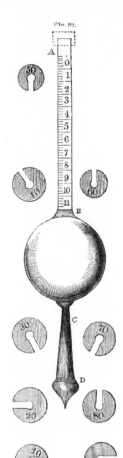

Adopted by the British government, in 1818, as the legal measure of alcohol volume, Sykes' hydrometer remained the standard until 1980.

of its kind. That is, until John Clarke's slightly more accurate copper "hydrometer and brandy prover".

The young Clarke was asked, in 1725, by the principals of a London distillery to create an instrument that would "ascertain the true strength of brandy, rum, malt, or molasses spirits without tasting the same, or trusting to the uncertainty or fallacy of the proof vial, the only method then made use of by the whole trade to discover whether any of the above mentioned liquors were proof or otherwise." Though it was still not perfect, this new hydrometer was quickly adopted.

Clarke went to his friend and advisor, experimental philosopher John Theophilus Desaguliers (1683-1744) to see if his new invention worked. The first one didn't. The hydrometer body was made of ivory, which absorbed too much liquor. The second one, made from copper, met with Desaguliers' approval, which the philosopher recommended for use in distillation in his contribution to the *Philosophical Transactions*, March and April 1730.

Adopted by the government in the 1740s, Clarke's instrument remained the standard until Bartholomew Sykes (or Sikes) devised a relatively more accurate apparatus. With the passing of the Hydrometer Act of 1818, Sykes' hydrometer was adopted by the British government and remained in use until 1980, with the established proof being "if the volume of the ethyl alcohol contained therein made up to the volume of the spirits with distilled water has a weight equal to that of twelve-thirteenths of a volume of distilled water equal to the volume of the spirits, the volume of each liquid being computed as at 51 degrees Fahrenheit."

Alcohol by Volume

ALTHOUGH THE BRITISH made headway in the establishment of liquor controls by the use of precision instruments, it was the French who more often than not perfected devices and methodologies for their use. Such was the case when French chemist and physicist Joseph Louis Gay-Lussac (1778-1850) determined the most accurate way to measure alcohol strength without relying on proof calibration.

Born at Saint-Léonard-de-Noblat, Gay-Lussac studied at the École Polytechnique and the École des Ponts et Chaussées, before he became a demonstrator for A F Fourcroy, a chemistry professor at the École Polytechnique. He was professor of physics at the Sorbonne from 1808 to 1832.

Joseph Louis Gay-Lussac's alcoholmetric table and hydrometer design remains the European standard longer after its invention in the 1820s.

The year after he started, Gay-Lussac met Geneviève-Marie-Joseph Rojot, a shop assistant. When he walked into the linen draper's establishment where she worked, she was reading a chemistry textbook under the counter. They soon married and went on to parent five children.

Around 1820, a French politician who wanted to tax wines and spirits based on alcohol content asked Gay-Lussac to develop an acceptably precise process. He delivered his calibrated alcoholometric table two years later, which measured the amount of ABV at a given temperature. To this day, all spirits are measured by either ABV or degrees Gay-Lussac) as well as by proof . But that's another story altogether. Gay-Lussac's precise system was the basis of the new 1824 law for wine and spirits taxation.

Inspired by his own discovery, Gay-Lussac partnered with Charles-Félix Collardeau, a Parisian scientific instrument maker, to design and manufacture a glass alcoholometer (AKA: proof and traille hydrometer), which they sold to the French government at five francs per unit. Today there is a Rue Gay-Lussac in nearly every French city.

The Right Place at the Right Time

ANOTHER REMARKABLE breakthrough lightened the taste of spirits and industrialised its production. Aeneas Coffey (1780-1852) patented the continuous distillation process and consequently made it easier to obtain greater quantities of higher-proof alcohol to meet the ever-growing demand for potable spirits.

The French led the way in the development of alembic stills and commercial spirits production from the 1300s to the 1600s, when pot stills designed by Nicholas Lefèvre and Möis Chabas allowed for greater quantities to be produced at a given time. But these spirits were collected at a low proof. If a stronger spirit was desired, the distiller put the distillate through a second and sometimes a third distillation to achieve higher strength in what was then called a common still.

This worked fine for eaux-de-vie producers, who did not mind waiting a few days or a week for a charge to finish its cycle. It also worked for Scottish and Irish whisky producers until 1788, when the British Parliament levied excise duties on spirits. (A distiller was taxed according to the height of his still and the number of stills he had in operation.) Gaugers were sent out to measure the stills, collect the appropriate tax, and investigate illegal operations. These tax collectors were not concerned about how the grain spirit was made or to what proof. They visited establishments to ensure a larger still had not replaced the one already taxed and that new stills had not been added to the operation.

Centuries after its invention, the alembic or common still continued to be improved primarily by French inventors who sought ways to increase output and strength.

Fig.44.

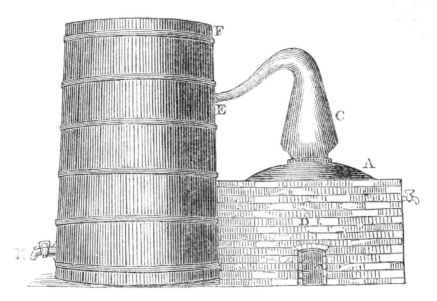

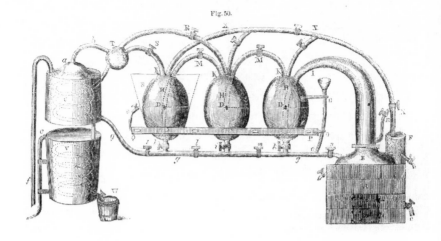

Fig. 50.

The still designs developed by French engineers Édouard
Adam (above) and Isaac Bérard (below) may have improved the
quality of distillate output but not the quantity that producers
demanded.

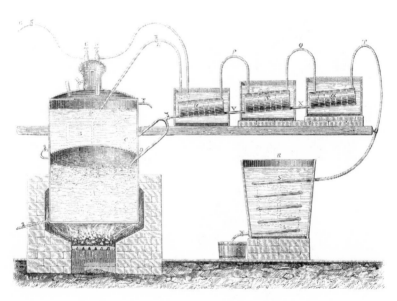

Fig. 234. — Troisième appareil distillatoire d'Isaac Bérard.

The whispers of a more efficient style of still were first heard in France. Édouard Adam and Isaac Bérard led the way, in the early 1800s, in the search for the perfect distillation method. But their ideas did not yield the increased production distillers demanded.

Baglioni conceived of the idea of continuous distillation and patented a design on 24 August 1813. His attempts at construction were not very successful and he ended up losing his rights to the concept when the government awarded a patent in the same year to Jean-Baptiste Cellier-Blumenthal (1768-1840) even though he did not provide a drawing with his application.

Interestingly enough, despite his attempts to expand his rights to the concept by applying for patents in the Netherlands and conducting trials of his design, he found no support for his project because it was not as efficient as his presentation had promised. It wasn't until Cellier-Blumenthal met Charles Derosne (1780-1846), in 1816, that a revised design and subsequent trials proved that continuous distillation was not only feasible but possible. Unable to raise enough funds to go into production, the inventor handed over his patent to Derosne.

It was also around this time that a company in Leith, Scotland developed the Scotch still, an apparatus that was wider than it was tall, exposing more surface area to heat

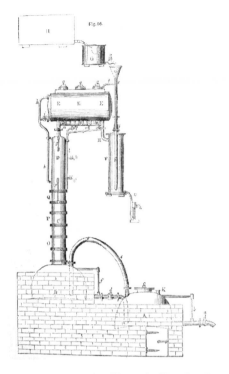

The work of Jean-Baptiste Cellier-Blumenthal and Charles Derosne proved that continuous distillation was not only feasible but possible when it was unveiled in the early 1800s.

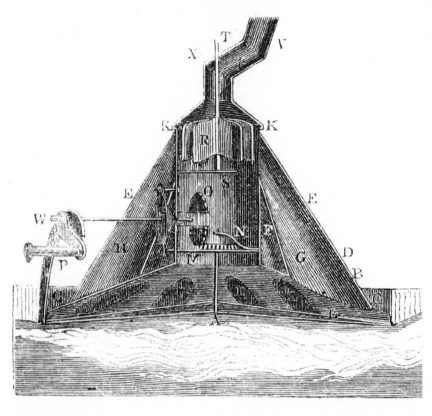

Fig. 46.

Wider than it was tall, the Scotch still kept more money in whisky distillers' pockets: the low height meant that less money went to excise tax and its increased output met with rising demand.

and less to the tax collector. The result: a distillation cycle that took place within a few hours instead of days or a week. The lowered height meant that distillers could produce more spirit without being taxed for the increased output. That was only temporary. The gaugers eventually caught on and new laws were enacted by British Parliament. In 1815, the licence duty was abandoned and excise tax was levied on the quantity of wash as well as the quantity of resulting distilled spirits.

Speed became the name of the game amongst Scottish and Irish distillers who were in hot competition to meet the rapidly rising demand for whisky. Through observation of the Scotch still, Sir Anthony Perrier of Cork, Ireland, developed a method, in 1822, that allowed the mash to flow gradually and continuously over the heat during distillation through a labyrinth of partitions. This meant small portions of wash received the greatest amount of heat, thereby increasing the amount of alcohol collected.

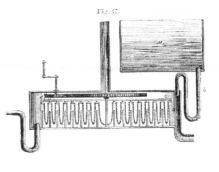

Observation of this device in the 1820s, inspired Robert Stein, owner of the Kilbagie Distillery in Clackmannanshire, Scotland. Stein created a device that produced spirit in a continuous stream so long as mash was fed through the column. Called a patent still or Stein still, its inventor received patents #5583 and #5721, in December of 1827, installing the finished design three years later at his cousin

Sir Anthony Perrier's condenser (above) increased the amount of alcohol distillers could collect off of a charge while Aeneas Coffey's column still design improved both the overall quality and quantity of distillate production.

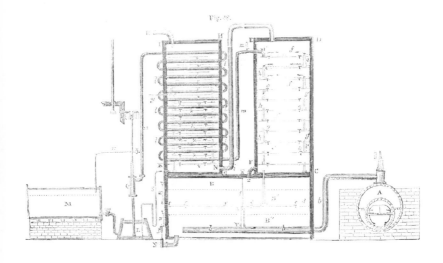

John Haig's Cameron Bridge Distillery in Fife. But it was not Stein's still that set the beverage alcohol industry ablaze. It was the observations of the Stein still conducted by Aeneas Coffey (1780-1852) that yielded the greatest result.

Coffey worked as a gauger in Dublin for a quarter of a century before he attended a demonstration of Stein's patent still. Born in Calais, France and educated at Trinity College in Dublin, Coffey had ample opportunities to observe all manner of still designs. Legend has it that he was severely beaten by moonshiners when he attempted to shut down illegal distilling operations in his territory. Because of his job, he knew how much could be produced in a given period of time. He also knew that the new continuous stills had a flaw: to obtain a higher proof spirit, receiving vessels had to be changed so multiple distillations could take place.

Tired of either his government job or the beatings that came with it, Coffey opened the Dock Distillery on Grand Canal Street in Dublin. The main feature of his operation was a customised still of his own design—or rather Stein's design with a minor modification. Coffey inserted two pipes into Stein's column still that allowed a greater portion of the aqueous vapours to re-circulate into the still instead of flowing into the receiver with the spirit, thus eliminating the need for multi-distillation and producing a spirit with a higher proof and lighter character. In 1830, he was granted Patent #5974 for his second design, a two-column continuous still.

Within five years of receiving his patent, Coffey had enough orders to warrant the establishment of Aeneas Coffey & Sons in London. (The company is still in operation today under the name John Dore & Co Limited) He closed

Dock Distillery four years later and devoted all of his time to building and installing stills in others' distilleries.

You could say that Coffey merely trumped Stein's original concept by perfecting it. But without Coffey's improvements and the overwhelming popularity of his column still, the Scotch whisky market might never have grown by leaps and bounds that it did during the two decades that followed his achievement.

Although Scottish highlanders were limited by politics and grain shortages to producing only small-batch, pot-distilled malt whisky, the lowland distillers were able to capitalise on Coffey's column still, producing huge volumes of a grain whisky that had a more accessible, lighter character. Demand increased exponentially over the next decade, inspiring Andrew Usher, in 1853, to create a blended whisky made from both malt and grain whiskeys. With his success, master blenders such as John Haig, John Walker, George Ballantine, John Dewar, and William Teacher, and James Chivas quickly followed.

Coffey's still eventually revolutionised the way that gin, vodka, and rum were also distilled, making spirits cheaper and more plentiful at a time when cocktails and mixed drinks were spanning their reach beyond the rich to the public-at-large.

There was, however, one more pivotal figure who vastly improved the quality and character potable alcohol while also achieving what seemed like an unattainable, yet ultimate goal: the collection of nearly absolute ethanol.

Purity of the Spirit

I N THE DAYS when Arab alchemists al-Jabir, al-Kindi, and al-Razi first distilled potable spirits during the 700s and 800s, no one ever collected pure alcohol. The knowledge did not exist. And early alembic designs were not capable. When the art of distillation was refined in France and then spread through Europe and the Americas between the 1200s and 1600s—and the world's major spirits categories were born—no one was able to refine the character or colour of the final product of distillation and ageing. Both seemingly improbable zeniths finally occurred after humankind fully embraced the sensual experiences of spirits during the 1700s to the point of mass commercialisation and government control. It was at this juncture that a missing element emerged: charcoal.

It was not an unknown substance. The process for making charcoal was mentioned in the *Book of Proverbs* and by Pliny during ancient times. But it wasn't until the late 1700s that this by-product of burning wood was found to be a useful element, which also became closely associated with the refinement of alcohol.

A chain of events led to this breakthrough. The father of modern chemistry Antoine Lavoisier (1743-1794) was the first person to determine, in 1789, that ethyl alcohol (AKA: ethanol) was a compound comprised of carbon, hydrogen, and oxygen, while he was making ether from a wine-based *eau-de-vie*. Seven years later, Swiss chemist Nicolas-Théodore de Saussure (1767-1845) defined its chemical formula as C_2H_5OH. Fifty years later, Scottish chemist

Archibald Scott Couper (1831-1892) made ethyl alcohol one of the first chemical compounds to have its molecular structure published.

It was all well and good that these scientists defined ethyl alcohol and identified its carbon component. However, it was the work of Johann Tobias Lowitz (1757-1804) that finally tilted the scales by finding a way to capture spirit in its purest form. Born in Goettingen, Germany, Lowitz was the son of German astronomer-geographer Georg Moritz Lowitz. After completing his education, Lowitz moved to Russia where he launched into a series of experiments with carbon, based on Lavoisier's writings.

The 28-year-old chemist discovered, in 1785, that charcoal adsorbed noxious odours from sick people, putrid meats, and rotting vegetables. Adsorption is the accumulation of molecules on the surface of a given material, creating a film of the adsorbate or accumulated molecules on the adsorbent's surface. Adsorption is different from absorption, in which a substance diffuses into a liquid or solid, forming a solution.

Lowitz found that the substance was excellent at removing the colour from liquids, particularly tartaric acid during its preparation: honey was transformed into a pure sugar by boiling it with powdered charcoal. By merely shaking corn-based spirit with powdered charcoal, fusel oils, and unpleasant esters were removed, improving the liquor's aroma and taste. In addition, any undesirable colour was quickly whisked away, producing a crystal-clear product. Not willing to stop there, he tested charcoals made from a variety of woods, documenting which served the best results for the desired purpose.

By 1793, Lowitz accepted a post in St Petersburg, Russia, as Professor of Chemistry at the St Petersburg Academy of Sciences. This academic appointment did not hinder by any means his obsession with charcoal's amazing effects. Within three years, he successfully collected pure ethyl alcohol by filtering the distillate through hardwood charcoal that was activated to increase its adsorption of undesirable particles and aromas.

Some Russian historians have written that at some time around 1780, Lowitz was commissioned by the tsar to complete this crucial study. There is not much documentation from the period to confirm that Tsar Catherine the Great was Lowitz's mentor or that he was specifically requested to focus on improving the purity and character of Russian vodka. However, there was a definite call to find a solution to the problem of unwanted and sometimes lethal congeners in vodka made not only by commercial producers, but also by home distillers by the barrelfuls.

On the other hand, it is well-documented that this unsung hero and pivotal figure of the late 1700s opened the floodgate to a bounty of improvements employed around the world in the way sugar and potable ethyl alcohol were produced and the way people lived in cities.

Lowitz's work caught the eye of a sugar refinery owner in the British-held Caribbean, in 1794, which led to the successful development of crystal clear sugar syrup. However, that was the only application of his work he potentially witnessed.

He died before Gruillon opened the first large-scale French sugar refinery, in 1805, to produce clear sugar syrup and white crystals by applying Lowitz's process.

T HAT SAME YEAR, Benjamin Delessert (1773-1847) employed charcoal in the production of spirits distilled from sugar beets to improve both appearance and aroma. Napoléon Bonaparte awarded him a Legion of Honour for his efforts. It didn't take long before charcoal filtration was adopted throughout France as the country stepped up domestic sugar production in an effort to compete with foreign imports, primarily from Brazil.

Not willing to rest on the laurels of his success at perfecting and manufacturing Cellier-Blumenthal's continuous still, Charles Derosne, designed a device that used bone-based, activated charcoal to filter impurities out of cane syrup. He and partner Charles-Louis Cadet de Gassicourt became the first, in 1811, to manufacture beet sugar in France. Twelve years later, Derosne and another partner Jean-François Cail built a filtration machine factory.

Cuba was an early adaptor of Derosne's defecator and possibly even his version of the continuous still. In addition to this miraculous invention, which heated, decanted, and clarified the cane syrup, a sugar mill in the Matanzas region purchased a number of labour-saving machines that were also manufactured by Derosne and Cail. In 1841, the mill was additionally out-fitted with a sugar mill that had a mobile mat and vacuum evaporators. Derosne himself came

Based on Lowitz's experiments with charcoal filtration, Charles Derosne's defecator revolutionised the sugar industry,

C. DEROSNE.

Defecating Cane Juice.

No. 4,108.

Patented July 10, 1845.

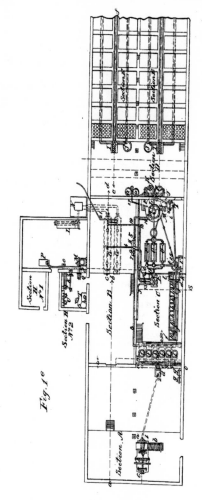

AM. PHOTO-LITHO. CO.N.Y. (OSBORNE'S PROCESS)

to Cuba to install all of his labour-saving devices and to train technicians on their operation.

The year before his death in 1846, Derosne patented his charcoal filtration invention in the United States and assigned the right to his Patent #4,108 to Joseph F Lapéra.

Eventually the work of Lowitz and Derosne, coupled with the employment of continuous stills led to the production of a smoother, silvery-hued liquor that became the signature of what we now know as Cuban rum.

BACK TO JOHANN TOBIAS LOWITZ for one moment. Aside from its effect on the sugar, vodka, and rum industries, his filtration process made massive strides in Britain for a completely different reason. Queen Victoria commissioned Royal Doulton, in 1835, to produce stoneware water purifiers fitted with manganous carbon filters that actually made Thames River water safe to drink. It was a major breakthrough in Europe where untreated water was the cause of typhoid, cholera, E-coli, and other fatal diseases (as well as the reason potable spirits consumption reached its peak during the Age of Enlightenment). Then, in 1854, John Stenhouse successfully used carbon filters to remove noxious and sometimes poisonous vapours from London's sewers, vastly improving the city's air quality and the population's overall health.

Potable public water supplies, made possible by a filtration method developed to improve potable alcohol, stimulated the first call for temperance from certain factions of the public sector as you will discover later on. Thus, the inventions and concepts that changed the alcohol industry during the Age of Enlightenment also transformed the quality of life for people living in urban environments. Consequently, the quality of life also changed for the rural population, who now travelled in droves to carve out livings amid the new industrial sprawl. Those who stayed at home also found their lives forever changed by the introduction of labour-saving and health-improving methods, often initiated by discoveries related to the spirits industry.

THE INDUSTRIAL REVOLUTION heralded the rise of quality spirits. Mixed drinks also improved in content and presentation as the scope of ingredients broadened. Additionally, ice became more widely available and replaced plain water as the balancing element. The world at large travelled further than its town limits thanks to increases in expendable income for the masses. Consequently, more people experienced the marvels of mixed drinks.

A few more essential steps in the evolution of spirits production took place just as the Industrial Revolution wound down and the Victorian Era went into full swing. Packaging also went through a similar series of advances.

The legislation that finally segregated Highland and blended Scotch from Irish whiskeys after the invention of the Coffey still was not the only division to take place in spirits categories. Many liquors found themselves in two camps once continuous distillation became the norm: Rhum, rum, ron, cachaça were also affected.

A new style of Cuban rum was initiated when Pedro Diago, owner of the Santa Elena plantation, experimented with ageing rums in terra cotta containers. This was quickly changed to maturation in wood barrels. Although continuous distillation was more than likely already in place in Cuba by the 1840s, Don Facundo Bacardí Massó added the final touch to this new process by blending Lowitz's charcoal filtration with Diago's ageing technique, creating a silver-hued, lightly aged spirit with a smoother character than its competitors. This was the birth of what we now know as Cuban rum.

Similarly, Lars Olsson Smith, a Swedish spirits manufacturer and politician, who was called *"Brännvinskungen"* [The King of Spirits] because of his domination during the late 1800s of spirits production in Stockholm, changed the way that vodka was made. He initiated the production of Absolut Rent Brännvin, in 1858, when he established an agency for a number of distilleries in Skania and Blekinge as well as a modern facility on Reimersholme. The distilleries that Smith installed there made him rich by producing spirits with an unusually low fusel value.

Smith was one of the first distillers to employ rectification as a means to clean a spirit. His best-selling product made by this means was marketed as *tiodubblat renat* [ten times purified]. This breakthrough ran the communal distilleries out of business and the city of Stockholm tried to hamper his business. Smith, however, placed his distillery in Reimersholme, outside the city limits, and sold his products from the Fjäderholm Islands (his Stockholm customers commuted there by boat). This brand was later renamed Absolut Vodka.

SALAMANDER!

Around 1831, a peculiar toast arose from students in Heidelberg, Germany, that continued long after the original meaning was lost, leaving thoughtful drinkers to speculate why they raised their glasses and shouted in unison: "Salamander!" In the mid-1800s, American officers in Washington were setting fire to their rum shots, and called it "making a salamander" but this was clearly not the origin. Some scholars suggested it came from the Hebrew schalo-mandri (hail to the man). However, the most likely answer was simply a corruption of a call in German to drink all together: *sauft all emit ein einander!*

Louis Pasteur's discovery of the pasteurization process not only changed the face of the milk industry, it also revolutionized beer and distillate production.

Similarly, during the 1870s, Lowitz's process came full circle back to Russia where Andrew Albanov improved the charcoal filtration process employed by Tsar Alexander III's appointed vodka maker, Piotr Arseneevich Smirnov. Using activated charcoal made from birch wood to create one of the world's most popular vodkas, the method became a standard for its production even to this day.

While serving as the director of the École Normale Supérieuere in Paris, French chemist and microbiologist Louis Pasteur (1822-1895) demonstrated that fermentation is caused by the growth of microorganisms that are introduced to liquids via spores carried on dust particles in the air. Based on this tenet, he and Claude Bernard successfully determined, in 1862, that liquids could be heated to a specific point to kill most of the bacteria and moulds that are already present. This was a breakthrough for milk production when it was first adopted. But in 1873, it also became a landmark discovery for brewing and distillation when, on 28 January, Pasteur determined that finished beer could be pasteurized at a temperature above 160 degrees Fahrenheit thereby making it less susceptible to harmful bacteria.

By the summer of that same year, he developed a safer yeast-making process that significantly reduced the harmful bacteria that led to poor fermentation results in the brewing and distillation processes.

T HE STAGE WAS SET, the actors were in place, and the curtain rose on the most momentous cultural shift in attitudes toward potable spirits and mixed drinks that anyone could have anticipated on any continent.

CHAPTER NINE

Heading for the High Road

AMERICA'S LOVE AFFAIR WITH COCKTAILS HITS ITS STRIDE

CONSUMPTION OF MIXED DRINKS rose to a fever pitch as the young United States gained its footing after the War of 1812. With a strengthening economy came the leisure time that allowed the public sphere to flex its muscles about the social condition in the new nation. With a profitable national and international trade in New England rum as well as a burgeoning bourbon and rye whiskey industry, it was natural for detractors to raise the cry for temperance.

ENGLISH BISHOP

1 fresh orange, quartered
and studded with 12 cloves in each
quarter and dusted with brown
sugar
750 ml port

Place orange quarters on a roasting
pan and place under the broiler in a
medium oven (350° F) until the juice
begins to seep out of oranges and
they are slightly brown. Place port in
a saucepan and warm the liquid under a low heat. Add the oranges and
simmer for about 30 minutes. Pour
into mugs and garnish with an orange slice and a grating of nutmeg.

RUM FLIP—VERSION II

1 quart ale
120 ml dark rum
4 whole eggs
120 ml demerara sugar
1 tsp grated nutmeg (or ginger)

Heat the ale in a saucepan; beat up
the eggs and sugar, add the nutmeg
and rum, and put it all in a pitcher.
When the ale is near to a boil, put
it in another pitcher, pour it very
gradually in the pitcher containing
the eggs, etc., stirring all the while
very briskly to prevent the eggs from
curdling, then pour the contents
of the two pitchers from one to the
other until the mixture is as smooth
as cream.

Drinks historian Dave Wondrich found one humor-
ous anecdote on temperance that he shared with us while we
were developing the 2006 New York exhibit of the Museum
of the American Cocktail. It seems that Dr Samual Latham
Mitchill was an advocate for libational restraint. He was a
United States Congressman and Senator from New York,
an attorney, professor, linguist, discoverer of laughing gas
(nitrous oxide), and travel writer responsible for New York
City's first guidebook. Mitchill gave a temperance lecture, in
1820, that categorized potent morning-after potions according to what negative effects were relieved by consumption
of what he called "antifogmatics".

According to this esteemed speaker, gum-ticklers
were taken upon wakening to warm the gums and remove
bad breath: a glass of gin, a dram of bitters, "raw" Slings, or
a "small horn" of distilled cordial.

Between dressing for the day and eating breakfast, a phlegm-cutter was taken to cleanse mucous from the
throat, relieved hoarseness, as well as ease breathing and
swallowing: Egg Nog, a stiff Mint Julep, Brandy Sling, or a
strong Holland Twist.

If these potions did not set you right, a gall breaker
was taken: Grog, Rum Flip, Sampson (rum and cider stewed
over coals), Roasted Apple Toddy, Punch, Bishop, Doctor
(rum and milk), or a simple cocktail of rum and honey with
a dash of bitters.

And when nothing else worked, a clear comforter
was the ultimate cure for what ailed thee: Hot Spiced Wine
with plenty of gin and whiskey, or the Cure-All (equal parts
of heated rum and brandy with a spoon of red pepper).

Go West

CLEARLY, Latham's efforts did more to spread bad remedies than to actually stem the tide of American alcohol consumption. The daily drink routine he described reached far beyond the city limits of New York, Philadelphia, or Boston, far beyond the "wild west" territories of Ohio, Kentucky, Tennessee, and Illinois. Particularly ambitious and/or desperate souls headed out to Colorado, Missouri, New Mexico, and California overland after Meriwether Lewis and William Clark discovered, in 1803, the bounty of the territory that had been acquired by President Thomas Jefferson from Napoléon Bonaparte in the Louisiana Purchase.

Mixed drinks followed the intrepid souls who braved the wilderness that lay westward beyond the banks of the Mississippi River. Fur trappers and fur traders were the first to break new ground. It didn't take long for saloons that were no more than tents, dugouts, or mud huts to rise up along the way. Saloon-keepers served up Hailstorm Juleps and Monongahela whiskey cocktails to the thirsty trappers when they ventured down from the craggy Rocky Mountains laden down with valuable furs. Trading posts and roadhouses gave way to villages and towns as waves of settlers arrived by covered wagon.

The Santa Fe Trail that led from Missouri to New Mexico had many pit stops along the road to perdition. Would-be prospectors, settlers, fur trappers, and carpetbaggers making their way to "El Dorado" (AKA: California), frequently found themselves at one such frontier establishment,

A popular drink in the California goldfields, in 1852, was called Porteree. It was made by adding a little sugar dissolved in water to a bottle of porter and stirring it in.

HAILSTORM JULEP

90 ml whiskey
2 tsp sugar
2 sprigs of mint
Place ingredients in a mason jar and fill with ice [brought down from the mountain glaciers]. Close the lid and shake vigorously 50 times. Remove the lid and drink from the jar. Or to create a hailstorm, use a style of mixing that was popular at that time and pour it between two mixing glasses, one held high above the other, before serving it.

(continued on the opposite page)

quenching their thirst at the United States Hotel in Santa Fe, New Mexico. Not quite a hotel, more of a roadhouse, the establishment's bartender was an east-coast transplant nicknamed "Long Eben".

While travelling with frontiersman Kit Carson, in 1848, journalist-artist George Douglass Brewerton encountered the bartender plying his craft, which he recounted in an April 1854 *Harper's New Monthly Magazine* article entitled "Incidents of Travel in New Mexico":

> *As I recollect the "United States Hotel" in the summer of 1848, it was a long, low adobe building, with white-washed walls, narrow windows, and earthen floors; its landlord and proprietor being a certain Mr Ebenezer Spindle, a man whose long arms, long legs, huge nose, and cadaverous countenance had made him the wonder of his neighbours, who had seen fit to particularize him in familiar discourse as "Long Eben" — as they said, "for short"— a diminutive which I shall ad-opt in alluding to him.*
>
> . . .
>
> *Upon entering the common room, I found "Long Eben" engaged in the concoction of a curious compound beverage, known among the initiated as a "gin cocktail" which being duly discussed and paid for by the consumer, I beckoned to mine host, and calling him aside, asked — with some trepidation, I must confess, in my blandest tones — if he could accommodate me with board and a room during my stay in Santa Fe.*

Although we have read a few accounts suggesting that this Gin Cocktail was made with vermouth (which would make it a very early Martini Cocktail) and know that vermouth had arrived in the west via the port of Galveston, Texas (a major point of entry for imported liquor in the

(continued from the opposite page)

nineteenth century), we have found no proof to support or refute this claim.

"Long Eben" was not the only colourful gentlemen presiding over the mixing of libations in the frontier. In his memoirs *Roughing It: 1860 to 1864*, Mark Twain aptly summed up the life of the Wild West bartender after his encounters further north:

> In Nevada, for a time, the lawyer, the editor, the banker, the chief desperado, the chief gambler, and the saloon keeper, occupied the same level in society, and it was the highest. The cheapest and easiest way to become an influential man and be looked up to by the community at large, was to stand behind a bar, wear a cluster-diamond pin, and sell whisky. I am not sure but that the saloon-keeper held a shade higher rank than any other member of society. His opinion had weight. It was his privilege to say how the elections should go. No great movement could succeed without the countenance and direction of the saloon-keepers. It was a high favour when the chief saloon-keeper consented to serve in the legislature or the board of aldermen.

Despite the prevalence of whiskey and rum in early American culture, many gin cocktails were born along the trail from New York to San Francisco. A particularly famous and controversial one was the Martinez. It was purportedly invented by Julio Richelieu at a bar on Ferry Street in Martinez, California. According to his brother-in-law John "Toddy" Briones, Richelieu divined the libation when a prospector asked him to create a new drink in exchange for a bottle of Jesse Moore whiskey. Or a bag of gold dust. Or a gold nugget.

Eye Opener,
Apple Dam,
Burgundy,
Haut Bersae,
Champagne,
Maraschino,
Tafia,
Negus,
Tog,
Shambro,
Fisca,
Virginia,
Knickerbocker,
Snifter,
Exchange,
Poker,
Agent,
Floater,
I O U,
Smasher,
Curacoa,
Ratafia,
Tokay,
Calcavalla,
Alcohol,
Cordials,
Syrups,
Stingo,
Hot Grog,
Mint Juleps,
Gin Sling,
Brick Tops,
Sherry Cobblers,
Queen Charlottes,
Mountaineers,
Flip Flap,
One-eyed Joe,
Cooler,
Cocktails,
Tom and Jerry,
Moral Suasion,
Jewett's Fancy,
Ne Plus Ultra,
Citronella Jam,
Silver Spout,
Veto,
Deacon,
Ching Chang,
Sergeant,
Stone Wall,
Rooster Tail,
Vox Populi,
Tug and Try,
Segars and Tobacco.

The story is a little far-fetched. Nevertheless, the legend of the Martinez was inscribed in drinks history for well over a century.

However, this tale becomes more perplexing when a passer-by reads the plaque, erected in 1992, that commemorates the Martini's birth on the northeast corner of Alhambra Avenue and Masonic Street in Martinez, California:

> *In 1874, Julio Richelieu, Bartender, served up the first Martini when a miner came into his saloon with a fistful of nuggets and asked for something special. He was served a 'Martinez Special.' After three or four drinks however the 'Z' would get very much in the way. The drink consisted of 2/3 gin, 1/3 Vermouth a dash or orange bitters, poured over crushed ice and served with an olive.*

An olive? Also, the gold rush was long over by 1874, and the valley was prospering with an altogether different golden harvest: wheat.

The Professor

ANOTHER PERSON who laid claim to the Martinez's invention was Jerry "The Professor" Thomas (1830-1885). We won't bore you with the a reiteration of historian Dave Wondrich's wonderful account of Thomas's life in his 2007 book *Imbibe! From Absinthe Cocktail to Whiskey Smash, a Salute in Stories and Drinks to "Professor" Jerry Thomas, Pioneer of the American Bar*. Go read it for yourself. We'll just state a few points about the greatest bar showman with the Cocktail's Golden Age to give you a glimpse.

MARTINEZ COCKTAIL

1 dash Boker's bitters.
2 dashes maraschino liqueur
30 ml Old Tom gin
120 ml vermouth.
2 small lumps of ice
Shake up thoroughly, and strain into a large cocktail glass. Put a quarter of a slice of lemon in the glass, and serve. If the guest prefers it very sweet, add two dashes of gum syrup.

INTERIOR OF THE "EL DORADO," GAMBLING HOUSE.
(On Kearney Street facing the Plaza, in 1849)

Born in Sackets Harbor, New York, Thomas learned his craft in New Haven, Connecticut as an assistant barman before departing on the barc *Annie H. Smith,* in 1847, to seek his fortune. Two years later, he made it south around the tip of South America and up to San Francisco, where he jumped ship and landed a job as first assistant to the principal bartender at the city's first and most popular "resort", A J McCabe's El Dorado at 750 Kearny Street across from Portsmouth Square.

In his 1933 book *The Barbary Coast: An Informal History of the San Francisco Underworld*, author Herbert Asbury wrote:

> Originally El Dorado was a canvas tent, but the
> tent was soon replaced by a large square room of rough
> boards, with a few private booths partitioned off with
> muslin, where a man whose mind was elsewhere than

The El Dorado, circa 1849, with a bartender throwing a drink.

on games of chance might entertain his inamorata of the moment.

Asbury was known to sensationalize or even fictionalize history, but in this case his description appears to be accurate. Taverns and hostelries across the west were sometimes built from the remains of the wagon that brought the proprietor there. It if was successful, he could eventually afford a proper structure. In its heyday, El Dorado beckoned miner-patrons "like a cool fountain beckons the thirsty wanderer in the desert." Baroque furniture, fine-cut glass mirrors, ten chandeliers, and "lascivious oil paintings of nudes in abandoned postures" delighted the eye along with the live singers, dancers, short-skirted "pretty waiter girls" (showing ankles was considered risqué at the time) who served up drinks, and the walrus-moustached "Michelangelo of Drinks" who cut a gigantic figure in his crisp white jacket: Jerry Thomas.

BLUE BLAZER

1 tsp superfine sugar dissolved in 120 ml boiling water
120 ml Scotch whiskey
Put the whiskey and the boiling water in one mug, ignite the liquid with fire, and while blazing mix ingredients by pouring them 4 or 5 times from one silver-plated mug to the other.

If well done this will have the appearance of a continued stream of liquid fire. Serve in a small bar-glass with a piece of twisted lemon peel.

THOMAS'S CLAIM TO FAME was a show-stopper drink called the Blue Blazer, which he reputedly never made unless the temperature dipped below 50 degrees Fahrenheit, which happens a lot in San Francisco. If someone came in suffering from cold or flu symptoms, he would make an exception to this rule. (The word "blazer" was a double entendre. At the time, it also meant to boast, which is appropriate for such a showy drink.) El Dorado patrons tried to confound Thomas "with the fanciest orders imaginable", but never succeeded. That's how he earned the monicker, "The Professor."

Some say Jerry tired of the Barbary Coast. Others claim a customer finally stumped him, requesting a drink that was common in Central America and he left in shame. Whatever story is true, he joined a minstrel show and headed down the south during the summer of 1850. By winter, he made his way to Central America and then home to New Haven, where he introduced Yale students to his expanded repertoire.

From there, Thomas travelled to South Carolina, Chicago, the Planter's House Hotel in St Louis, where he reputedly invented the Tom & Jerry. (More about this drink in the next chapter.) But then, Planter's House also claims to be the birthplace of Planter's Punch and the Tom Collins.

What is more plausible is that the Planter's Hotel in Charleston, South Carolina was the birthplace of Planter's Punch. Built in 1809, the place hosted wealthy and powerful guests to this coastal port, where Caribbean rum was cheap to import. Since Jerry worked there before heading to St Louis, he probably brought the recipe with him.

In New Orleans, Thomas opened his own establishment for a while, and where he picked up the recipe for the Crusta from Santina, a celebrated New Orleans café owner. Returning to New York, he took the head bartender slot at Boss Tweed's Metropolitan Hotel: the city's second luxury hotel, an Italian palazzo-styled structure built on the former site of Niblo's Garden at Prince Street and Broadway.

Author Herbert Asbury noted in the 1929 edition of *The Bon-Vivant's Companion* that Thomas "left the Metropolitan, in 1859, to brave the dangers of a transatlantic voyage, but he was both seasick and homesick, and in less than a year he was again in New York." Some reports say

CREMORNE GARDENS.—THE ORCHESTRA.

Nestled on the banks of the River Thames in London's Chelsea district, the Cremorne Pleasure Gardens was an eden of frivolity that flourished from the mid-1840s to the late 1870s.

that he took a "grand tour" to Liverpool, London, and Paris, but we could not find a passport application nor passenger list to back this allegation. We did, however, discover that, in 1859, "a genuine Yankee professor" made a guest appearance mixing drinks at the American bar in London's Cremorne Pleasure Gardens. Yes. It was Jerry. Amongst the garden's many delightful entertainments were a few American imports, including an American-style bowling green and an American-style bar. The Bowling Saloon opened, in 1858, and lasted through two seasons.

When the 30-year-old Thomas returned to his beloved New York, he opened a high-profile bar at 622 Broadway and then did what no bartender had done by that point. In 1862, he published the first book to contain cocktail recipes (ten of them): *The Bar-Tenders' Guide: A Complete Cyclopaedia of Plain and Fancy Drinks, Containing Clear and*

Reliable Directions for Mixing All the Beverages Used in the United States, Together with the Most Popular British, French, German, Italian, Russian, and Spanish Recipes, Embracing Punches, Juleps, Cobblers, etc etc in Endless Variety.

The cocktail list consisted of Bottle of Brandy, Brandy Cocktail, Champagne Cocktail, Fancy Brandy Cocktail, Fancy Gin Cocktail, Gin Cocktail, Japanese Cocktail, Jersey Cocktail, The Cocktail, and Whiskey Cocktail.

The one concoction attributed to Thomas that the book did not contain was the Martinez. That libation appeared in Thomas's third revision, printed in 1887, which was renamed *The Bartender's Guide and the Bon-Vivant's Companion*. (It also did not contain a Martini, which is sometimes attributed to him.)

The only reason that we know that "The Professor" mentioned in this August 1866 London newspaper advertisement (above) was Jerry Thomas is because when he opened his own American bar at 33 Leicester Square (below), he made certain that the public knew that he was the New York "Professor" who had quenched Londoners' thirsts at the Cremorne Pleasure Gardens.

NEW YORK ITS SQUARES: BIRD'S-EYE VIEW

Another thought about Thomas's relationship to the Martinez: It was very possible that someone travelling from the east stopped in at the United States Hotel in Santa Fe, discovered Long Eben's Gin Cocktail, requested the same be made in Martinez, and the bartender there (whoever he or she was) renamed it after the town. The drink's notoriety was assured all the way to the coast after Brewerton's accounts were serialised in one the nation's most famous periodicals.

The American Civil War (1861-1865) changed the tide of Jerry's life when a military draft was called in New York, in 1863, the young and able-bodied Thomas on the top of the draft list. Not being of the mind to take up the rifle and do his service, Jerry high tailed it westward back to San Francisco by covered wagon. First, he found a slot at the Occidental Hotel, which had opened on New Year's Day 1863, on Montgomery Street between Sutter and Bush. His signature drink there was his Blue Blazer. A year later, he headed eastward to Virginia City, Nevada, where he plied his craft in the burgeoning boom town at sprung up with the discovery of silver.

The fighting ceased. The Union was victorious. And Thomas returned to New York, operating a saloon at 937 Broadway with his brother George. Aside from a jaunt to London to opened a bar, Thomas stayed put. He even got married.

An inheritance squandered on the stock market, a few failed business ventures, and a taste of gambling left slowly sapped Thomas's fortunes by the 1870s. He was forced to close up his business, sell what little he had, and work at less stellar "resorts". He dropped dead from heart failure, in 1885, at the age of 55 and was laid to rest at Wood-lawn Cemetery in the Bronx.

We recently had an epiphany about the origin of some of Thomas's famed concoctions. But first, let's talk about the man who first detailed the proper setup and maintenance of a bar operation .

CHAPTER TEN

The Dean

THE LIFE & TIMES OF HARRY JOHNSON

ACCORDING TO THE PREFACE of the 1882 "reprint" of his bartending manual, the "Dean of Bartenders" Harry Johnson (1845-1933) had written an earlier edition in 1860, making his the first modern cocktail book. Was this part of a rivalry with Jerry Thomas, putting his book ahead of the Professor's? Was it simply a story he'd told to land jobs and decided to stick with? Or was it the truth?

Like Thomas' 1862 *The Bar Tenders Guide*, *Harry Johnson's Bartenders' Manual* does not carry a recipe for a Martinez or a Santa Fe Gin Cocktail. However, it does feature a recipe he called the Martini and a few others that are much akin to what we now call a Dry Martini.

Johnson's book also covered something Thomas's did not: He devoted 159 pages of his 286-page book to advice on the operation and management of a quality bar, from

With his distinctive *moustache and dramatic signature, Harry Johnson cut a dashing figure in the world of saloons and bars.*

Harry Johnson's knowledge of the bar business grew over the years and so did the number of pages he devoted to the subject. The 1882 edition contained about 15 pages; whilst the 1888 edition provided 29 pages of insights. By the 1900 editions, 139 to 159 pages covered every aspect of the business.

negotiating leases, to hiring and keeping staff, to selecting glassware, to accounting practices, to lists of recommended brands of spirits and food items that every bar should stock.

Front and centre he detailed how a bartender should dress and conduct himself when he was on duty, how he could obtain a position, how to collect money from a customer, and how employers and employees should conduct their business.

So, who was this man who in his own words stated that: "There was published by me, in San Francisco, the first Bartender's Manual ever issued in the United States ..... As a proof, ten thousand (10,000) copies of the work were sold at a price much larger than the present cost within the brief period of six weeks"?

Harry Johnson was born on 28 August 1845 in Königsberg in German-held Prussia (now known as Kaliningrad, Russia). Aged seven years old, he and his family sailed, in 1852, on the SS *Speculant* from Hamburg and settled in California.

According San Francisco bartender and historian John Burton, Johnson worked, in 1858, at The Eagle. The saloon was perched on Pacific Avenue at the edge of the

Barbary Coast district. A bar owned by a J H Johnson at 95 Pacific was listed in the city directory, but no mention was made of the establishment's name. It is possible that he started there, but Harry himself said that he was mixing drinks at the Union Hotel by the time he was 15 years old. As Harry put it: "The drinks I invented and the way I mixed them attracted many patrons to the bar, and I had so many requests from other bartenders to how I made this or that drink that I wrote a little book which I called the 'Bartenders' Manual'."

Word got around about Harry. In 1869, just after he moved to Chicago to open a bar that was "generally recognized to be the largest and finest establishment of the kind in this country," the 23-year-old Harry was contacted by New Orleans bar owner Le Boeuf to take part in a national bartending competition. (Harry later stated that his invita-

Situated a few doors down from the sailing vessel that was converted into the Niantic Hotel, the Eagle Saloon attracted numerous patrons to its bay-side location on the Barbary Coast.

WHISKEY COCKTAIL.

3/4 glass of fine shaved ice
2 dashes of gum syrup
2 dashes Boker's bitters
2 dashes curaçao
120 ml whiskey
Stir up well with a spoon and strain it into a cocktail glass, putting in a cherry or a medium-sized olive, and squeeze a piece of lemon peel on top, and serve. This drink is without doubt one of the most popular American drinks in existence.

tion came because of his book.) Mixologists from St Louis, Cincinnati, Boston, and New York took up the challenge.

Each competitor went behind the bar and arranged his *mise en place* to suit himself. A dozen judges—made up of industry folk, lawyers, judges, and businessmen—stepped up to order, each asking for his favourite drink. Then it was Harry's turn.

Judge Wilson led up a party of a dozen men and instead of giving him orders for Cocktails, Flips, and Juleps, the judge said, "Well, Master Harry, you can just mix us a dozen Whiskey Ccocktails, and we'll see what you do with an order like that."

Harry placed a dozen glasses in two rows of six each and then built a pyramid of cocktail glasses on top. "The glasses under the top one were nearly covered over, you see," Harry explained, "but I arranged so that there was a little crack left uncovered in the mouth of each glass." He mixed up a dozen cocktails and strained them using a pair of large mixing glasses without spilling a drop. After the jury cheered him, he went on to make a round of a dozen Mint Juleps.

As you can imagine, Harry won the prize: a $1,000 USD in gold and a solid silver tumbler and mixing spoon.

He went back to Chicago and enjoyed a run of extremely good luck until the Great Fire of 1871 put an end to his establishment and to his good fortune. That turned around quickly when he met and married his wife Bertha (affectionately known as "Birdie") in Chicago. She was born in Germany in March 1852 and emigrated, in 1873, to the United States. They were married that same year.

Opposite:

Harry Johnson won a bartending competition in New Orleans using this complex straining and service presentation.

PLATE No. 3.

HARRY JOHNSON'S STYLE OF STRAINING MIXED DRINKS
TO A PARTY OF SIX.
Copyrighted, 1888.

Johnson became a naturalized citizen two years later and according to his chapter entitled "Why Bartenders Should Have Their Own Union for Protection and Association," he went to New Orleans in an attempt to unionize the profession. He was very cognizant of the fact that there was a wide economic gap and equally gaping rift in the treatment of bartenders from establishment to establishment that needed to be addressed.

The Johnsons moved to Philadelphia, in 1876, where he worked as head barman at the Grand Hotel during the Centennial Celebration. Two years later, we find him at Delmonico's in New York, earning $100 USD per week, managing both the bar and the wine cellar. It was there that he hosted Ulysses S Grant, who was so legendary in his love of compound libations that one news headline from around that time read "Grant Lingers Around Long Branch, Bartenders Weary of Making Fancy Drinks". Harry also served Russian Grand Duke Alexei Alexandrovich a Sherry Flip. He recounted years later that his receipts averaged $600 USD a day.

In 1881, the International News Company asked Johnson to revise and enlarge his book. The publisher printed 50,000 copies the following year, which it paid him for in advance. With that money plus savings from his job at Delmonico's, he opened the 14-foot-wide Little Jumbo at 119 Bowery, near Grand Street. He obtained a five-year lease on the property from John Callahan for a cost of $2,500 USD (equivalent to about $56,500 USD in today's currency).

He decked out the venue with fixtures and furnishings that were uncommon for the neighbourhood. His friends told him he was crazy to open such an expensively furnished bar in the Bowery. But he did.

Former patrons of his at Delmonico's strolled over on their way home to the elevated train. They brought friends. Little Jumbo was a show place. It was also located at one of the elevated train stops.

Harry worked long hours to make his new bar succeed, mixing his creations whilst his staff served up straight drinks. He would relieve his night barman at 7 AM on Saturday and work through until 4 AM Monday morning. From 1 AM until 4 AM on Saturday, he stood outside to turn away any customers who looked "rough" or drunk or underage. He personally kicked out any who caused trouble. He took pride in only selling top-shelf spirits. He later commented, "I was told that I couldn't follow those rules on the Bowery, but I did."

When not crafting creations or managing the bar, Johnson taught the valets of wealthy gentlemen how to stock

The Third Avenue Elevated Train ran the length of the Bowery on Manhattan's Lower East Side, right above Little Jumbo.

a private bar and to make mixed drinks. A New York correspondent for the *Pioneer Press* reported, in 1885:

> *The newest affectation in this line is the private*
> *bartender. He is not an importation from England, but*
> *wholly, so far as I can learn, a New York production.*
> *. . .The idea is said to have been original with Alfredo*
> *Talharin, a rich young Brazilian, who had known only*
> *the harsh and primitive distillations of his native land*
> *before coming to New York to spend the winter.*

Knowing that he would soon return to his home in Buenos Aires, he put his valet "under the instruction of Harry Johnson, noted among New York able drinkers as a mixer of complicated beverages." Word got around town amongst the city's dandies. And the correspondent noted that "already a dozen valets of distinguished dudes have become proficient, and their masters' rooms are provided with cabinets from which the newest cocktails and the queerest mixed drinks are turned out."

Bowery Beer Gardens & Bar Rooms

AROUND THE TIME OF PROHIBITION, when New Yorkers pined for the decadent days of the 1880s and 1890s, they commonly reminisced that the Bowery was "the liveliest mile on the face of the earth." New Yorkers who had never seen the Bowery in its prime yearned for it. When Hollywood—run by transplanted New Yorkers—began putting those reminiscences on screens across the country, it became a national obsession. *Angel of the Bowery*, *The King of the Bowery* (starring Mae West), *Bow-*

ery Boys, and *The Bowery Bishop* are just a few of the nearly 50 motion pictures that focused on the Bowery or its denizens that were made before the 1950s. But during Harry's Bowery days, not every New York citizen appreciated the neighbourhood's nefarious reputation.

Temperance and social reform were hot topics of conversation throughout the city. The Gilded Age of Jerry Thomas's heyday had given way to the Progressive Era, which lasted throughout Johnson's career in New York. The Anti-Saloon League, the Women's Christian Temperance Union, and the Prohibition Party were organised in those years, campaigning hard for the closing of saloons and "resorts" across the nation. Famed *New York Sun* reporter Julian Ralph tallied, in 1884, an average of six saloons to the block along the Bowery. In his 1890 exposé *How the Other Half Lives: Studies Among the Tenements of New York*, photojournalist and social reformer Jacob A Riis reported that a sixth of the city's saloons were there. The 1878 installation of the Third Avenue Elevated Train along the Bowery sent the neighbourhood into a gradual but steady decline. Harry's place was a diamond in a dark well.

The introduction of lager beer to the American public, in 1842, saw a tidal wave of German beer gardens and saloons arise in and around the Bowery by the 1880s, much to the dismay of Irish saloon-keepers. Blamed for the city's 1861 Draft Riots and for most gang and organised crime activity in the Lower East Side and the Bowery, Irish immigrants fought a long hard battle to gain even a toehold in the city.

WHY BEER GARDENS?

When the weather is too hot, we take it for granted that we can head to a cool bar and soak up the air conditioning. A century ago, that was not an option. So, to cool off people headed to beer gardens built in park-like settings and even on rooftops.

Before Prohibition, the United States was awash in beer gardens. Over three million Germans arrived in the United States in the 19th century. The beer garden was just one of the customs they brought with them. Unlike the Irish bars that had proliferated before them, these were family-oriented and drinking was just one of the attractions. Minstrel shows and other theatrical acts, food and music were also on offer for the multitudes that filled these gardens. One of the most famous was Castle Garden, which opened in Castle Clinton at Battery Park on the southern tip of Manhattan. The US Army decommissioned it as a fort in 1821. It opened as Castle Garden 3 July 1824, built on a grand scale. It hosted Swedish opera singer Jenny Lind's first American performance. European dancer Lola Montez performed there. Finally, in 1855 it was taken over by the government as an immigrant processing center. The beer garden legacy lives on in one famous name: Madison Square Garden. Plus, the Bohemian Hall and Beer Garden in Astoria, New York, opened in the early 1900s is still open as of this writing.

But German saloon-keepers had successfully organized, in 1872, to protect their interests from the drive to re-enforce the old "Sunday clause" of the state Excise Law. In 1885, Mayor William Russell Grace sided with this special-interest group and sought to amend the Excise Law "so as to permit the sale of ale and beer on Sunday, except between the hours of 10 AM and 4 PM. (Hotel bars, restaurants, and private clubs had already figured out how to dodge the law by exclusively serving drinks in their guest-only spaces and private dining rooms.)

A flood of German immigration hit American shores in the 1860s, settling primarily in New York and Pennsylvania. During the 1800s, eight million Germans sought a new life in the land of the free. More than just about any other ethnicity, they dominated nineteenth-century American bar operations. Think of it. Willy Schmidt, Harry Johnson, and George Kappeler were not the only Germans who plied their craft in New York's famed watering holes.

Between 1860 and 1900, the number of bartenders and saloon owners west of the Mississippi rose from under 4,000 to nearly 50,000. Forty percent were recent immigrants, and 25 percent of those were of German descent. Thirty percent of saloon proprietors in Colorado were German and no doubt knew the proper use of a *doppelfassbecher* as well as the joys of quaffing *vermut*. And if they didn't, according to the *San Antonio Express* in 1886, there were a number of bartending manuals printed in English and German for them such as Harry Johnson's *Bartenders' Manual*. With that large a niche audience, Harry's book must have flown off the shelves.

T HE IRISH FINALLY GAINED political power, in 1872, when Tammany Hall—the Democratic Party's political machine—elected its first Irish "boss", John Kelly. And they had the ear of City Hall when Tammany member Abram Stevens Hewitt was elected New York City mayor, in 1886, defeating economist Henry George and the young widower Theodore Roosevelt. Hewitt staunchly campaigned against the city's vice and red light districts, particularly the Bowery. During his term, a ban on the sales of beer and liquor on Sundays was introduced. But with every saloon boasting a busy side or back door the law was impossible to enforce.

In his 1887 book *Recollections of a New York Chief of Police: An Official Record of Thirty-Eight Years Patrolman, Detective, Captain, Inspector and Chief of the New York Police*, George W Walling recounted the difficulties faced by police on the beat:

> *Let the police do what they may in the matter of making arrests for violations of the excise law, they cannot stop them. Suppose, in the first place, a policeman, in citizen's clothes, enters a saloon on Sunday and sees beer and spirits sold freely. He arrests the bar-tender, who is taken before a magistrate. The law says that if the accused demands a trial by jury it must be granted him, the amount of bail being fixed at $100. Then the case goes to the General Sessions, where it is placed on file, never to come up again probably while he lives. Why? Because I suppose there are not far from twenty thousand such cases on file there now, and the machinery of the court of General Sessions is totally inadequate to deal with them.*

Why Sundays? Most men worked a six-day week, and Sunday was the only full day left for drinking at sa-

"A small proportion of the Omaha bartenders are "book men"—that is, they have studied receipt books and gleaned nearly all they know about the business from that source. But a larger number of them are men who have grown up behind the bar. They commenced in the business by opening the saloon in the morning, sweeping out, cracking ice, squeezing lemons and performing the thousand and one other menialities which fall to the lot of the salon boy. Gradually the novice grows up in the business, its mysteries slowly, but surely unfold themselves to him, and he is finally able to . "throw a cocktail" with the dexterity of an old-time bartender." —*Omaha Daily Bee*, 26 September 1886

loons. Thus, proprietors made their best money on the Lord's Day.

With all eyes on the Bowery and its saloons, even Harry had a run-in with the law. D J Whitney, counsel for the Society for the Prevention of Crime, and a few companions walked into Little Jumbo on a Sunday. Whitney ordered a soft drink and some of his friends ordered whiskey. Johnson confronted him and said, "It may be offensive to your friends to drink whiskey. If so, tell them not to do it. They don't need to do it to prove that I am violating the excise law. I admit it."

Dumbfounded, Whitney asked Harry to come to his office the next day. Rather than indicting him, Whitney told him to "preach to other publicans to keep orderly places" like Little Jumbo.

From Bar to Hotel

AN ARTICLE in the 29 July 1895 edition of *The World*, titled "Side Doors: Open All Over the City to Those in the Secret and with Money" sets the scene for the reappearance of Harry. That year, the city's drinks trade pried open a loophole in the Sunday excise law:

> *One wet hour closed the dry day. When last midnight came saloons all over town that had been deserted through the day threw open their doors, and white-coated bartenders served the thirsty who had long waited for something cool and refresh them.*
>
> *In front of many saloons a long line had formed. Many men who naturally would have been in bed long before waited for that single hour, from Sunday midnight to 1 AM Monday, which is not covered by the law,*

and when it is legal to sell anything that a man wants to buy. Along Park Row, the Bowery, Third Avenue, Houston Street, in the Tenderloin and uptown saloons had an extraordinary business.

But Harry was no longer on the Bowery. After his lease ran out, he opened a place in the basement of former mayor Grace's office building at One Hanover Square. There he served lunch and drinks. Naturally, Mr Grace was a daily customer. Harry republished his manual—this time with illustrations—and continued to train "publicans". (Ironically, the restaurant that has occupied that space since 1972 is called Harry's Steak, opened by Harry Poulakakos, who is not a blood relation, but had also worked at Delmonico's for over a decade before launching his own restaurant which is now owned and operated by his son Peter.)

By 1896, Harry's workload had worn him down. He handed day-to-day operations over to his staff. Then, he and Bertha went to Europe for a rest, thinking he would never own another bar again.

One cold December day after his return, in 1897, Harry walked up Broadway and stopped for a drink at Trainor's Hotel and Restaurant at 33rd Street. He knew the owner from his Little Jumbo days. Squat and rotund, with sandy hair and moustache, James Trainor had a reputation for running a respectable establishment during daylight hours, and employing local "toughs" to tend bar overnight. This plan had two flaws: occasionally a respectable customer would wander in at the wrong time. If that customer ran afoul of the staff, they would throw him out—hard—and it would make the newspapers. Also, the toughs began lining their pockets with Trainor's revenues.

Trainor's Hotel was situated at the heart of New York's shopping and nightlife action, the Tenderloin.

So when Trainor spotted Harry in the bar, he told him that he wanted to sell the place. He encouraged Harry to look at his books, which disclosed that Trainor was losing $27,000 USD a year due to staff embezzlement. Trainor went to the barber shop for a shave. When he returned, Harry wrote him a deposit for $50,000 USD and took possession of a five-year lease on the place.

Opened in 1873 by James Trainor, the establishment was one of the city's best known cafés and hotels. According to a 1909 article in *The New York Times*: "It was Trainor's place that gave the name 'Tenderloin' to the section of the city where dandies went to trip the life fantastic. It is said that Inspector Williams, coming to the Tenderloin as Captain of the West 30th Street Station ate his first meal as precinct commander at Trainor's. The next day he went back to Mulberry Street on business, and to some of his associates is said to have remarked: 'I am through with chuck steak; it is tenderloin for me where I am now,' and since that day the district has been best known as 'The Tenderloin.'"

That same year, the Raines Law was passed, on 23 March, in the New York State Legislature. Amongst its many provisions, it prohibited the sale of alcohol on Sunday except in hotels. The state considered any establishment to be a hotel if it had ten rooms for lodging and served at the very least sandwiches with its liquor. Thus, Harry's old Little Jumbo became known as the Little Jumbo Hotel. Dozens of saloons added small furnished bedrooms and applied for hotel licences. At least Harry acquired a legitimate, landmark hotel.

A notice in the 2 December 1897 edition of *The World* announced that "Trainor's Hotel [at 1289-1291 Broadway] was sold yesterday by James J Trainor to Harry Johnson, who formerly conducted a resort on the Bowery, and the latter took immediate possession" for a reported price of $120,000 USD (about $3,175,000 USD in today's currency).

The 1888 *Illustrated New York: The Metropolis of To-Day* best describes what Harry purchased:

> *The results have borne out Mr Trainor's sound judgment, for this quiet strictly respectable house is fully patronized by the best classes of the travelling and city public, who truly appreciate economical accommodations of this kind in the business centre of the city. A large restaurant 100 feet in depth is attached and very handsomely fitted up, and where meals are served at moderate prices. The catering is liberal and the cooking first-class, and the majority of the guests dine here, in addition to a heavy outside patronage. The bar (distinct from dining room) is splendidly fitted up, and is fully stocked with purest and best of wines and liquors. It*

Harry Johnson's passport application bears his distinctive signature as well as a full physical description.

should be recollected that Trainor's Hotel is so central that elevated railroad trains and street cars to all parts of the city can be taken from its door.

An item in *The New York Times* on 26 April 1898 referred to the establishment as Johnson's Hotel. Another article from that same year noted that Harry Johnson of

Trainor's Hotel bailed out Sergeant "Buck" Taylor, a former member of Theodore Roosevelt's Rough Riders who had been arrested and unjustly accused of defrauding another hotel keeper. (Taylor's friends rallied and paid off his outstanding bill at Morrison's Hotel for him, then pleaded with the management to drop the charges.)

Harry didn't stay for the full term of the lease. In 1899, he sold out to E A Morrison, a dry-goods merchant, with a profit of $113,000 USD plus the proceeds on the sale of the lease.

Johnson began to lead a very stable personal life. City directories and the Federal Censuses from 1900 through 1925 find the Johnsons living at 352 West 117th Street, after arriving there with a 17-year-old German servant named Rose Schacht. The building, named The Endymion was erected in 1900 half block away from New York's verdant Morningside Park and Columbia University's campus, a very respectable neighbourhood in its time. The building featured six- and seven-room, *en suite* apartments fitted with hot water, steam, and windows that faced the outside. "Hall service" and an elevator made this accommodation more posh that the standard Manhattan living space. The building even supplied ice.

BUT THAT'S NOT THE END of Harry's story. His most audacious project placed him on Columbus Circle at the turn of the century. The 19 May 1901 edition of *The New York Times* reported that the plans "for Pabst Grand Circle Hotel and Park Theatre were filed . .

A showcase for theatrical productions including the Broadway hit The Wizard of Oz *and home to Johnson's private art collection, the Pabst Grand Circle Hotel was a proving ground for one of Manhattan's preeminent restaurateurs, Johnson's nephew Paul Henkel.*

.by Architect John H Duncan" for an estimated build-out cost of $450,000 USD (about $12 million USD in today's currency).

Johnson went into partnership, on 27 February 1902, with Mathias Bock, a caterer from the Arion Club. (Located at 59th Street and Park Avenue, this German-oriented private club occasionally hosted dinners for up to 1,800 of its members.) The Johnson & Bock Corporation became proprietor of the Pabst Brewing Company's second Manhattan hotel venture. Although it was set to open in 1902, the Pabst Grand Circle was unveiled to the public on 12 January 1903 at Eighth Avenue and 58th Street. With an unimpeded view of Central Park, the complex consisted of the New Majestic Theatre, a café and dining room, roof garden, and a hotel. An art gallery on the café floor contained paintings valued at $150,000 USD (about $4 million USD in today's currency) which were "the personal property of Harry Johnson."

Thirty-six flambeau gas torches on the cornice gave the edifice an imposing façade. The Louis XIV Room on the second floor was fitted with more paintings, backgrounded by regal red velvet and finished oak wainscoting touched with gold. Huge gold sunbursts embellished the ceiling at a cost of $20,000 USD (about $500,000 USD today).

Columns throughout the building were fashioned from Levant marble with bronze caps. The back bar featured polished brass brackets which accentuated an impressive collection of glassware. Food service included an à la carte menu even in the evenings, a rarity at the time. An eight-piece orchestra entertained diners and imbibers, led by David Blimberg.

Johnson hired his nephew Paul Henkel as managing director, the city's youngest person to hold the position. An aspiring journalist, Paul was talked into entering the hospitality trade by Harry, first working at the gargantuan Pabst Hotel on 125th Street in Harlem and then with his uncle.

With an ear for music, Henkel hired a song-and-piano act billed as Berlin and Snyder to play in the café. Among the patrons to hear the duo was Lee Shubert who hired Irving Berlin as a singer in the Shubert musical *Up and Down Broadway*. Ted Snyder became the publisher of Berlin's first big hit, "Alexander's Ragtime Band", and later became a partner in the music publishing firm, Watterson, Berlin, and Snyder.

During the opening of the art gallery at the Pabst Grand Circle Hotel, featuring $150,000 USD in oil paintings belonging to Harry Johnson, it was estimated a thousand bottles of Champagne were served. Paul Henkel, the manager, commented that it led to "an all-time high in art criticism." The erotic nature of the art collection was hinted at as many of the paintings were reputed to have frames like keyholes.

T

HE INAUGURAL PRODUCTION at the Pabst Grand Circle's theatre, The Majestic, staged on 21 January 1903, was the Broadway premiere of Frank Baum's musical adaptation of his best-seller *The Wizard of Oz*. It was an overnight hit. The 15 August 1903 performance made even bigger headlines in *The New York Times*. The famed tea merchant and yachtsman Sir Thomas Johnstone Lipton arrived not so quietly at the theatre with a group of yachting friends. Onlookers gathered to shake hands or just to get a glimpse of the America's Cup most famous loser. Three policemen had to escort him safely to the door through the exuberant mob. But even the production company had all eyes on Sir Thomas, especially when actress Lotta Faust looked up from the stage at his box and sang the musical's "popular 'Sammy' song" with a few twists in the lyrics:

> *Tommy, Oh! Oh! Sir Tommy.*
> *You're a dandy, from your feet up.*
> *Tommy, when you come cruising, we scared*
> *of losing*
> *That blessed cup.*

After several encores, Lotta added a new line in her final reprise:

> *Tommy, Oh! Oh! Sir Tommy.*
> *When you come wooing, there's something doing,*
> *Around my heart.*

The audience's roars of approval were deafening after each an every verse. Then finally, Lipton "rose from his seat and tossed a large bunch of American Beauties on the stage."

With this kind of cachet, you can well imagine that Johnson's venture did a heavy trade. But his involvement didn't last for long. The business had huge overhead: $20,000 USD per year in rent alone. Plus, profits from beer sales went directly to Pabst. What was worse: Johnson slipped and fell in the hotel just after it opened. His injuries were bad enough that he travelled to Germany for treatment. He signed power of attorney to Henkel.

The company was unable to pay $3,207 USD for goods sold to it between December 1903 and February 1904. The firm of Johnson & Bock was forced to file for bankruptcy. By the time Johnson returned, his only job was to quit-claim on the lease and to sign over his half of the interest to Eugene Schliep to clear his portion of the company's $45,000 USD debt.

This downturn took some of the wind out of Harry's sails. He did not go abroad again until 1907. When he did, the 62-year-old hotelier/mixologist did not mention an occupation on his passport application. On his next trip, in 1909, he called himself "a gentleman of leisure". He did the same the following year, and spent time living in London, Paris, and Berlin.

Paul Henkel became manager of Keen's Chop House around the time it began allowing women in the restaurant. And he was responsible for expanding it (and at one point came up with the odd idea of keeping chickens on the roof to ensure fresh poultry). He went on to operate the Kaisserhof Restaurant, a sprawling German restaurant directly across the street from the old Metropolitan Opera House at the corner of Broadway and 39th Street, with uncle Harry checking in on his progress. Henkel owned a share

Keen's may claim they have allowed women to dine there since 1905, but that didn't mean women could eat in any room in the restaurant. In 1908, Paul Henkel faced two lawsuits, each demanding $10,000 USD, from a pair of suffragettes he refused to serve in the main dining hall, which was for men only. Upon being refused service, one of the women launched herself onto a chair and gave an impassioned equal rights speech. It's said she had the support of the 200 men in the room until she began a "scathing denunciation" of men and of Henkel in particular. In his defense, he later pointed out the ladies had not been refused service at Keen's, just not in that room.

in the Keen's Chop House chain, with outlets at the ostentatious Ansonia on the Upper West Side and two venues in midtown Manhattan: He was often referred to as Keen's owner. When he sold his share in the Keen's enterprise, he took office as the president of the city's Society of Restaurateurs, an organization that he helped to found in 1913. He even publicly announced to Humphrey Bogart and Errol Flynn that unless they behaved in New York restaurants, they'd be tossed out of all of them. But now we're getting ahead of ourselves.

I N OCTOBER 1913, Johnson moved to Berlin, citing his health as the reason for his departure. He didn't return until 1916. This was at the height of the First World War. Although the US had not yet entered into the conflict, there was a rising anti-German sentiment. Newspapers in New York and other cities published lists of inhabitants names and addresses, labelling them as "Enemy Aliens," effectively inviting neighbours instigate hostile actions. US President Woodrow Wilson issued a proclamation, in November 1917, that restricted the employment and travels of German males over the age of 14 who were living in the United States. The *New York Times* reported that the order directly affected 130,000 men in the Greater New York and northern New Jersey regions.

This would explain why he clearly states on his 1916 passport application that he was born in "Königsberg, Germany of American parents" and that he lived in London, Amsterdam, and Paris in recent years.

Anti-German nativism and encroaching Prohibition probably convinced the 70-year-old Harry to lay low and enjoy his twilight years in relative peace and anonymity. He travelled to Europe again in 1920, declaring on his passport that he was a salesman. By 1925, he was back home on 117th Street with Bertha.

Five years later, it appears that his beloved "Birdie" passed away. The 1930 Federal Census shows the 87-year-old Johnson living at 576 Monroe Street in Brooklyn in a home that he purchased for $7,500 USD. The changing face of the Morningside district and the Great Depression may have forced his move. Continued anti-German attitudes as stories of the Fascist rise to power reached American shores may have forced him to claim that he was of Scottish descent on that census report.

But the concerns of an old bartender living in New York City soon passed. Harry Johnson died at the age of 89 on 26 February 1933 and was buried in Green-Wood Cemetery in Brooklyn.

There were no flowery obituaries published at his passing as there were for Jerry Thomas and Willy Schmidt, who preceded him to the grave. The city and the country were still living with Prohibition. Harry had outlived most of his customers. And sadly, his body did not carry him a few months further to witness Repeal: an act his nephew fought hard to bring about, even leading a delegation to Washington to meet with President Herbert Hoover in March of 1932. But his work did live on. The next year, Charles E Graham & Company of Newark, New Jersey, republished Johnson's book for the next generation of bartenders to peruse.

DID HARRY JOHNSON write a successful bartending manual in 1860? He says he did, but no one has discovered a single copy. No one has found a minute mention in any newspaper about his book. It was never even referenced in another book. Does this mean it did not exist?

Yet, when International News Company published his 1882 edition, it printed 50,000 copies entitled "New and Improved": a clear indication that this was a massive revision of his earlier work. Would a publisher use such a title if they had not seen a copy of the earlier edition? Perhaps, though it is not likely. So, how is it possible that there is no proof the book existed? Could all traces of a book disappear in our modern centuries?

Let's consider another cocktail book for a moment. The author was Emil Lecaire. He was a New Orleans bartender, considered to be among the best in town. He worked in the Crescent City for over 30 years. And in 1905 he published a cocktail book. His book contained 843 recipes for drinks from around the world: mostly imported formulas that had been adopted as American drinks, but also quite a few that he considered outstanding that had never been mixed, according to him, on American soil. He was also a collector of obscure spirits from around the globe and wrote about the native spirits and drinking habits of various cultures.

Are there copies of Emil's book floating around? We've never heard of a single one. In fact, if not for a single 1905 article that appeared in a single newspaper, his book and his name might have been lost and forgotten forever.

Emil wrote his book 55 years after Harry Johnson allegedly wrote his first edition. From 1860 until the great earthquake and fire of 1906 that levelled the city, San Francisco had a number of major conflagrations. Thus a complete and comprehensive document archive does not exist. We will never know the truth of Johnson's first book.

WHY THEN IS HARRY JOHNSON so an important figure in drinks history? The "Dean", Harry Johnson, secured his vaunted position by creating the earliest published record of the word "Martini" and its recipe. But more importantly, the lessons in his bartenders' manual about service and are as viable today as they were over a century ago. As Harry said:

> *I am not boasting, but I'm glad of the chance to say that it takes training to be a publican and that a publican's chances for success are just in proportion to his observance of business rules. And the best of those rules are to keep an orderly place and sell good stuff. Oh, yes, it does not hurt if he knows how to mix drinks properly.*

For this lesson alone, we are most grateful.

Gin & Something in It

THE MARRIAGE OF GIN AND VERMOUTH had overtaken the classic Gin Cocktail in the public opinion polls while Thomas and Johnson were in their heyday.

As we mentioned earlier, French (read: dry) vermouth made by L Noilly Fils & Company had arrived in the

TURF COCKTAIL

3/4 full of fine shaved ice
3 dashes orange bitters
3 dashes maraschino liqueur
2 dashes absinthe
120 ml French vermouth
120 ml Plymouth Gin
Stir up well with a spoon, strain into a cocktail glass, putting in a medium size olive, and serve.

TUXEDO COCKTAIL.

3/4 glass full of fine-shaved ice
2 dashes maraschino liqueur
1 dash absinthe
3 dashes orange bitters;
120 ml French vermouth;
120 ml Old Tom gin;
Stir up well with a spoon, strain into a cocktail glass, putting in cherry, squeeze a piece of lemon peel on top and serve.

BIJOU COCKTAIL.

3/4 glass filled with fine shaved ice;
30 ml green chartreuse
30 ml Italian vermouth
30 ml Plymouth gin
1 dash orange bitters
Mix well with a spoon, strain into a cocktail glass; add a cherry or medium-size olive, squeeze a piece of lemon peel on top and serve.

US as early as 1844—in New Orleans. But sensing a potential market because of the massive migration of Italians to the United States, Sardinian vermouths made an appearance at the 1853 New York Exhibition.

Born in 1861, the year Sardinia—including Turin—became part of a unified Italy, Alessandro Martini, Teofilo Sola, and Luigi Rossi formed a company that produced a sweet vermouth. It met with such acclaim, the partners began exporting their product, in 1867, to New York and London.

Harry Johnson's book offers a glimpse of the effect imported vermouth and even its primary botanical—wormwood—had on the development of mixed drinks during the early days of the cocktail's Golden Age. Vermouth quickly took its place among the most essential mixers of the era. The Vermouth Cocktail, the Manhattan, Gin and Wormwood, the Trilby, the Morning Cocktail, and seven key drinks—the Bijou, the Silver Cocktail, the Turf Cocktail, the Tuxedo Cocktail, the Marguerite, Bradford à la Martini, and the Martini—heralded the nuptials between gin and vermouth.

We'll digress about the Martini later. For now, let's head back to San Francisco in the 1860s to pick up the rest of our story.

CHAPTER ELEVEN

Stories from the Bar

GREAT MIXOLOGICAL MOMENTS

The Peruvian Punch

BOTH JERRY THOMAS AND HARRY JOHNSON cut their teeth as bartenders along San Francisco's "Cocktail Route". Besides the El Dorado, the burgeoning city sported numerous other "resorts" that offered imbibers cocktails: Parker House, Dennison's Exchange, the Verandah, Rising Sun, Fontine House, the Mazourka, the St Charles, the Aguila de Oro, the Empire, Arcade, the Varsouvienne, the Ward House, the Alhambra, the Rendezvous, the Bella Union, and the Pacific Club. All were within walking distance of each other. Kearny Street, leading up to the Barbary Coast from the financial district was where young gents made the rounds, in the 1880s, for more than just cocktails:

> *The greatest beauty-show on the continent was the Saturday afternoon matinee parade in San Francisco. Women in so-called "society" took no part in this function. It belonged to the middle class, but the "upper classes" have no monopoly of beauty anywhere in the world. It had grown to be independent of the matinees. From two o'clock to half-past five, a solid procession of Dianas, Hebes and Junos passed and repassed along the five blocks between Market and Powell and Sutter and Kearney [sic] -the "line" of San Francisco slang. Along the open-front cigar stores, characteristic of the town, gilded youth of the cocktail route gathered in knots to watch them. There was something Latin in the spirit of this ceremony—it resembled [a] church parade in Buenos Ayres. Latin, too, were the gay costumes of the women, who dressed brightly in accord with the city and the climate. This gaiety of costume was the first thing which the Eastern woman noticed—and disapproved. Give her a year, and she, too, would be caught by the infection of daring dress."*

Another San Francisco showman bartender who Herbert Asbury described as second only to Jerry Thomas, held court at the Bank Exchange and Billiard Saloon between the 1860s and 1870s. His name was Duncan Nicol. The bar featured ten billiard tables, and a painting by Paul Emil Jacobs of Samson and Delilah that was purchased for the bar at auction, in 1853, for $20,000 USD, which is over $550,000 USD in today's currency. The painting drew more than a few comments from patrons, including Mark Twain (He thought Delilah's scissors were too modern).

Nicol's fancy drinks were also a major attraction. One concoction in particular immortalized him, which employed a spirit imported from Peru. A stopping point on the long voyage from New York to San Francisco via Tierra del Fuego and Peru, pisco brandy was a wild hit in the city by the bay. A glass of Nicol's Pisco Punch commanded a hefty price of 25 cents, which people were more than happy to pay. Ironically, Nicol did not create the Pisco Punch himself. He started work at the Bank Exchange, in 1854, but the drink was already being made by another bartender there named John Torrence.

The recipe was passed on to Nicol and he continued to mix the famous drink up until Prohibition closed the Bank Exchange Saloon, which had even withstood the 1906 earthquake and fire.

Torrence and Nicol (who passed away at age 72, in 1926, two years after enrolling in an automobile repair course) are said to have taken the original recipe with them to their graves. However, the same cannot be said for John Lannes, the Bank Exchange's bar manager prior to its closing.

For a "long lost" recipe, it even emerged one other time in San Francisco. In 1934, the first post-Prohibition shipment of pisco—100 cases of Peru's finest—arrived in the city. The first one was opened by Hollywood bombshell Dorothy Lamour to great fanfare. At the time the newspapers declared that Duncan had revealed the recipe to his brother, and he intended to see the drink revived.

Pisco Punch was not the only classic born in San Francisco. Great bars and bartenders were flourishing, much as they are today. No commentary on San Francisco mixing would be complete without a look at the Honour-

PISCO PUNCH

"1. Take a fresh pineapple. Cut it in squares about 1 by 1.5 inches. Put these squares of fresh pineapple in a bowl of gum syrup to soak overnight. That serves the double purpose of flavoring the gum syrup with the pineapple and soaking the pineapple, both of which are used afterwards in the Pisco Punch.

"2. In the morning mix in a big bowl the following: I/2 PINT (8 OZ.) OF THE GUM SYRUP, PINEAPPLE FLA-VORED AS ABOVE 1 PINT (16 OZ.) DISTILLED WATER 3/4 PINT (10 OZ.) LEMON JUICE 1 BOTTLE (24 OZ.) PERUVIAN PISCO BRANDY "Serve very cold but be careful not to keep the ice in too long because of dilution. Use 3 or 4 oz. punch glasses. Put one of the above squares of pineapple in each glass. Lemon juice or gum syrup may be added to taste."

able William T Boothby—better known as "Cocktail Bill" Boothby.

He began his career as a minstrel in New York, but soon found himself bartending across the United States before he settled in San Francisco and penned the first of a series of highly-successful cocktail books.

His "honourable" title came when he was elected, in 1894, to the California State Legislature. He represented the 43rd—or Tenderloin—district. Then became chairman of the City's Crimes and Penalties Committee. He also declared himself a staunch suffragist based—as he put it—on the number of women in his district, coupled with his desire to be re-elected.

We could delve deeper into his career and creations, but it is the cover of his first book that interests us. In particular, it is the way he uses a metal two-part cocktail shaker, holding one half above his head and letting the liquid fall into the other.

Enter the Mixologist

THERE IS NO QUESTION—unless someone finds a cocktail recipe from the late 1500s—that the shaker came before the cocktail. That is when the shaker first appeared in its basic modern form. It was called a *doppelfassbecher*: a double-barrel beaker that was used presumably for drinking toasts rather than mixing drinks. It was common in Germany during the sixteenth and seventeenth centuries, made of silver, brass, or gold. This should not be confused with the *doppelscheuer*, interlocking silver wine goblets that were made around the same time.

The *doppelfassbecher*'s design was much like the two-part shakers of today: two metal cups of almost equal size—one slightly taller than the other—included a lip that locked it into place with the other. Even the height and width was sometimes very similar to classic cocktail shakers. But this is not a coincidence.

Religious persecution, during the 1600s, drove massive German emigration to Britain. But the German-British connection went all the way to the throne.

From the 1714 coronation of Hanoverian prince George I to the present day, every king, queen, or consort has descended from or married with German ancestry. Thus, the *doppelfassbecher* made its appearance in Britain, in the late 1700s, particularly in London. Many examples made in Sheffield, a city renowned for its metalwork, can be found. And it was in Britain that the *doppelfassbecher* met the cocktail and became the cobbler mixer.

By the mid-1800s, cobbler mixers were purveyed by Farrow & Jackson Limited of London—wine and spirits merchants who also billed themselves as engineers of all sorts of bar and cellar fittings. Unlike the *doppelfassbecher*, this bar tool did not have a pattern of barrel staves etched into it. However, it still retained the horizontal bands around it that represented barrel hoops. These early cobbler mixers are the obvious missing link between modern all-metal two-part shakers and the sixteenth-century originals.

An 1856 article in the *Brooklyn Daily Eagle* gives an early glimpse of the cobbler mixer's place behind the bar:

The barkeeper and his assistants possess the agility of acrobats and the prestidigitative skill of magicians. They are all bottle conjurors.—They toss the drinks about; they throw brimful glasses over their heads; they shake the saccharine, glacial and alcoholic ingredients in their long tin tubes...

The earliest references to cocktail shakers that we have found appeared, in 1868, in two British publications. The first, from *Meliora: A Quarterly Review of Social Science*, notes that: "This endeavour to get up a system of stimulation has given rise in America to the manufacture of 'cocktail' (a compound of whiskey, brandy, or champagne, bitters, and ice), dexterously mixed in tall silver mugs made for the purpose, called 'cocktail shakers.'"

In the British periodical *Notes and Queries*, from that same year, we found the earliest description of cocktail shaker's use:

An 1882 economics lesson from Fort Wayne, Indiana: "People who contemplate indulging in the just at present expensive luxury of strawberries should remember that if you buy a cocktail at a saloon you get five strawberries with the liquor thrown in. Buy the berries by the box and you only get them at the same rate."

What is a cocktail-shaker? I never possessed a pair of "cocktail-shakers" myself, but a young officer in the Blues [the Union army during the American Civil War] a fellow-passenger in a Cunard steamer in which I crossed the Atlantic in 1865, did possess, and was very proud of, a brace of tall silver mugs in which the ingredients of the beverage known as a 'cocktail' (whiskey, brandy or champagne, bitters and ice) are mixed, shaken together, and then scientifically discharged—the "shakers" being held at arm's length, and sometimes above the operator's head—from goblet to goblet, backwards and forwards, over and over again, till the requisite perfection of homogeneousness has been attained. These are the "cocktail shakers" and our friend in the Blues was so great a proficient in the difficult art of goblet-throwing, and the compounds he made were so delicious, that ladies on board, who in the earlier stages of the voyage had been dreadfully sea-sick, were often heard to inquire, towards two PM, whether Captain—— was going to make any "cocktails" that day.

From the description, the young officer combined the ingredients, shook them in the shaker, then separated the cups and used them as throwing glasses to give the mixture a series of finishing throws. This is particularly interesting since most bartenders at that time were masters of throwing, but none was noted for shaking drinks.

A cuillère à pilon from Louis Fouquet's book, Bariana.

T HE BARSPOON appears to have evolved in apothecaries from the French *cuillère medicament* [medicine spoon] to the *cuillère à pilon* [pestle spoon] to its modern incarnation.

The glassware became more sophisticated: Tumblers and flip glasses were replaced by wine glasses and coupes. Garnishes of seasonal fruits and herbs were arranged like floral bouquets. Repertoires grew as barmen found themselves mixing for politicians, literati, financiers, artists, and actors.

A new name was coined for these creative barmen who plied their trade coast to coast and across the Atlantic: mixologist. *The Knickerbocker: New-York Monthly Magazine,* literary home to Washington Irving, Robert Louis Stevenson, and Nathaniel Hawthorne, featured in the sixth instalment of the fictional serial "The Observations of Mace Sloper" a conversation overheard in a New Jersey hotel, appearing in the July 1856 issue:

The mixologist of tipiculars directored me to apart-
ment XC, which, being exceedingly weary, I did uncan-
delized. Yet if you desire illuminosity- . . .

Mixed drinks were as much a part of daily routine as they had been in colonial times. The only difference was that public opinion was shifting. A correspondent from *The New York Times* was quoted, in 1856, in London's *Weekly Dispatch* as lamenting that:

> *Every sentence a man utters must be moistened with a julep or a cobbler. All the affairs of life are begun and ended with drinks. Is a project of any kind to be started the first word is 'Let us go to the Astor and talk it over.' So capitalists leave their quiet offices where one would suppose business would be more easily transacted and take themselves to a reeking bar, where they stupefy themselves with liquors fearfully and wonderfully made.*

Was it a lucrative business for the owners of those establishments? The correspondent further noted that: "A well-known proprietor opened an uptown hotel and bar room the other day. On the opening day he took in over $400 [USD] at the bar alone and his gross receipts on the entire establishment for the first week were $16,000 [USD]."

Across the Atlantic, three distinctive drink repertoires took shape that are the subject of our next chapter.

Cooling Cups & Dainty Drinks

THE DEVELOPMENT OF EUROPEAN COCKTAILS

AMERICA WAS NOT THE ONLY COUNTRY to experience a surge of passion for creative liquid cuisine. Cross-cultural influence increased during the nineteenth century. Sure, the British Sling became an American Cocktail with the addition of bitters when America adopted the word "cocktail" a few of decades earlier. British compounds such as a Flip and the European-born Julep also made their way into the American lexicon. But the international exchange went far afield from these obvious points.

A drink that Jerry "The Professor" Thomas claimed to have created was the Tom & Jerry. The name was not original. Those were names of the protagonists that British

TOM & JERRY

(Mixologist Audrey Saunders of New York's Pegu Club adapted this classic recipe for modern palates.)

BATTER:
12 eggs
3 tbs pure vanilla extract
60 ml Bacardi 8 rum
4 dashes Angostura Bitters
1 kg granulated sugar
1 tsp ground cinnamon
0.5 tsp ground cloves
0.75 tsp ground allspice
0.5 tsp ground nutmeg
Beat yolks separately. Add vanilla extract, rum, sugar, and spices. Beat whites until stiff. Fold into batter and refrigerate.

SERVICE:
1 gallon milk
750 ml Bacardi 8 rum
750 ml Courvoisier VSOP
Heat milk to just before boiling. Stir batter. Pour 60 ml batter into a toddy mug. Add 30 ml rum and 30 ml cognac. Fill with hot milk. Garnish with a little grated nutmeg.

sports writer Pierce Egan (1772-1849) used to satirise the raucous meanderings of rich, young Georgian bucks, who came for the season to carouse with the "sporting community" and theatre set in London. A journalist and pop culture chronicler when he himself wasn't fraternising with the sporting crowd, Egan published the monthly journal *Life in London*. His best-known story series appeared a year after he launched in 1820: *Life in London, or The Day and Night Scenes of Jerry Hawthorn Esq and his Elegant Friend Corinthian Tom*. Egan's characters Tom and Jerry became synonymous with the term "rabble-rouser". Some legends have it that to promote his popular tales, Egan devised a batter-based, hardy version of a rum-and-brandy flip called Tom & Jerry. We haven't confirmed that such was the case.

But what we do know is that Tom & Jerry was a term used to describe a low-class tavern, taken from the earlier term "Jerry shop" that predated Egan and his work. Further, Tom & Jerry was the name of a drink that made it to the American press long after William Moncreiff's stage adaptation of Egan's work, *Tom and Jerry, or Life in London*, was hit in London's West End in 1821 and on New York's Broadway, beginning in 1823.

In *The Rambler in North America : 1832-1833* it is noted that: "As to the rest, it was agreed by the majority of the good people of Tallahassee, to go drinking and stimulating with mint-julep, mint-sling, bitters, hailstone, snow-storm, apple-toddy, punch, Tom & Jerry, egg-nogg—and to remain dram drinkers and tipplers if not absolute drunkards, in spite of the machinations of the Temperance men."

And in Britain, an physician documented in the 1833 *Origins of the Cholera in Manchester* that someone "had been drinking Tom & Jerry in very large quantities . . .". A decade later, Tom & Jerry was a familiar old classic, as was noted in *The Symbol and Odd Fellows Magazine* that:

> *Time was when upon the front of the old house, just beside the inner door, for portico it boasted not, might be read upon the worn black board, in characters large as a modern theatre bill, "Flip," a long concocted beverage, whose ancient "half mugs" are fast giving place to the more refined "Tom and Jerry" . . .*

Soyer's Nectar & Other Delights

French celebrity chef Alexis Benoit Soyer revolutionized the culinary world with a health-minded redesign of the standard restaurant kitchen and opened London's first American-style restaurant bar.

LONDON'S MOST FAMOUS French chef of the period, Alexis Benoit Soyer (1810-1858), was another mixed drinks champion. At the height of his career, Soyer earned more than £1,000 per year as the Reform Club's chef: an outrageous sum of £100,000, if calculated in today's market. He created the sumptuous Reform Raclettes of Lamb still served in London's Reform Club. He designed the template for what would become the standard "modern" kitchen. He built an efficient, portable soup-kitchen that was stationed at the Royal Barracks in Dublin and fed 26,000 Irish Potato Famine victims daily. He developed commercial products such as Soyer's Sauce and Soyer's Nectar. He also created fanciful potables that

SOYER'S NECTAR COBBLER

Scrape 45 ml of crushed ice into a collins glass. Add 120 ml madeira and the contents of a bottle of Nectar over all.

NECTAR CLARET COBBLER

Is excellent after dinner, and should be made as above, only with double the quantity of claret, and one pinch of finely-grated cinnamon.

NECTAR MARASQUINO COBBLER

Proceed the same as above, only adding a 60 ml of maraschino and the same of brandy and pour the Nectar over.

Soyer's nectar bottles copied the design and shape made famous by the Schweppe Company.

may sound all too much like the 1970s through 1990s: Jelly Shots and blue drinks.

First the blue drinks. The popularity throughout Britain of Schweppe's fizzy drinks in glass bottles inspired Soyer to team up with the Carrera Water Manufactory & Company to create his own branded sparkling water, a sparkling lemonade, and a new soft drink: Soyer's Nectar. Composed of raspberry, apple, quince, and lemon juices, spiced with cinnamon, and tinted bright lake blue, the carbonated drink was a trendy hangover cure for novelty-obsessed Victorians. By 1850, *The Sun* declared it far better than Sherry Cobbler. *The Globe* recommended adding a tot of rum and dubbed Soyer the "Emperor of the Kitchen". His own advertisements suggested that "It may also be taken just previous to going to bed, with a glass of wine, such as Sherry, Madeira, etc, or of any spirit or liquor mixed in it, and drinking as much of it as possible as a draught." The same promotion included recipes for three types of Cobbler.

In his 1851 runaway best-seller, *The Modern Housewife or Ménagère*, Soyer offered up recipes for Gold Jelly, made with eau-de-vie de Danzig; a Maraschino Jelly imbued with quartered fruits; and Rum-Punch Jelly.

This concept was grabbed up by Jerry "The Professor" Thomas and was crafted into a sherbet-with-cognac and Jamaican rum #28 Punch Jelly. The American mixologist commented in his 1862 *The Bar-Tender's Guide* that: "This preparation is a very agreeable refreshment on a cold night, but should be used in moderation; the strength of the punch is so artfully concealed by its admixture with the gelatine, that many persons, particularly of the softer sex have been tempted to partake so plentifully of it as to render them somewhat unfit for waltzing or quadrilling after supper."

Author Ruth Cowen related another of Soyer's contributions to the drinks world in her 2006 biography *Relish: The Extraordinary Life of Alexis Soyer:* his introduction of an American-stye bar in the configuration of a six-star restaurant. The same year that Prince Albert opened the Great Exhibition of 1851 and its fabulous Crystal Palace in Hyde Park, Soyer opened Soyer's Universal Symposium of All Nations where the Albert Hall now stands.

Reached via a wooden staircase in the building that was once Gore House, Soyer created an experience that would be grand spectacle today. Each room was lavishly decorated: one as a Chinese boudoir, another as a grotto, another a dungeon. One room boasted a table covered by a 400-foot-long tablecloth that sat 500 people. Amongst these settings he opened The Washington Refreshment Room with a beverage menu that offered up 40 different concoctions, including Hailstorms, Mint Juleps, and Brandy Smashes plus some of Soyer's own inventions such as his Nectar Cobblers and Soyer au Champagne.

Although he had interviewed "an eccentric American genius, who declared himself perfectly capable of compounding four [cocktails] at a time, swallowing a flash of lightning, smoking a cigar, singing 'Yankee Doodle', washing up the glasses, and performing the overture to the *Huguenots* on the banjo simultaneously", he selected a West Londoner named William York to head his bar. Was that American Jerry Thomas? It's highly unlikely as he had sailed from New York for San Francisco in 1849, and did not visit London until

GIN PUNCH

(Based on Jerry Thomas's 1862 adaptation of Alexis Benoit Soyer's punch, listed as #11 Gin Punch.)

240 ml London dry gin
120 ml maraschino liqueur
juice of 2 lemons
grated peel of 1 lemon
120 ml simple syrup
240 ml sparkling water
or champagne
Add all ingredients to a punch bowl. Stir and fill with ice. Garnish with fruits of the season.

PUNCH JELLY

(Our modernized version of Punch Jelly uses Soyer's Gin Punch as its base. Thomas used Punch à la Ford.)

240 ml boiling hot water
4 envelopes powdered gelatin
or
12 leaves gelatin
Gin Punch recipe (see above)
Dissolve gelatin in hot water, stirring thoroughly. Strain into a bowl through a China cap or cheese cloth and a fine sieve. Add punch mixture and stir. Pour into a glass baking dish to about 25 mm deep. Refrigerate overnight. Cut into 25 x 25 mm squares. Serve three squares on a up-turned stemmed cocktail glass. Garnish with a thin slice of lemon.

SOYER AU CHAMPAGNE

1 tbs French vanilla ice cream
6 dashes maraschino liqueur
6 dashes orange curaçao
6 dashes brandy
Build ingredients in a champagne flute and fill with champagne. Garnish with an orange slice and a cherry.

Soyer's highly efficient camp stove was such a success at improving soldiers' diets on the battlefield, the design was adopted by the British forces and employed—unchanged—well into the 1980s.

1859 (at which point he was impressed enough with Soyer's work to include six of his recipes in his 1862 book).

The Universell Symposium closed before the year was out due to massive financial complications. It left Soyer free to join his close friend Florence Nightingale in the Crimea, where he devoted his remaining days to developing military cooking equipment designed to provide healthy, efficiently-prepared meals for the troops. His Soyer Stove was readily adapted by British military personnel around the world. The unchanged design was used during the 1982 Falkland War. You can even see a cluster of them in the Michael Caine film *Zulu*.

INFLUENCED BY THE INFLUX of so-called American concoctions by 1869, William Terrington wrote *Cooling Cups and Dainty Drinks*. With an ad for the Wenham Lake Ice Company, located on the Strand, and its ice safes printed on the back cover, the book surveyed wines, spirits, cordials, liqueurs and syrups, bitter drinks, wine cups (which included cocktails), and punches. It was a physical manifestation that American-style drinks, chilled over ice, made in-roads into London trendsetter psyches.

Felix William Spiers' and Christopher Pond's The Criterion Restaurant and Theatre, opened in 1874. Amid the opulent marble and mirror décor it sported an American bar in its prime Piccadilly Circus location.

London authors of *Drinking Cups and Their Customs* Henry Porter and George Roberts sniffed, in 1863, at the colonial intrusion into British drinking habits:

> For the 'sensation-drinks' which have lately travelled across the Atlantic we have no friendly feeling . . .we will pass the American bar . . .and express our gratification at the slight success which "Pick-me-up," "Corpse-reviver," "Chain-lightning," and the like, have had in this country.

Generally, British tastes were not attuned to the sweet offerings of the American cocktail menu nor the tooth-numbing coldness at which they were served.

Pinkers

PINK GIN was more attuned to the British palate. At 1862 Great London Exposition, locals were introduced to a cornucopia of imported inventions and advanc-

PINK GIN

2 dashes Angostura bitters
1 part London dry gin
1 part water
Coat the glass with the bitters by swirling it in the glass. Then add the gin and water.

es. Don Carlos Siegert arrived from Trinidad, exhibiting his father's digestive bitters, Amargo Aromatico, which he now called Angostura Bitters. A good marketer, the young Siegert paid close attention to all the ruckus about cocktails before unveiling his presentation: He passed out samples of bitters mixed with gin and a splash of water: a drink that legend says a Royal Navy ship's surgeon then used to combat stomach complaints and fatigue on ship crews while they were abroad. Naval officers called it "Pinkers". Londoners called it "Pink Gin".

Over the course of the next two decades, Siegert showed off his bitters in a similar manner in France (1867), Austria (1873), the United States (1876), and Australia (1879). The campaign worked.

Gimlette's Gimlet

BRITISH NAVAL OFFICERS encouraged another new taste trend, too. From the 1840s to the 1860s, if you wanted to preserve lime juice for future use, you fortified it with 15 percent rum—a semi-functional and wholly unpalatable mixture. In 1867, Lauchlin Rose of a prominent Scottish shipbuilding family from Leith, Scotland, perfected and patented a non-alcoholic preserved lime juice cordial that was considerably more attuned to British tastes.

GIMLET

1 part Rose's Lime Juice Cordial
2 parts London dry gin
Shake over ice, strain, and serve.

Luck had it that same year the Royal Navy ordered ships to carry limes instead of lemons to prevent scurvy amongst the crew. A powerful lobby by British colonial lime-growers made this happen. (Later it was discovered limes contain significantly less Vitamin C than lemons, much to the dismay of ships' surgeons and economy minded captains.) Meanwhile, it took a few years for Rose and his company to perfect the packaging: 1879 to be exact. Rose's Lime Juice Cordial is found in most Prohibition-era recipes for the Gimlet.

"But credit for mixing the first juice with gin," according to journalist Paul Clarke, "is typically given to a surgeon Sir Thomas D Gimlette, who joined the Royal Navy in 1879, and retired in 1913 as Surgeon General. Popular lore has it that Gimlette, an officer, induced his mess mates to take their anti-scorbutic by mixing it with gin, and the new concoction was named in his honour."

Another theory figures that Gimlette was concerned about officers' daily gin ration and hoped that diluting the gin with lime juice would flavourfully reduce its overall consumption. One point is certain, by 1877, Rose's Lime Juice Cordial was already available as far away as the American state of Wisconsin.

And Even More Bitter Truths

TWO SUCCESS STORIES take us back to Torino, Italy. Born in a small town in Lombardy, Gaspare Campari (1828-1882) moved to Torino at the age of 14, where he hoped to learn the art of making liqueurs. He spent a number of years working as an apprentice and then *maitre licoriste* at the then-famous Pasticceria Bass and at the opulent Ristorante del Cambio in Piazza Carignano.

TORINO-MILANO
1 part Campari
1 part Carpano Antiqua
Build ingredients in a rocks glass filled with ice. Top with soda water and garnish with a slice of lemon.

Legend has it that he tried his hand at making an American-style cocktail around 1856, adding soda water and a couple of lumps of ice to a glass of sweet vermouth. All the while Campari spent his off hours developing a bitter liqueur that combined 60 different herbs, spices, and fruits, plus a vibrant red colorant called "cochineal crimson E120."

He introduced his bitters, in 1860, into his American-style apéritif. It met with such rave reviews that Campari launched commercial production of his bitters in Milan. Two years later, Campari permanently settled in Milan and opened his own café where he served his signature drink, dubbed the Torino-Milano.

Remember the Torinese café where Carpano introduced his vermouth in 1786? That same establishment was the birthplace of another drink: Punt e Mes. The story goes that a group of stock exchange agents were taking their *aperitivo* there one day in 1870, discussing the day's business. One of them wanted vermouth with an added half measure of cinchona essence. It became another of the city's best sellers.

Les Cocktails du Paris

THE FRENCH WERE SEEMINGLY unaffected by the onslaught of the American cocktail—at least until 1862.

The improvements wrought by James Black and James Watt in the design of the steam engine meant steamships were able to cross the Atlantic much faster than sailing ships by the mid-1800s. This boosted international trade

The caption of this cartoon which appeared in an 1890 edition of the British magazine Punch reads: "The Phylloxera, a true gourmet, finds out the best vineyards and attaches itself to the best wines."

beyond anyone's wildest dreams. It also introduced invaders of the most insidious kind to new shores.

The grapevine-eating aphid, phylloxera, arrived in France in 1862. These small parasitic insects travelled on American rootstock imported via steamship by a Monsieur Borty, who installed the plants in his Rhône valley vineyards. It took less than one season for the phylloxera to inundate the valley and cross into the next and the next and the next. The grape harvests and the wine industry were decimated in less than a decade. By 1870, there were reports around the world of the decimation of French vines.

Parisian drinking customs shifted wildly as evidenced by one American visitor who was quoted in an article in *The New York Times* on 17 February 1886:

Drunkenness used not to be a French vice; but what with the destruction of the vines by phylloxera the manufacture of brandy out of beet root and potatoes, the beer devoid of malt and hops, which floods the cafes, and the drugged wine, the race is going to the dogs in the towns. The ability which makes the Frenchman a great artist, renders him unable to resist the noxious effects of alcohol on the nervous system. When the artisan earning good wages goes to dine at a gargote he begins with a nip of vermouth or absinthe, which is at once an irritant and a stimulant. Then he drinks half a litre of "manufactured" wine, in which there is not a drop of grape juice. After his coffee he takes a pousse café of beet root or potato brandy, on which he pours a chasse café, and finally a rincette. The rincette is all that remains in the carafon or brandy decanter of the liquor, which is thrown into the coffee cup to rinse out the sugar at the bottom.

Sure, Le Bar du Grand Hotel Paris near the Opéra Garnier, opened along with the hotel in 1862. But people generally drank things other than cocktails despite the lack of wine and eventually brandy.

The Miracle of Mariani

THE NEXT YEAR, French chemist Angelo Mariani (1838-1914) launched Vin Tonique Mariani, an infused Bordeaux. Not many alcoholic beverages could boast a Vatican Gold Medal. But Mariani's could. Pope Leo XIII and Pope Saint Pius X thought the elixir was a beneficial tonic for the body, brain, and nerves.

Born in Pero-Casevecchie, Corsica in 1838, Mariani became intrigued with coca leaves after moving to Paris. Paolo Mantegazza's studies of the coca plant, in 1859, intrigued him. Albert Niemann's naming and isolation of cocaine the next year fascinated him. At the youthful age of 25, Mariani capitalised on his fascination, marketing a patent medicine called Vin Tonique Mariani à la Coca de Perou in 1863.

Bordeaux wine infused with three varieties of coca leaves in the bottle, Vin Tonique Mariani was immediately applauded as a an ideal stomach stimulant, an analgesic on the air passages and vocal chords, appetite suppressant, anti-depressant, and treatment against anaemia. Two or three claret-glassfuls daily to be taken 30 minutes before or immediately after a meal was the recommended dose. Each fluid ounce contained six milligrams of the active ingredient, cocaine.

French chemist Angelo Mariani developed and manufactured a wine infusion that led to the invention of Coca-Cola.

Mariani did not stop with a simple success. From his laboratory in Neuilly-sur-Seine, he also developed Elixir Mariani, a spirits-based version with three times the active ingredient. Next, he made Pate Mariani and Pastilles Mariani, intended to strengthen the vocal chords. Gargles, sprays, and a tea infusion were next. But none of them received half the attention of Vin Tonique Mariani.

Kings and queens, popes and presidents, scientists and inventors, writers and dancers loved Vin Tonique Mariani. Testimonies filled 15 leather-bound published volumes. At one point he boasted in advertisements that he had "over 7,000 written endorsements received from eminent physicians". That number continued to rise. Before the turn

Vin Tonique Mariani was sold throughout Europe and North America to the highest, mightiest, and most influential minds at the turn of the century.

of the century, Mariani had offices at 41 Boulevard Haussmann in Paris, 83 Mortimer Street in London, and 87 St James Street in Montréal. Some historians claim that Mariani took to growing coca plants along the banks of the River Seine in Paris so he could keep up with the demand without waiting for South American shipments to arrive. And the demand was high. In Canada, Vin Mariani was even sold by the Hudson's Bay Company.

Success always invites competition. Copycat products were born: Coca des Incas and Vin des Incas were just the French competitors to Mariani's fortune.

In 1884, pharmacist John S Pemberton launched Pemberton's French Coca Wine in Atlanta, Georgia. Another overnight success would have been in the making, if it hadn't contained wine. The Klu Klux Klan forcefully lobbied for prohibition in Atlanta. The law was enacted in 1885. Pemberton was pressed to reformulate his product, replacing wine with cola extract and soda. Coca-Cola was born.

The high cocaine content of Pemberton's product as well as other American competitors forced Mariani to increase his dosage to 7.2 milligrams per ounce for US export. Mariani opened an office at 52 West 15th Street in New York to protect his interests.

The century turned and became apparent to many in Europe and the US, that cocaine addiction was a very real, very serious hazard. Coca-Cola was forced to denature its coca extract in 1904. Two years later, the Pure Food and Drug Act forced Mariani to claim there was no cocaine, only coca leaves in his product. The curtain closed on American sales of Vin Tonique Mariani with the passage of the 1914 Harrison Act that further controlled the sale of any product containing coca leaves or cocaine.

It made little difference to Angelo Mariani. To maintain his export share, he had already denatured the coca leaves' content to zero-levels of cocaine. Then, three months before the first shot was fired in the First World War, the chemist died and was buried at Père-Lachaise, taking the secret of his marvellous wine with him. His heirs carried on with the business as best they could. Removing the word "*vin*" from the name in the 1930s, they created Tonique Mariani, a pale flower against its ancestor, which remained on sale in French pharmacies until 1963. But this is just one of many points of interest in the French history of drink.

Vin Tonique Mariani had numerous rivals, from Coca des Incas to Pemberton's French Coca Wine, which eventually became Coca-Cola.

MARK TWAIN lamented in his 1869 travelogue *Innocents Abroad*, that advertising the existence of cocktails in a Parisian establishment didn't mean there would be cocktails as he knew them:

> *We ferreted out another French imposition—a frequent sign to this effect: 'ALL MANNER OF AMERICAN DRINKS ARTISTICALLY PREPARED HERE.' We procured the services of a gentleman experienced in the nomenclature of the American bar, and moved upon the works of one of these impostors. A bowing, aproned Frenchman skipped forward and said: "Que voulez les messieurs?" I do not know what "Que voulez les messieurs?" means, but such was his remark.*
>
> *Our general said, "We will take a whiskey straight."*
>
> *[A stare from the Frenchman.]*
>
> *"Well, if you don't know what that is, give us a champagne cock-tail."*
>
> *[A stare and a shrug.]*
>
> *"Well, then, give us a sherry cobbler."*
>
> *The Frenchman was checkmated. This was all Greek to him.*
>
> *"Give us a brandy smash!"*
>
> *The Frenchman began to back away, suspicious of the ominous vigour of the last order—began to back away, shrugging his shoulders and spreading his hands apologetically.*
>
> *The General followed him up and gained a complete victory. The uneducated foreigner could not even furnish a Santa Cruz Punch, an Eye-Opener, a Stone-Fence, or an Earthquake. It was plain that he was a wicked impostor.*

He must have been. A July 1851 article, translated from a French newspaper, appeared in the *New York Tribune*, stating that:

Sherry cobblers have arrived at Paris—direct from New York. In fact, they have been here long enough to be quite domesticated, and to have turned many an honest penny for the Cafe when they are exhibited.

That was more than a decade before Twain and his companions arrived in the City of Lights. By then, Rue Saint-Michel in Paris's Fifth Arrondisement was the location of two bars that were popular with Latin Quarter intelligentsia: Taverne du Pantheon and Sherry Cobbler. Odd name for a Parisian establishment? Not really.

The November 1867 issue of *Harper's New Monthly* noted that the American Restaurant at the 1867 Exposition Universelle cracked open 500 bottles of sherry in a single day and transformed them into Sherry Cobblers for one franc per serving.

Humorist Alphonse Allais (1854-1905) was devoted to the Sherry Cobbler—both to the establishment and to the drink. Well, he was devoted to cocktails in general. In his 1895 collected tales *Deux et Deux Font Cinq*, Allais employs the character of Captain Cap, whose real name Albert Caperon, as a pretext for talking about cocktails and making political states such as "bureaucracy is like germs: we do not negotiate with microbes. It kills. "

In his story "The Perfect Cocktail", Captain Cap shows how well-versed he is in the importance of quality ice in a drink:

> — *Where does this ice come from?*
> —*From the Auteuil factory, sir!*
> —*The Auteuil factory? It is perhaps wonderfully equipped to provide some scalding water to the Parisian population, but it has never known the first word about ice making. You can go tell them that from me . . .*

SHERRY COBBLER
(Use a large bar-glass.)
240 ml sherry
1 tbs superfine sugar
1 slice of orange cut up into quarters
2 small pieces pineapple
Fill the glass nearly full of shaved ice, then fill it up with sherry wine. Shake up, ornament the top with berries in season, and serve with a straw.

—But, sir!

—Besides, I know the only ice really worthy of the name is picked up the winter in the Barbotte!

—Ah!

—Yes, Barbotte! Barbotte is a small river which throws itself in Richelieu, who Richelieu throws itself into Saint-Laurent . . . And you know the name of the small city which is in the confluence of Richelieu and of Saint-Laurent?

—Don't believe I do, sir . . .

—Ah! You are not well up on your geography, you other Europeans! It is a small city which is in the confluence of Richelieu and Saint-Laurent. It is called Sorel. Do not confuse this with Sorel in Canada with the very pretty and very appealing Cecil Sorel or with Albert Sorel, a distinguished and very kind new academician! Swear be not confused!

—Really, sir!

—Then, give me your nasty Auteuil factory ice.

French wine may have run out. But fortunately, there was still a plentiful supply of Spanish sherry. (It took another decade or so for the phylloxera aphids to consume Spanish vineyards.) There were also innumerable French liqueurs and cordials with which to play.

One could always order a Pousse-Café, literally a liqueur or cordial with after-dinner coffee. But now a new form emerged that demonstrated the barman's skill at layering a drink and his ability to determine which liqueur or cordial had a lower relative density than another. Another French layered after-dinner creation, Pousse L'Amour, was equally fanciful.

An aside: Not all of Twain's experiences with European cocktails and mixed drinks were as harrowing as those he wrote about in Paris. In a 2 January 1874 letter to his wife

POUSSE CAFÉ

cognac
crème de cacao
green crème de menthe
curaçao
maraschino liqueur
Parfait Amour
raspberry syrup or grenadine
Layer ingredients one on the other in the order given in a sherry glass or a pousse-café glass.

POUSSE L'AMOUR

Put an egg yolk into a wine-glass. Half cover it with maraschino liqueur. Add a little vanilla cordial, and some brandy.

Livy while touring Britain, Twain wrote enthusiastically about a cocktail that a surgeon in Chester recommended he take "before breakfast, before dinner, and just before going to bed" made of Scotch whisky, a lemon, some crushed sugar, and Angostura Bitters. After asking Livy to procure all of the ingredients and place them in the bathroom for his return, he added: "To it I attribute the fact that up to this day my digestion has been wonderful—simply perfect."

A Temperance Breeze

THE SEEDS OF TEMPERANCE sprouted during the Nineteenth Century in response to the rapid growth and expansion of the bartending trade in both sides of the Atlantic. Commonwealth countries were the first to promote moderate consumption, not prohibition: Canada and Australia were early adaptors. Powered primarily by religious or labour groups, Britain's middle-class teetotaller movement, which began in 1832, was the only one that promoted total abstinence from alcohol. They were not endorsed by the church or labour or political groups, even after the state of Maine passed a prohibition law in 1851. Counties in the state of Georgia followed suit, in 1885, as we mentioned earlier.

Australia and Norway, Italy, plus Denmark and Poland made valiant attempts to control the amount of liquor their citizens consumed. But none of them managed to build popular support or strict enough legislation and their efforts were eventually dropped. The cocktail entered its Golden Age and no one wanted to miss out on the fun.

The United States was not the only country to attempt Prohibition, nor was it the first. Others have included:

Canada
1901 to 1948 (on Prince Edward Island; Saskatchewan 1915 to 1925; Alberta 1916 to 1924; All provinces except Quebec by 1917; Quebec 1919 to 1920)

Australia
1910 to 1928 (only in the capital, Canberra)

Russia
1914 to 1925

Iceland
1915 to 1922 ("strong" beer (over 2.25 percent) was prohibited until 1989, despite ten attempts at repeal.

Norway
1916 to 1927

Puerto Rico
1917 to 1933

Finland
1919 to 1932

US Virgin Islands
1920 to 1933 (included in the US ban)

Ironically, Germany is not on this list. Martin Luther (1483 to 1546), father of Protestantism, is also credited with launching the first modern European temperance movement. (Obviously, it failed.)

CHAPTER THIRTEEN

Enter the Golden Age

THE RISE & DEMISE OF THE COCKTAIL

GRAND STYLE, grand hotels, grand banquets, and radical artistic movements marked the 40-year period surrounding the world's entry into the twentieth century. It was, in many ways, a golden age for culture, the arts, cuisine, and cocktails. The western hemisphere enjoyed its first taste of relative peace and prosperity; capitalists and industrialists made jobs and money more available to the general populous.

Thanks to the steam engine that was inspired by whisky distillation, the late nineteenth century was highlighted by the availability of speedier, easier travel. More people were on the move than ever before.

In Britain, Isambard Kingdom Brunel set the standard for railway architecture when he designed the Great Western Railway and its two main stations: London's Paddington and Bristol's Temple Meads. For the convenience of travellers, Brunel installed bar counters, where men could stand while sipping a refreshment or nibbling a sandwich. He built the Great Western Hotel in Bristol to accommodate passengers overnight. The new railways were not his only obsession. Even before the Great Western was officially opened, Brunel designed the first large-scale transatlantic steamship, capable of crossing from port to port in 29 days.

On the Continent, the Orient Express offered travel from Paris to Istanbul without changing trains. In the United States, George Pullman offered affluent travellers a "palace car" accompanied by a dining/kitchen car, a lounge car with a bar, and a sleeper car. Fred Harvey built restaurants and hotels to serve rail passengers. He even operated the dining cars on a few rail lines.

Growing international tourism spurred the global interest in cocktails. As more information became available about American and British cocktails, regional repertoires emerged. Frank Newman's 1900 *American-Bar, Boissons Anglaise et Américaines Telles Qu'on les Prépare* and Louis Fouquet's 1896 *Bariana: Receuils Pratique de Toures Boissons Américaines et Anglaises* featured dozens of seasonal cocktails designed for French patrons—not just tourists—such as Whisky Flash (the name was very likely a typographical error in his book or taken from someone else's, as flash was frequently a misprint of the word "flask" around this time).

N° 84 WHISKY FLASH
CLEAR GLASS C
Place some small ice cubes in a silver goblet, add 1 tsp superfine bar sugar, 10 ml lemon juice, 20 ml pineapple syrup, finish with equal parts Scotch whisky and water. Shake hard, strain into a glass and serve.

While researching his translation and annotation of Fouquet's book *Mixellany's Annotated Bariana*, mixologist Charles Vexenat tested each of the French master's recipes and discovered that far from parroting American and British recipes, Fouquet chronicled the birth of a unique liquid cuisine that added touches of familiar regional ingredients to foreign concoctions. Other countries followed suit.

The 1891 International Electrotechnische Ausstellung (an electro-technical exposition) held in Frankfurt am Main sported an American-Bar Pavilion. Hamburg already had two American bars by then. Carl A Seutter's 1909 *Der Mixologist* demonstrated the way the cocktail was adopted for the German palate.

No stranger to the art of serving apéritifs, Italy embraced cocktail culture as part of its daily ritual. Venice's Royal Hotel Danieli opened an American bar by 1896, according to an anonymously published *A Summary History of the Palazzo Dandolo Now Royal Hotel Danieli* (Venice 1896):

> *Opposite the grand stairs is a luxurious smoking*
> *room, its walls hung with rich material, and furnished*
> *in Oriental comfort and style, with an American bar*
> *leading out of it.*

Opened in 1887 by Tigran Sarkies and his brothers Arshak, Aviet, and Martin, Raffles Hotel in Singapore opened with a Bar & Billiard Room, frequented by literary luminaries such as Joseph Conrad and Rudyard Kipling (later by Somerset Maugham, and Noël Coward). Due to its popularity, the bar room was expanded in 1907, giving bartender Ngiam Tong Boon a better theatre for crafting the Million Dollar Cocktail and the Singapore Sling, sometime around 1910.

An American wigwam was erected in the midst of the American Exhibition at the 1873 Weltausstellung [World's Fair] held in Vienna, Austria. With a dozen native American bartenders inside working behind three circular bars, crowds of curious Austrians were served up frosty American mixed drinks.

As one correspondent reported, "ten cobblers were drunk for every julep, cocktail, sling, smash, fix or champarello."

The straws were an especially popular novelty. The bar in the Rotunda started with a stock 300,000, but was obliged two restock two more times by the time the reporter arrived.

Ladies slipped them into their hair in place of hair pins, to be reused on any drink they might encounter later that could fit through a straw..

MILLION DOLLAR COCKTAIL

30 ml gin
1 tsp Italian vermouth
1 tsp French vermouth
120 ml fresh pineapple juice
1 dash egg white
1 dash Angostura bitters
Shake all ingredients over ice. Strain into a chilled highball glass.

SINGAPORE SLING

30 ml dry gin
15 ml cherry brandy
120 ml fresh pineapple juice
15 ml fresh lime juice
10 ml Cointreau
10 ml Bénédictine
10 ml grenadine syrup
1 dash Angostura bitters
Shake all ingredients over ice. Strain into a collins glass. Garnish with a pineapple slice and a maraschino cherry.

French chef Régis Cadier founded Grand Hôtel Stockholm, in 1874, after presiding over the Royal Palace kitchens for King Oskar I. He opened Sweden's first American bar, in 1899, when the hotel reopened after a major renovation and reconstruction.

N *Marketing the Trend*

NATURALLY, as people started moving at a faster pace, marketing-minded entrepreneurs came up with line extensions to satisfy the modern man on the go. G F Heublein and Brothers of Hartford, Connecticut capitalized on this concept, in 1892, distributing the first commercially bottled cocktails. The brand line included a Martini, Manhattan, whiskey, Holland gin, Old Tom gin, York, and vermouth, sold under the slogan: "A better cocktail at home than is served over any bar in the world".

A wonder of the modern age emerged, in 1897, thanks to foresight of a pair of clever alcohol marketers: Sir Thomas Dewar and his United States agent Frederic Glassup. The world's first moving-picture commercial "Dewar's—It's Scotch" was projected on an outdoor canvas screen erected overlooking New York's Herald Square. Directed by Eric S Porter, who also produced *The Great Train Robbery*, the 30-second silent flick was a major sensation. An article appearing in the August-September 1897 issue of *Phonoscope* magazine commented:

> *A very interesting and novel exhibition is now being given on the roof of the building at 1321 Broadway, facing Herald Square. Animated films are shown illustrating advertisements. The pictures were all by the In-*

ternational Film Co, 44 Broad Street, and attracting the attention nightly of thousands of people.

It wouldn't be the only or last time Sir Tommy made headlines with his marketing genius. The largest mechanical sign erected in pre-World War Europe advertised Dewar's Scotch, in 1911, across 68 feet of London's Thames Embankment.

High financial liquidity at the turn of the century meant more grand thinkers had more time to think, to create, and to get paid for the privilege of thinking. People with marketable ideas took the stage.

French celebrity chef Georges Auguste Escoffier took over where Alexis Benot Soyer left off, modernising the service of classic cuisine and championing the installation of an American bar at London's Savoy Hotel.

BORN NEAR VILLENEUVE-LOUBET, Georges Auguste Escoffier (1846-1935) was one of those lucky souls who was born at the right time and positioned himself in the right place. Creator of such gastronomic delights such as Tournedos Rossini and Pêche Melba, Escoffier elevated the art of cooking to a revered profession throughout Europe, adapting *haute cuisine* master Antonin Carême's recipes and presentation techniques to the "modern" kitchen.

Escoffier organized his efforts into a *brigade de cuisine* system: a hierarchy of responsibility. From bottom to top, a person could work up from *plongeur* (dishwasher) to *apprenti* (apprentice) to *commi* (junior cook) to *cuisiner* (cook) to *chef de partie* (senior cook) to *sous-chef de cuisine* (deputy kitchen chef) to *chef de cuisine* (kitchen chef). Or the person could aspire to one of many speciality categories: *saucier* (sauce maker and sauté cook), *rôtisseur* (roast cook), *poissonnier* (fish cook), *entremetier* (entrée prep), *garde manger* (pantry supervisor), *pâtissier* (pastry cook), *boucher* (butcher), *aboyeur* (announcer/expediter), or *communard* (staff cook).

He also replaced the practice of serving all courses of a meal at once (*service à la française*) with *service à la russe*, serving each course in the order printed on the menu.

After he made his reputation throughout France, Escoffier and manager César Ritz, in 1890, opened Richard D'Oyly Carte's Savoy Hotel on the Strand. (D'Oyly Carte made a fortune producing the operettas of W S Gilbert and Arthur Sullivan as well as owning the Savoy Theatre on the Strand.) When the Savoy reopened after its retrofit, in 1898, it sported an American bar with Frank Wells as its first head barman, according to former Savoy barmen Peter Dorelli and Joe Gilmore.

D'Oyly Carte also purchased Claridge's Hotel, in 1893, and commissioned the designer of Harrod's department store, C W Stephens, to rebuild the hotel from the ground up. Reopening, in 1898, it also featured an American bar in its renovation. But it also possessed a very unusual touch: a female bartender named Ada Coleman. According to historian Gary Regan, Coleman's father was a steward at the London golf club where D'Oyly Carte regularly played after he was introduced to the sport by baritone Rutland Barrington, who started in many Savoy productions.

When Ada's father passed away, a club member (possibly Richard D'Oyly Carte himself) gave the young woman a job as a bartender at Claridge's. She honed her craft there until 1903. Then, Rupert offered her the head bartender position at the Savoy. (D'Oyly Carte took over his father's seat as hotel chairman and opera company director two years earlier when the great impresario and entrepreneur passed away.)

"Coley", as she was affectionately called, served the hotel's celebrity-royalty driven roster which included Mark Twain, Prince William of Sweden, and actor-producer Sir Charles Henry Hawtrey, who named one of Coley's creations: the Hanky-Panky Cocktail.

HANKY PANKY COCKTAIL

2 dashes Fernet Branca
1 part Italian vermouth
1 part dry gin
Shake well and strain into cocktail glass. Squeeze orange peel on top.

In a 1925 edition of *The People* magazine, Coleman herself recalled:

> The late Charles Hawtrey ... was one of the best judges of cocktails that I knew. Some years ago, when he was overworking, he used to come into the bar and say, 'Coley, I am tired. Give me something with a bit of punch in it.' It was for him that I spent hours experimenting until I had invented a new cocktail. The next time he came in, I told him I had a new drink for him. He sipped it, and, draining the glass, he said, 'By Jove! That is the real hanky-panky!' And Hanky-Panky it has been called ever since.

Just as Escoffier turned the gastronomic world on its ear by streamlining *haute cuisine*, the new breed of mixologists did the same with cocktails. While Jerry Thomas devoted only ten recipes to the cocktail genre in his bartender's guide (and insisted the Crusta would gain more prominence than the cocktail in future generations) mixologists of the Golden Age expanded the simple three-to-four-ingredient shaken-or-stirred equation to dozens of creations made with different base spirits, liqueurs, cordials, fortified wines, syrups, and juices.

Streamlined cocktails made more sense as American bars filled to the brim every day with new, curious customers. Careful attention to ingredient proportions and a balance of flavours won them back as regulars more than the ability to make a flaring Blue Blazer, or a labour-intensive Shrub, Punch, Cup, or Crusta.

The Only William

NEW YORK BARTENDER William Schmidt, nicknamed "The Only William", commented in his 1892 book *The Flowing Bowl* that:

> *Mixed drinks might be compared to music: an orchestra will produce good music, provided all players are artists; but have only one or two inferior musicians in your band and you may be convinced they will spoil the entire harmony.*

The Only William receives much less attention from historians today than Jerry Thomas and Harry Johnson, yet it could be argued that he was far more famous in his lifetime than either of them.

Born in Hamburg, Germany, William gained fame there as a bartender, and would later state that it was not entirely true that the best bartenders are Americans, or that the best fancy drinks are of American origin. He was quick to point out that he mastered his craft in Hamburg. He also noted that "The finest mixed drinks and their ingredients are of foreign origin. Are not all of the superior cordials of foreign make?"

William, with his small face and giant moustache, arrived, in 1869, in Chicago. By 1873, he took charge of opening the Tivoli Garden with 16 bartenders under him. He was renowned for his acrobatic bartending feats: throwing flaming and non-flaming drinks in graceful arcs. He was even better known for his ability to create drinks that would even convert people who swore they liked nothing stronger than lemonade.

He moved to New York in 1884, where he tended bar at the Bridge Saloon. This may have been its name or simply a geographic monicker, as it was at the Manhattan end of the Brooklyn Bridge and was pulled down a few years later to make way for bridge approaches.

The "Only William" orchestrated some of new York's finest cocktails and mixed drinks with a blend of impromptu creativity and remarkable pride for the cocktail's European origins.

After 20 years behind bars in the US, Schmidt took his first holiday and returned to Hamburg, in 1889, to visit his elderly parents (who were aged 90 and 92 at the time; they passed away the following year). Upon his return to New York, he took on a business partner and opened a place on Broadway near Park Row. When his partner died shortly after, the bar was sold. He stayed on as bartender, through several years and different owners. Eventually the bar was moved to 58 Dey Street, one door west of Greenwich Street, a site that is precisely at the heart of Ground Zero today, as the buildings on that part of Dey Street were torn down to make way for the World Trade Centre.

William was renowned for creating new drinks. And at one point he was estimated to have invented a new one daily. He even created a "$5 cocktail" at a time when drink prices hovered around 15 cents. Sadly, that recipe is lost. He was credited with an encyclopedic knowledge of the classics, but he preferred talking with his customers, then inventing new drinks on the spot to suit their tastes and moods.

He authored two books: *Fancy Drinks and Popular Beverages* published by Dick & Fitzgerald (who also published Jerry Thomas' book), in 1891, and a much larger volume, *The Flowing Bowl,* published by Charles L Webster & Company the following year. Two books from different publishers in such a short time? Not exactly. *Fancy Drinks and Popular Beverages* simply contains the mixed drink chapters from *The Flowing Bowl*, which is a much larger book.

Despite packing hundreds and hundreds of recipes into his book(s), many of his drinks never made it in. These were often created when a journalist writing about drinks asked him for a classic and, without telling the writer, he created them on the spot. Drinks like the Svengali Cocktail and The Angelus made only into newsprint.

William achieved fleeting international fame. Another William—William II, the last Emperor of Germany and King of Prussia—came across a recipe by Schmidt named Hohenzollern Punch, after the Emperor's family name. Schmidt created it in honour of Prince Henry, the emperor's son, who was due to visit New York for the launch of

SVENGALI

1 part French Brandy
1 part absinthe
1 part French vermouth
2 dashes gomme syrup
Combine all ingredients in a glass with cracked ice. Stir and serve.

THE ANGELUS

30 ml Old Tom gin
2 dashes orange bitters
2 dashes curaçao
1 dash gomme syrup
1 dash absinthe
1 dash Italian vermouth
Combine all ingredients in an ice-filled mixing glass. Throw or stir. For "an appetizing" variation substitute absinthe for the Old Tom gin.

his free-spending father's new yacht. The emperor clipped a copy of the recipe from a German newspaper. He read it aloud with great amusement to guests who were enjoying digestifs in his drawing room and sent it to his son in New York after writing the words: "*Schrecklicher katzenjammer an morgen!*" ["Oh, what a headache in the morning!"] across the back.

Schmidt was unperturbed. He replied via the national newspapers that: "I will venture to say some royal bartender spoiled my decoction." Made properly, he said, "it will put music in his soul, and charm him into a state of gladness and soft hilarity." And no *katzenjammer*.

US Ambassador to Germany Andrew Dickson White said, "It was a terrific brew, which only a very tough seaman could expect to survive."

The press enjoyed bestowing other people named William with his sobriquet. Senator William Daly, of Hudson County, New York became "The Only" William when his gubernatorial campaign became too outlandish. US newspapers began referring to former Prime Minister of the United Kingdom William Gladstone as "The Only" as well.

Schmidt retired in October 1904 rather than submit to the wage cut proposed by the bar's owner. Why the owner would have pressed such an acclaimed barman out of the business might be answered in the fact that his obituary, one year later, listed his cause of death in the State Hospital on Ward's Island as senile dementia.

Another answer might be found in the changing attitudes of the time. As William said:

> *A man in my profession should never forget he is a gentleman. However well he may mix a drink, much of*

HOHENZOLLERN PUNCH

In a large bowl mix 2 parts St. Croix rum, 8 parts brandy, 10 parts Rhine wine (liebfraumilch), 10 parts Rhine wine (Ashmanhauser), 1 part curaçao, 1 part chartreuse (yellow), 2 parts sherry wine, 2 parts sauterne, 4 parts moselle, 2 parts port and 3 parts chambertin. Mix thoroughly and add some sliced fruit--to wit, pineapple, oranges and preserved cherries--and one large piece of ice. When all is ready, pour into same six bottles of extra dry champagne and serve to 25 persons. Take the white of two dozen eggs, well beaten, and put on top, with German and American flags at the sides and the name Hohenzollern in middle in all colours.

SHAMROCK PUNCH

Created for Sir Thomas Lipton, and sent to him, bottled, along with an invitation to "come and have some more" at Schmidt's bar.
1 litre Scotch Whisky
1 litre champagne
720 ml strong tea
juice of 1 lemon
225 gr sugar
60 ml maraschino
60 ml curaçao
60 ml green chartreuse
480 ml sherry
480 ml brandy
Combine all ingredients. Mix in sliced banana, pineapple and orange. Serve in small sherry glasses.

ICE TRUST COCKTAIL

(Note: crème de menthe was much drier when William invented this drink, in 1900, which is now called the Stinger.)
1 part brandy
1 part white crème de menthe
Shake well with cracked ice and strain into a cocktail glass.

BROADWAY ZEPHYR

1 part sherry
1 part rum
4 parts Rhine wine
1 tsp lemon juice
Shake well with cracked ice and strain into a cocktail glass.

WHISPER OF THE FOREST

(A ladies drink)
Place two tall mint sprigs in a tall glass. Fill with crushed ice. Add a tablespoon of fine sugar, and the juice of half a lemon. Add equal parts rum, sherry, and claret. Mix thoroughly with a long handled spoon. Slightly dampen two straws and place them against the outside of the glass allowing the capillary action to hold them in place.

"...and the concoction is served to milady on the veranda."

the flavour is lost unless he serves it with politeness. But politeness has been dying out with the coming in of the quick lunch and the quick drink. They want speed, not quality, these days. And how can a true artist put soul into his productions is no time is allowed to him?

His obituary described the experience of sitting at his bar that was clearly written by a man who had been there many times, "To watch the 'Only William' at work was an education, and to hear his commentaries on the drink in the process of formation was to excite the appetite beyond all words. His drinks were creations. In his nimble fingers and his fervid heart there dwelt the genius of one of the earth's eccentric benefactors.

"And then the next day. Where again is such a man who can be the sponsor of such a day-after feeling that William by his deftness guaranteed? Where are the 'Broadway Zephyrs,' 'Ambrosia Ambrosialized,' the 'Pleasant Surprise'? They are no more, for the 'Only William' is dead, and all Park Row mourns."

The Continuing Case of the Martini

WITHOUT QUESTION, the undisputed king of cocktails is the Martini. Clean, clear, and simple, the Martini has a life of its own. The story of its birth and its name, however, are probably the most convoluted of all drink origins.

Over a decade ago, we tried to pin down not only the Martini's creator but the truth of the drink's name. What we ended up with, at first, was a laundry list of contenders as well as competing tales of the name's provenance.

We have never been convinced that the Martinez was the Martini's parent. It was more likely a sibling. The bitters, maraschino, Italian vermouth, gomme syrup, and Old Tom Gin—a style of spirit distilled with macerated sweet botanicals—are very close to the Gin Cocktail documented by William Terrington in his 1869 *Cooling Cups and Dainty Drinks*, which used ginger syrup instead of gomme syrup. We think the Gin Cocktail was the Martini's mother. How could we say that?

Harry Johnson's 1882 Martini Cocktail (mislabelled Martine Cocktail on the accompanying illustration)

Although it was misspelled in the caption, the Martini made its appearance in recipe and drawing in Harry Johnson's landmark book.

PLATE No. 13.

Danziger Goldwasse.

Yolk of a fresh cold Egg.

Chartreuse (yellow).

GOLDEN SLIPPER.

MARTINE COCKTAIL.

Copyrighted, 1888.

KAPPELER'S MARTINI

Half a mixing glass full fine ice
1 dashes orange bitters
1 part Tom gin
1 part Italian vermouth
a piece lemon-peel.
Mix, strain into cocktail-glass. Add a maraschino cherry if desired by customer."

Who was the first person to call a Dry Martini a Dry Martini? Jaques Louis Muckensturm, author of Louis' Mixed Drinks, was born 1 May 1877 in Turckheim, Alsace, a border region renowned for its food and drink that was swapped back and forth between Germany and France in virtually every skirmish (five or six times in 133 years). He arrived in Boston in 1891, aboard the ship La Bourgogne, accompanied by his parents and siblings. He worked as a waiter and hotelkeeper, before opening his popular namesake French restaurant, Louis, at 15 Fayette Court in Boston.

follows the basic Gin Cocktail equation. So does his Marguerite Cocktail, which substitutes anisette for curaçao. In this same book, however, the Martini also experiences a transformation.

Called the Bradford à la Martini, the drink called for Tom Gin, a few dashes of orange bitters, and vermouth. Not a speck of liqueur is to be found. Instead, the recipe calls for the peel of one lemon to be placed in the mixing glass.

Similarly, in George J Kappeler's 1895 *Modern American Drinks*, the Martini calls for orange bitters, lemon peel, and equal parts Old Tom Gin and Italian vermouth.

By the late 1800s, imbibers and mixologists alike seemed to find the Martini's real bones. Dashes of additional sweetness were unnecessary to achieve balance. Gin, vermouth, and citrus notes from the orange bitters and lemon peel rang out with a clear voice. Orders became common for a Martini made with Italian vermouth, a Dry Martini made with French vermouth. Martini. Not Martinez.

There was a time when cocktailians proclaimed that the drink was named after the breech-loading, lever-actuated Martini-Henry rifle, which was placed in service by British forces in 1871 and remained until 1904. The fact is that this rifle was partly blamed for the defeat of British troops during the 1879 Anglo-Zulu War in South Africa. Although 150 British soldiers had successfully defended Rorke's Drift against thousands of Zulu warriors using the same weapon, this state-of-the-art rifle for its time frequently became non-functional in the blazingly hot African climate. Besides possessing a heavy "kick" or recoil when fired, the action tended to overheat and foul after heavy use, eventually making it difficult to move the breech block and reload the rifle. Thirteen hundred British troops were killed in Zululand because of this mechanical flaw.

We are not convinced the cocktail's name stemmed from this allusion. It still seems more likely that heavy competition in the vermouth market on American shores led to the call.

But why call it a Martini or a Bradford à la Martini? Dwell on some historical facts. Although Noilly Fils & Cie exported French vermouth to New York as early as 1844, before the company changed its name to Noilly-Prat, no one thought to call the blending of gin and Noilly vermouth a Noilly.

The exportation of Martini vermouth by the Martini, Sola & Cia to New York, beginning in 1867, seems to coincide with the emergence of the Martini. The company went nose-to-nose with Noilly-Prat to gain the American market, in 1900, when it introduced its Extra Dry Vermouth. It is very likely the Martini cocktail took its name from the brand of vermouth. This is not as romantic a story as the cocktail being born in Martinez (or created by Jerry Thomas, or being named after the Martini rifle, or created by Martini di Arma di Taggia at the Knickerbocker Hotel in New York, or at the Savoy hotel in London to cite a few of the standard tales). However, it seems the most plausible potential origin of the Martini cocktail's name. Martini advertised heavily in the United States, and even launched a campaign around 1904 reminding drinkers that a real Martini cocktail could only be made with Martini vermouth.

In the final decade of the nineteenth century there were still champions of a sweeter Martini recipe. San Francisco bartender William T ("Cocktail") Boothby put one

GIN COCKTAIL

2 parts gin,
2 parts curaçao,
1 tablespoonful of bitters,
1 part ginger syrup
8 parts of ice; mix with a spoon;
moisten the rim of the tumbler with
juice of lemon

MARTINI COCKTAIL

Fill the glass up with ice
2 dashes gum syrup
3 dashes Boker's bitters
1 dash curaçao or absinthe, if
required;
1 part old Tom gin;
1 part vermouth.
Stir up well with a spoon; strain it
into a fancy cocktail glass; put in a
cherry or a medium-sized olive, if required; and squeeze a piece of lemon
peel on top, and serve.

MARGUERITE COCKTAIL

Fill glass 3/4 full of fine-shaved ice
3 dashes orange bitters
2 dashes anisette
1 part French vermouth;
1 part Plymouth gin;
Stir up well with a spoon, strain into
a cocktail glass, putting in a cherry,
squeeze a piece of lemon peel on top
and serve.

BRADFORD À LA MARTINI

3/4 glass of fine-shaved ice
4 dashes orange bitters
peel of one lemon into mixing glass
1 part Tom gin
1 part vermouth
Shake well with a shaker, strain into
a cocktail glass, put a medium-sized
olive into it and serve.

MARGUERITE

1 dash orange bitters
1 part Plymouth gin
1 part French vermouth
Stir up well with a spoon, strain into
a cocktail glass, squeezing a piece
of lemon peel on top and serve.

N° 18 MARTINI COCKTAIL

GLASS D
4 dashes orange bitters
2 dashes absinthe
3 dashes curaçao
3 dashes crème de noyaux
30 ml gin
30 ml Italian vermouth
Mix, strain into the glass, garnish
with a lemon zest and serve.

MISS MOLLY

(The name's origin was reported
lost by 1898)
1 part Plymouth Gin
1 part French vermouth
1 dash orange bitters
Stir up well with a spoon, strain into
a cocktail glass.

in his 1891 book *Cocktail Boothby's American Bartender* (changed in title in its 1908 fourth edition to *World Drinks and How to Mix Them*) commenting that: "This popular appetizer is made without sweetening of any description, as the Old Tom Cordial gin and Italian vermouth of which it is composed are both sweet enough." (By 1930, when a revised and expanded version of his tome was published, the book listed eleven different Martini styles, ranging from non-specific to dry to medium, to sweet, to special.)

The Dry Martini rapidly gained overwhelming public approval. A Marguerite that was more streamlined than Johnson's version appeared in Thomas Stuart's 1896 book *Stuart's Fancy Drinks and How to Mix Them*, where it was featured in the "New and Up-to-Date Drinks" section:

The United States was not the only place in which the Martini made an appearance. A Parisian barman at The Criterion on Rue St-Lazare, Louis Fouquet, recorded his take on the Silver Bullet in his 1896 *Bariana* with an interesting twist:

It is pretty obvious that in the United States the popularity of this liquid equation soared sky high. Between 1900 and 1910, annual French vermouth sales tripled from 25,000 cases to 75,000 cases. Martini & Rossi responded to this lucrative market by exporting Extra Dry Vermouth.

In 1897, the Alaskan gold rush was in full swing and the Martini cocktail took on another new name as people across the States toasted the allure of easy riches. This report appeared in *The New York Journal*:

> *The Klondike cocktail has made its appearance in*
> *a dozen first class bars downtown. It is made preferably*
> *of gin, with vermouth and orange bitters—really along*

the lines of the Martini, but the "Klondike suggestion"
is given by a floating piece of lemon or orange peel cut
into a disk and just the size of a $20 gold piece.

There was even a recipe that was called Miss Molly, although, by 1898, no one could ever remember why.

So, why did the Martini start out as a sweet drink and go dry? And where did the olive come from? These were both products of the same well-documented flavour trend in the late 1800s away from sweet drinks and sweet garnishes. The cherry had once graced many Martinis, not in recipes but in every day service:

" . . .the girl was fishing in the bottom of her Mar-
tini glass for the cherry at the very minute James was
telling me how religious she was and how she sang in
a choir and all that nonsense."

(This passage from the 7 October 1906 edition of New York's *The Sun* is also the earliest reference to a Martini glass that we have found.)

Now, the olive was king, and the drinks were dry. As one bartender remarked at the time: "No one but a fool or a farmer has his drinks sweetened." However, there is one classic that never willingly welcomed an olive.

The Equally Strange Case of the Manhattan

VERMOUTH and its inclusion in mixed drinks was a result of the advancements made in transportation during the Industrial Revolution. Cheaper transatlantic travel offered Carpano, G&L Cora, the Dettone Brothers and other Sardinian companies the opportunity to display their Torino vermouths at the 1853 New York Exhibition. It also meant that more German émigrés could continue their homeland's tradition of vermouth in their new American home.

We've already explained how many American bartenders were of German descent. Aromatic bitters and American whiskeys had already established themselves from coast to coast. And preserved cherries were a traditional favourite in mixed drinks since colonial days. All of these Manhattan ingredients converged on the island with the same name in the late 1800s. But where and when?

It is possible, as William Mulhall said in his 1923 *Valentine's Manual* that: "The Manhattan cocktail was invented by a man named Black who kept a place ten doors below Houston on Broadway in the sixties…" Approximately ten doors below Houston Street, at that time, was the Metropolitan Hotel, which was built adjoining the popular watering hole, Niblo's Garden—a grand Broadway theatre and beer garden that was immortalized by poet Walt Whitman, and where P T Barnum launched his career. The site was also remembered as the 1860 home of the Japanese Embassy, in whose honour another local bartender, Jerry Thomas, created the Japanese Cocktail.

What did bars like those owned and operated by Thomas and Johnson look like on the inside? They were true spectacles: shrines to drink and art. To attract customers, the better places lined their walls with art that now hangs in some of the world's top museums. Bouguereau's *Nymphs and Satyrs* once hung among many other paintings in the Hoffman House. Its proprietor Edward Stokes paid $10,010 USD for it at the time, or roughly $250,000 USD in today's currency: a fraction of the painting's current value. Both Thomas's and Johnson's personal art collections were reputed to be massive. But we digress.

What is really more important: Where a drink was first mixed or where it secured its place in history.

The Manhattan Club opened in 1865. The club's archives remember that the drink was invented there. However, the club secretary was certain that another drink born there was the one destined for immortality: the Sam Ward (yellow chartreuse over crushed ice in a cocktail glass, rimmed with a long thin lemon twist).

What about the whole Samuel Tilden story? There are too many questionable or outright mythical elements for this tale—that young socialite Jennie Jerome created the drink to salute Tilden—to be true. On the evening of 29 December 1874, a party was held at the club for Samuel Tilden and William Wickham, then-governor of New York State and mayor of New York City, respectively. They were the Democrats' great hopefuls. Tilden was also a prominent member of the Manhattan Club.

MANHATTAN

3 parts rye or bourbon whiskey
1 part sweet vermouth
1 dash Angostura bitters
Stir with ice. Strain into chilled cocktail glass. Garnish with a cherry or lemon twist.

NOT A DROP SPILLED

An 1893 race between the waiters from the Delmonico's and Hoffman House restaurants, and those from Cafe Savarin took place in 1893, with each waiter carrying a Manhattan cocktail on a silver tray. Though only the winner got a prize, all competitors got to enjoy their cocktails after the race. But the cocktail was moving a lot faster than a sprinting waiter. By 1895, Manhattans were being served in Japan, Korea, and the Straits of Magellan.

The club's food and drink was said to rise above the finest New York restaurant of its time, Delmonico's: Save for the ice cream, which they bought directly from Delmonico's. The wine cellar was renowned. So, it would be likely that the club's bar was of the same calibre.

The night of the Tilden event, one Republican reporter raved about the food and drink. Although his exact words are lost, it is very possible he mentioned the Manhattan Cocktail. However, neither he nor anyone else who recorded the evening's events mentioned any member of the Jerome family—or for that matter any woman let alone Jenny Jerome Churchill—attending the event.

If it was born there, the Manhattan would have been created by the club's bartender. Drinks created by members were normally acknowledged. Take for example the Manhattan à la Gilbert (whiskey, French vermouth, and Amer Picon), or the previously-mentioned Sam Ward. The Manhattan could have made the club's cocktail list as early as 1865 when the club opened or any time prior to 1874.

However, if you recall the date of Angostura Bitters' arrival in New York, it would be impossible for a Manhattan made with Dr Siegert's finest to have been created until later. The club's original recipe? Equal portions whiskey and vermouth, with dashes of orange bitters. No garnish is listed. (It is interesting to note that by the turn of the century, there was a panic amongst California olive and cherry growers that garnishes were a fading fashion in New York. Bartenders were no longer automatically garnishing drinks, unless a customer asked. And the fruit growers were scrambling to reverse the trend.)

The Manhattan was first mentioned in the 3 September 1882 edition of the *Sunday Morning Herald* from Olean, New York:

> *Talking about compounders of drinks reminds me of the fact that never before has the taste for mixed drinks been so great as at present and new ideas, and new combinations are constantly being brought forward. It is but a short time ago that a mixture of whiskey, vermouth and bitters came into vogue. It went under various names—Manhattan cocktail, Turf Club cocktail, and Jockey Club cocktail. Bartenders at first were sorely puzzled what was wanted when it was demanded. But now they are fully cognizant of its various aliases.*

However, this 1887 encounter by a *London Court and Society* reporter (possibly marking its arrival across the pond) is more entertaining:

> *When you visit the [Buffalo Bill Cody] Wild West Show beware of too many cocktails. These, indeed, are not "pisen," [poison] but they are insinuating and fatal. There is one in particular which must be approached cautiously, and then only by men who have been under fire; it is called the "Manhattan Cocktail." Its component parts are, I believe, rye whiskey, vermouth, Angostura bitters, ice, lemon and crushed sugar. Probably there are several other ingredients. Those I have mentioned, however, indicate the "pisen" as one which will work almost imperceptibly on the human animal, reducing him eventually to the consistency of a pulp. In any match between a man and a Manhattan Cocktail you must recollect always that it is about ten to one on the cocktail.*

FIZZMAKER RAMOS' RECIPE

1 tbs superfine sugar
3 or 4 drops of orange flower water
juice of one-half lime
juice of one-half lemon
45 ml Old Tom gin
white of one egg
one-half glass of crushed ice
2 tbs of rich milk or cream
30 ml seltzer
Shake till milk-like in air-tight
shaker and strain.

The Shaker Boys to Mister Bullock

I
T'S TIME TO ADDRESS another portion of the cocktail story. Famed colonial American tavern-keepers Samuel Fraunces of Fraunces Tavern and Cato Alexander of Cato's Inn may have formed the vanguard of African-American involvement in the development of the American bartending industry. But little—in fact, nothing—has been narrated beyond that point.

Throughout the history of the industry there were African-American bartenders, but the story has always been skewed in favour of every other ethnicity. One of the first glimpses anyone has of African-Americans behind the bar in the nineteenth century brings us to the story of the Ramos Gin Fizz.

Author Stanley Clisby Arthur documented in his 1937 book *New Orleans Drinks and How to Mix 'Em* that Baton Rouge native Henry C Ramos invented this classic, creamy concoction that as like "drinking a flower".

Henry Charles Ramos, a first generation Louisiana native—his parents emigrated from Germany—arrived, in 1888, in New Orleans from Baton Rouge. He purchased the Imperial Cabinet Saloon at the corner of Gravier and Carondelet streets from Emile Sunier. He also bought a house on Rampart Street at the edge of the French Quarter for his growing family, and he set to work.

For The Stag, Ramos had metal business cards with calendars printed on the reverse.

"ONE AND ONLY ONE"
Ramos' Original Gin FIZZ PHIZZ

"The Stag"
H. C. RAMOS, LTD.

712-714 GRAVIER STREET New Orleans
OPPOSITE ST. CHARLES HOTEL

The saloon shared space with The Old Hickory Restaurant. (Some historians say that the invention took place at Meyer's Restaurant, but no one seems to give a location for this place.) There he remained until, in 1907, he purchased The Stag Saloon, across the street from the Gravier entrance of the St Charles Hotel. In a city where business is built on friendships and connections, it isn't too much of a surprise that he bought it from a fellow member of the Elks, Tom Anderson.

It was there that Ramos's "New Orleans Fizz" gained notoriety. Customers patiently waited up to 20 minutes to observe and savour the creations that were shaken by his army of up to 35 "shaker boys".

Henry Carl Ramos (1856/1857-1928), was photographed for Southern Buck, *the magazine of the Elks of Louisiana.*

Three years after Ramos opened this establishment, he was asked by the Louisiana Grand Commandery of the Knights Templar to supply a crew of six "shaker boys" and his recipe as representatives of the Crescent City's delegation to a Templars convention held in August 1910 at the Congress Hotel in Chicago. Just as creamy and irresistible as those found at The Stag, the drinks, their preparations and presentation made quite a spectacle. As a *Washington Post* reporter explained:

> The bartender mixes the fizz and then he hands the shaker and glass to one of the boys.
> The boy pushes the glass and shaker firmly together, starts it a-shakin' and then he leans back against the

RAMOS GIN FIZZ

1 tablespoon superfine granulated sugar
3-4 drops orange flower water
juice of a half a lime
juice of a half a lemon
45 ml dry gin
1 egg white
45 ml heavy cream
1 squirt seltzer water

Mix in a tall bar glass in the order given; add crushed ice, not too fine as lumps are needed to whip up the froth on the egg white and cream. Use a long metal shaker and remember this is one drink that needs a long, steady shaking. Keep at it until the mixture gets body -- "ropy" as some experienced barkeepers express it. When thoroughly shaken, strain into a tall thin glass for serving.

wall. Soon he is sound asleep, but the shaking goes mechanically, as regularly as the strokes of the pendulum. Sometimes when a boy goes too soundly asleep, the expert mixer takes one shaker out of his hand before he can wake up, puts a fresh one in, and there he stands, as sound asleep as he'll ever be, a-shakin' and a-shakin', while the grateful crowd on the other side of the improvised bar partakes of the product of his somnolent industry.

This description comes from an age of open prejudice, when the word "boys" did not necessary define age but ethnicity. Ramos's shaker boys were African-American. Though they were relegated to the position of bar back in this instance, bartending was one of the few industries where a black man in the United States could rise to a position nearing equality.

In his sixties when Prohibition unfolded, Ramos elected to retire. However, this was not the end of his fizz. He shared the recipe. And when he passed away, his formula appeared as a footnote to his obituary in *Time* magazine. Of course, Prohibition did not stop the fizz. It headed south of the border in the hands of former Ramos employee A N Bulliard, who opened the Cadillac Bar in Nuevo Laredo, Mexico, much to the delight of thirsty Texans on the northern banks of the Río Grande. Bulliard was joined by Pat Perry who had worked in New Orleans at the Sazerac Bar, The Stag, the Grunewald Hotel (which would later become the Roosevelt), and the St Charles Hotel bar. The former manager of Jannsen's restaurant in New Orleans also came to work there. Some of them later returned to the north side of the border, opening another Cadillac Bar in San Antonio, and both establishments are still open as of this writing.

When the United States regained its sanity with Repeal, drink historian Phil Greene tells us that the drink's popularity soared when Louisiana Senator Huey Long first re-introduced the drink in New York accompanied by bartender Sam Guarino.

"The Kingfish", as he was called, gave a press conference at the Hotel New Yorker, blasting President Franklin Delano Roosevelt's New Deal to lift America out of the Great Depression. However, the highlight of the day came when Sam demonstrated how to make a Ramos "New Orleans style".

Long's recipe, as reported by The New York Times differed slightly. "A noggin of gin, the white of one egg, two drops of orange flower water, dash of vanilla, one-half glass of milk with a little tincture of cream, pulverized sugar, a small dash of seltzer, and lots of ice. Shake well for ten minutes."

A deluge of letters to the editor and articles in the national news were quick to point out that the original recipe contained no vanilla (no one commented on Long's opinion of the President). Even Long's bartender Guarino publicly concurred. He then recommended both lemon and lime juice. Long's final word on the subject was that his recommendation for vanilla extract was only to be applied "if you couldn't get orange flower water."

"We saved the Ramos fizz for the American people during Prohibition," Long concluded. "I'm performing a public service showing you how."

Knowing a great thing when it gets publicity, The New Orleans Roosevelt Hotel not only served up the city's creamy classic, it trademarked the drink's name in 1935. The introduction of the blender in the same decade, of course, made the drink easy to produce without the employment of shaker boys. While suggesting a blender might ring of blasphemy to a purist, it makes a superb Ramos.

RAMOS'S SHAKER BOYS presented one end of the spectrum as the world entered the First World War. Heading up the bars at the prestigious Pendennis Club of Louisville, Kentucky and then the St Louis Country Club in Missouri for 25 years before he published his cocktail tome was the African-American mixologist Tom Bullock. His replete talents were famed throughout the American heartland. Former US President Theodore Roosevelt sampled Bullock's Mint Julep—Kentucky Style, in 1913. Financier and grandfather of US President George H W Bush, George Herbert Walker, scribed a glowing personal introduction to Bullock's landmark 1917 book *The Ideal Bartender*.

Tom Bullock (1873-1964) mixed drinks for American elite politicians and businessmen at the prestigious Pendennis Club just before Prohibition.

It is proper, when a person steps up to the bar, for a bartender to set before him a glass of ice water, and, then, in a courteous manner, find out what he may desire.
—Tom Bullock, *The Ideal Bartender*

Containing both virgin and spirituous recipes, Bullock's book demonstrates the artistry involved in serving the sophisticated patrons of American private clubs. This point between private valet and hotel mixologist required intuition and sensitivity to the desires of well-heeled, well-travelled, prominent pillars of society.

Take for example Bullock's presentation of both a Blackthorne Cocktail and a Blackthorne Sour, appealing to those who favoured bitters and those who preferred the trendier citrus style.

Similarly, Bullock's work experiences in Kentucky and Missouri offered him an opportunity to present a few styles of julep, including the Mint Julep and the Overall Julep.

When Prohibition was enacted two years later, Bullock fell into obscurity as did many of his contemporaries. But his dedication to his art lives on in the rediscovery of his recipes.

OBVIOUSLY the high level of professional pride demonstrated by so many of the bartenders of this era went beyond presentation. In the Golden Age, mixology was a matter of culinary creativity. Even barware got more elaborate as mixologists demanded and manufacturers answered with fancier hawthorne and julep strainers for use with two-piece shaker sets. Barspoons with longer handles that were ideal for stirring and muddling in taller mixing glasses came on the scene along with. Glassware went upscale. Stemmed cocktail glasses and cocktail coupes dominated the wine glasses and tumblers.

Although Jerry Thomas and William Terrington predicted that the Crusta would supersede the Cocktail in popularity, it faded from the menu along with the Sangaree, Cobbler, Flip, and Negus.

BLACKTHORNE COCKTAIL

Fill mixing glass 2/3 full shaved ice
1 dash lemon juice
1 tsp gomme syrup
20 ml vermouth
20 ml sloe gin
1 dash Angostura Bitters
2 dashes orange bitters
Stir; strain into cocktail glass and serve.

BLACKTHORNE SOUR

Fill large bar glass
2/3 full shaved ice
4 dashes lime or lemon juice
1 tsp pineapple syrup
2 dashes green chartreuse
45 ml sloe gin
Stir; strain into claret glass; ornament with fruit and serve.

MINT JULEP—KENTUCKY STYLE

Use a large silver mug
Dissolve one lump of sugar into
15 ml water
Fill mug with fine ice
90 ml old bourbon whiskey
Stir well; add one bouquet of mint and serve. Be careful to not bruise the mint.

OVERALL JULEP—ST. LOUIS STYLE

Use a large mixing glass;
fill with lump Ice
90 ml rye whiskey
90 ml dry gin
60 ml imported grenadine
juice of half a lemon
juice of half a lime
Shake well; pour into tall, thin glass;
add one bottle imported club soda and serve.

WHITE LADY COCKTAIL NO. 1

1 part lemon juice
1 part white crème de menthe
1 part Cointreau
Shake well and strain.

WHITE LADY COCKTAIL NO. 2

2 parts dry gin
1 part Cointreau
1 part lemon juice
Shake well and strain.

BLUE RIBBON COCKTAIL

6 parts gin
1 part white crème de menthe
1 part Cointreau
Add 6 drops of Breton cooking dye;
when shaken together, this dye gives
a nice blue colour.

Around 1900, gin and whiskey rickeys were all the rage. The trouble was, with such a sudden surge in demand for limes the few that were available toward the end of the season were expensive. Using them cut into the bars' profits. One customer watched as an uptown New York bartender appeared to use the same half lime for four rickeys. He grabbed the lime in protest and discovered it was made of India rubber. More than one bartender substituted a wave of the rubber lime and a tablespoonful of bottled lime juice for each drink late in the evening once drinkers were "bibulous" and not paying attention.

In the United States, the *National Police Gazette* ran a weekly column that featured cocktail creations from every corner of the country. Good, bad or down right horrible, a bartender could get his name, his establishment's name, and his drink recipe published alongside the latest news about pugilists, racehorses, and true crime. The publication even sponsored a mixologist's recipe competition at the turn of the century, and later issued the *National Police Gazette Bartenders Guide*.

Two Harrys & a Pete

FAST, CHEAP INTERNATIONAL TRANSPORT by the 1910s, leads us to the story of two Harrys and a guy named Pete.

A Scottish from Dundee, Harry McElhone already had a decent reputation as a mixologist when Milton Henry asked him, in 1911, to work at the opening of his new cocktail bar in Paris. A former American jockey Henry went into partnership with a Manhattan bar owner known simply as Clancy. They dismantled Clancy's bar and wood-panelled walls and transported the entire assembly to Paris. On Thanksgiving Day that year, the New York Bar opened its doors at 5 Rue Daunou in the Opèra district. The place filled with racing car enthusiasts and American tourists making grand tours of Europe. For a couple of years during the First World War, the place was managed by another former American jockey Tod Sloan. In fact, it was known for a while as Tod Sloan's Bar. Then it faltered until Henry's ex-wife Nell McGee bought the place, in 1917, at the height of American involvement in the Western Front. She hired Charlie Herrick as manager and renamed it the New York Bar. A haven for British and American troops, the joint was hopping once again.

But Harry wasn't there yet. He took a post, in 1912, behind the legendary Oak Bar at New York's sumptuous Plaza Hotel. When the First World War ended the Golden Age's decades of relative peace, Harry returned home to Britain and enlisted in the Royal Naval Air Service.

While he was at the front, a fashionable London nightspot opened in 1915: Ciro's Club on Orange Street. The venue sported Europe's fanciest sprung dance floor. At war's end, Harry became the establishment's head barman, then manager and half owner. That same year, he published *Harry's ABC of Mixing Cocktails*. Ciro's was where he created his first version of the White Lady and the Blue Ribbon Cocktail. (He revised the White Lady, in 1929, replacing crème de menthe with gin.) He stayed there for the next four years, creating the seeds of the century's most remarkable cocktail repertoire.

By 1923, McGee was tired of hosting rich kids and disillusioned ex-doughboys who hadn't gone home after the war. She offered McElhone the New York Bar. He accepted.

Novelist F Scott Fitzgerald had his first Dry Martini there along with a host of McElhone's original creations and drinks that he popularised such as the Monkey's Gland Cocktail. Composer George Gershwin put the finishing touches on his "An American in Paris Suite" on the downstairs piano. Harry played towel holder to novelist-adventurer Ernest Hemingway's boxing bouts at the Montmartre

MONKEY'S GLAND

30 ml London dry gin
30 ml fresh orange juice
2 tsp grenadine
2 tsp absinthe
Shake ingredients over ice. Strain into a cocktail glass.

Sportif in his off hours. Everybody who was anybody ended up at "Sank Roo Doe Noo."

Who's 75 Is It Anyway?

A CHAMPAGNE COCKTAIL sparkling with zesty lemon juice, dry gin, and a hint of sugar, the French 75 is one of those enigmatic drinks whose origins perplex cocktail historians. Was it invented by Harry McElhone at his New York Bar (as some people say), around the corner at Henry's Bar, or Ciro's Club in London? The answer introduces us to a number of fascinating characters and a device that single-handedly won the First World War.

Let's start with the French 75 for which the drink is named. Adopted by French military forces in March 1898, the Canon de 75 mm Modèle 1897 field gun was a quick-firing cannon with a hydro-pneumatic long recoil mechanism that kept it perfectly still during a firing sequence. It did not need to be re-aimed after each shot. So it could deliver, on target, 15 high-impact rounds per minute within a 5-mile range. That sort of reliability made it popular not only with French military personnel during the First World War, but with the American Expeditionary Forces and British anti-aircraft fighters. In 1914, a non-commissioned German officer who was a prisoner of war incarcerated at Montpellier commented: "Your batteries demolished in a few minutes entrenchments that our soldiers had spent days in constructing. The majority of the men defending them were killed, and the rest fled. With such a cannon you can go to the world's end."

The term "French 75" or "75" or "Soizante-Quinze" became synonymous with "hard-hitting". Legend has it that such was the case when a pilot in the Escardille Américaine flying unit named Raoul Lufbery poured cognac into a glass of Champagne because he wanted something with a kick to it. He christened his libation after the 75.

But wait! In Robert Vermiere's 1922 *Cocktails—How to Mix Them*, the "75" Cocktail has nothing to do with Champagne. And as Vermiere noted: "It has been called after the famous light French field gun, and was introduced by Henry of Henry's Bar fame in Paris."

Henry! You mean Harry of Harry's New York Bar, don't you? No. We mean Henry. Henry Tépé, who was a bartender at the Chatham Hotel on Rue Daunou, across the street from the New York Bar. Henry picked up stakes and opened Henry's Hotel, in 1890, taking most of his clientele with him around the corner to Rue Volney. As British writer Basil Woon recounted in 1926, "During the war Henry's was frequented by the American Ambulance unit drivers and by American aviators. It is now exclusively inhabited by persons who remember when the Eiffel Tower was only knee-high to the [Palais du] Trocadero [built for the 1878 Paris World's Fair]."

Too bad that Henry didn't stick around to see his formula gain notoriety. Before the Armistice was signed, "Henry himself had been indelicate enough to commit suicide in 1917 by jumping out of a second-story window, landing on the glass roof of the restaurant." The "75" Cocktail made its way around the corner to 5 Rue Daunou by the 1920s and into the hands of Harry McElhone, who enhanced the drink with a delicate twist—a couple of dashes of ab-

VERMIERE'S "75" COCKTAIL

Fill the shaker half full of broken ice
and add:
2 dashes of grenadine
1 tsp lemon juice
1 part calvados
2 parts London dry gin
Shake well and strain into a cocktail glass

MCELHONE'S "75" COCKTAIL

1 tsp grenadine
2 dashes absinthe or anis-del-oso
2 parts calvados
1 part gin
Shake well and strain into a cocktail glass

JUDGE JR'S THE FRENCH 75

2 parts London dry gin
1 part lemon juice
a spoonful of powdered sugar
[read: superfine sugar]
cracked ice
Fill up the rest of a tall glass with
Champagne!

sinthe. His version appears in his 1924 edition of *ABC of Mixing Cocktails*.

Hey. What happened to the Champagne? It got shipped off to the US, appearing in Judge Jr's 1927 *Here's How* as "The French '75'".

Prohibition was in full swing in the States. However, that didn't stop sippers from savouring French 75s at Sherman Billingsley's Stork Club, which first opened in 1929 at 132 West 58th Street and even had its own moonshine still. The watering hole for a bevy of American celebrities whose appearances in the club's Cub Room were chronicled by the "orchidaceous oracle of cafe society" Lucius Beebe in his nationally syndicated column "This New York". It is from his pen that a glimpse of truth falls. The "75" Cocktail and the French 75 are two animals from different continents.

As Beebe explained in his 1946 *The Stork Club Bar Book*: "In the same family as the various versions of champagne cocktail is the celebrated French 75, an elixir which, if it did not actually have its origin in the first of the German wars, at least came to the general attention of American drinkers at that time and was immediately enshrined in the pharmacopoeia of alcohol artistry in the United States upon the conclusion of hostilities in 1919."

In London's American Bar at the Savoy Hotel, American barman extraordinaire Harry Craddock added the French 75 to his 1930 *Savoy Cocktail Book* repertoire. This is not surprising: 90 percent of his clientele were American tourists, expats, and international businessmen who had no doubt sipped a few in New York.

Back in Paris, even Harry McElhone succumbed to the calls of his American regulars at "Sank Roo Doe Noo".

By the 1940s, the bar offered the French 75 instead of Henry's potent potion with a distinctive European touch of anise, following Frank Meier of the Paris Ritz Hotel who, in 1936, published a Soizante-Quinze in his book *The Artistry of Mixing Drinks.*

By the 1950s, Americans equated the French 75 with Paris as evidenced when 6,500 guests entered San Francisco's civic auditorium to celebrate its symphonic conductor Pierre Monteux's 75th birthday. The space was transformed into a gargantuan Parisian café in honour of the maestro's home land, complete with Boston Pops Orchestra conductor Arthur Fiedler directing a set of light-hearted waltzes and ditties against a backdrop of the Eiffel Tower and a springtime City of Lights. The side walk tables were overflowing with French 75s.

But enough about this sparkling beverage. Let's get back to Harry.

Buzz Buzz

ON A COLD DECEMBER EVENING IN 1924, a group of journalists were gathered around Harry's bar talking shop when a colleague strolled through the saloon doors and commented that it looked like "a fine company of international bar flies."

The phrase tickled Harry's ear. He proposed that an association be formed and the group agreed. A 100 signatures were taken by him and journalist Oscar Odd McIntyre that night. One hundred of Harry's regulars formed a "secret organization devoted to the uplift and downfall of serious drinkers."

Some legends say that before leaving Harry's that evening, journalist Carl Dennewitz, pasted dead flies on sugar cubes. Members pinned these onto their jackets before they left Harry's and headed around the corner to the Chatham Hotel, Henry's Bar, the Ritz Hotel's bar, Lew Hauser's, Freddie Payne's, and ended up at Zelli's in Pigalle.

They became known as the "Parisian Bar Flies" but they were not very good at keeping a "secret" organization secret.

O O McIntyre published in his nationally syndicated newspaper column in the United States a list of special rules. Then, he devised the bar flies' secret handshake. When two bar flies happened to meet in a bar (or somewhere else) without knowing if the other person was a real International Bar Fly, they were never to rush at each other, asking if the other was a member. First the person had to smile and walk towards the other, pretending to hold a glass of brandy in his left hand. With his right hand he had to sweep his right shoulder as if chasing a fly. If the other person was really a bar fly then he repeated the same gestures. Then both people had to imitate the buzzing of a big fat fly without forgetting to raise their right foot up 20 centimetres off the floor. Finally each had to shake the other's right hand with their fingers tucked up as if they were holding a big pint of "ginger beer" or a full glass of "White Horse" whiskey.

The rules:

Members must buy, if not at the moment, sometime.
What is a decade among friends?

Any member caught cutting out paper dolls after a bad night must hand in their resignation.

Those who come to the Trap at 5 am and are able to play a ukelele without a rehearsal are eligible for life membership.

Members bumping their chins on the bar railing the act of falling are suspended for 10 days.

Members who have the idea that they can wallop [prizefighter Jack] Dempsey are notified that there is a plastic surgeon on duty day and night close to our traps.

It is respectfully suggested to Bar Flies that they do their weeping in the toilet , and also bring their own mops.

Back slapping after six drinks should be tempered with mercy. Remember many BF's have false teeth.

Those seeing cerise cats with purple cars should keep it to themselves. Traps are not zoological gardens.

Those sniffing about "the best little woman in the world" and staying for another round must pay for it.

Remember, nothing is on the house but the roof.

A few years later, McElhone published the official Fly Traps list in *Barflies and Cocktails, 300 Recipes*, which he dedicated to McIntyre. This global drinking atlas offered thirsty travellers with cash an incredible itinerary to the world's best bars:

Fly Trap No 1: Harry's New York Bar, Paris
Adlon Hotel Bar, Berlin,
Alcazar Bar, Madrid
Ango-American Bar, Buenos Aires
Bols Stube, Cologne
Carlton Hotel Bar, St Moritz
Casino Bar, Cannes
Casino Bar, Dieppe
Celtic Bar, Dinard

Chez Victor, London
Ciro's Club, London
Club de Constantinople, Constantinople
Embassy, Riga
Embassy, La Gaue
Golden Goose Hotel, Prague
Grand Hotel Bar, Leicester
Grand Hotel Bar, Vienna
Great Eastern Hotel Bar, Calcutta
Harry's Restaurant, Deauville
Hotel Cecil Bar, London
Hotel Europaisher Hof, Dresden
Hotel Majestic Bar, Grenoble
Jungfrau Hotel, Interlaken
Karapanos Buildings, Athens
Knickerbocker Bar, Monte Carlo
Lausanne Palace Hotel Bar, Lausanne
Murray's Club, London
New York Bar, Nice
New York Bar, Zurich
Palace Hotel, Rio De Janeiro
Papeeto Tahiti, East-Indies
Plaza Hotel Bar, Rome
RMS Belgenland, round the world trip
Regina Tea Rooms, Stuttgart
Roberts Hotel Bar, Qoute
Royal Automobile Club, Sao Paolo
Royalty Bar, Bordeaux
SS Minnedosa, C.P.R.
SS Olympic, afloat at sea
Sloppy Joe's, Havana
St George Hotel Bar, Algiers,
Taj Mahal Hotel Bar, Bombay
Taverne Max, Dunkirk
The Mint Bar, Juarez, Mexico
The Scots Cote de Marioz, Aix-les-Bains

At first, the brotherhood didn't accept female members. But when they did, the brotherhood was graced with the presence of International Butterflies—as they were called—such as French film actress Michèle Morgan plus American gossip columnist and famed hostess Elsa Maxwell.

The Bloody Mary's Bloodline

THE FIGHTS ARE ENDLESS over another drink connected to The New York Bar—the Bloody Mary. Was it a hangover cure created by an American entertainer visiting in Palm Beach, Florida? Was it a final toast crafted and named in a Parisian bar? Or something else?

Our story begins with the tomato. Tomato juice in particular. It's no surprise that barman Fernand "Pete" Petiot would have heard about this phenomenon. Born on 18 February 1900 in Paris where tomatoes had been used in cooking since the 1730s, he would have been more familiar with them than the average American.

Tomato juice was on French menus and ordered as early as 1914. It was available when Petiot took a job, in 1920, at the New York Bar: three years before it became Harry McElhone's New York Bar.

Then the vodka arrived the same year. This is where the blood line fight associated with the Bloody Mary's birth begins.

Purveyor to the Romanov Tsar Alexander III, Piotr A Smirnov built a remarkably successful vodka distillery, beginning in the 1860s, which captured over half of the Moscow market within two decades. He died in 1898 and his widow passed away the following year, leaving five sons to run the enterprise. Sergei and Alexey sold their interests, in 1902, leaving Piotr, Nikolai, and Vladimir to continue operations. Piotr became the sole owner two years later when the remaining brothers released their rights and successfully managed the company until his death in 1910.

In a US court case filed in September 2000 by the Pierre Smirnoff Company of Lwów, Poland against UDV North America, it was noted that Piotr's wife Eugenia was sole inheritor of the distillery, which she managed until the 1917 October Revolution. The distillery was confiscated and placed under state control on 22 November 1917.

But Eugenia married an Italian diplomat and fled to Italy before that fateful day, in all probability knowing that the fall of the Tsarist Empire signalled personal disaster. They eventually settled in Nice, France. But she was not the only Smirnoff to emigrate to France.

Vladimir Smirnov also took flight before the Winter Palace in St Petersburg was stormed by the Bolsheviks. Revolutionary guards found him in the Ukraine and arrested him for being in cahoots with the tsarist regime and the White Army. He was sentenced to death and taken before a firing squad four times just to terrorize him. He finally escaped his captors, on 18 February 1918, with the aid of White Army forces.

This is where the facts get murky. According to his research, historian Prince Valerian Obolensky places Smirnoff in Paris a few months later, where purchased a distillery on 2 May. But as of yet we have not been able to support this claim.

Documents from the 2000 US court case state that Vladimir relocated to Constantinople, where in 1920, he established a distillery under the title "Supplier to the Imperial Russian Court, Pierre Smirnoff Sons." Considering that few aristocratic Russians settled in Turkey but many made their way to France, it would be no surprise if the enterprising Vladimir exported his product to Paris.

Moving to Lwów, in 1924, he opened another distillery. Then he opened yet another in Paris a year later under the name "Ste Pierre Smirnoff Fils" or "The Company of the Sons of Peter Smirnoff." Finally, he changed the spelling of his name from Smirnov to Smirnoff, as it was then the popularly accepted spelling in French.

Eugenia first learnt of Vladimir's use of the family name and trademarks when the Parisian distillery was opened. Naturally, she was upset that Vladimir reneged on his buy-out agreement with his late brother and consequently herself. But she could not prove her claim. The documentary proof was left behind in now-Communist-controlled Russia. Vladimir continued his operations without restraint.

WHILST SMIRNOV hawked his vodka around Paris, it was inevitable that he would walk through the saloon doors at the New York Bar where the young Fernand "Pete" Petiot worked. In a 1972 interview with *The Cleveland Press* reporter Al Thompson, Petiot explained that the first two patrons to try his creation "were from Chicago, and they say there is a bar there named the Bucket of Blood. And there is a waitress there everybody calls Bloody Mary. One of the boys said that the drink reminds him of Bloody Mary, and the name stuck."

A similar story mentioned one of the customers by name. In Petiot's obituary which appeared in a 1975 edition of the *San Francisco Chronicle,* it states that:

> *Petiot was said to have been experimenting with vodka after having been introduced to it in Paris in 1920. He settled on a mix of half vodka and half tomato juice then introduced the drink where he worked at Harry's New York Bar which was frequented by American newspaper correspondents and bankers. An American entertainer Roy Barton, provided the name, saying it reminded him of a Chicago club, the Bucket of Blood.*

Who was this entertainer named Roy Barton? He is listed as the composer of "Alabama Shuffle", "American Rag", and a few other ragtime compositions from the genre's 1920s heyday in New Orleans' infamous Storyville district. Born in the Big Easy, jazz and especially ragtime flourished amid the clubs and bars that sprung up between the licensed brothels frequented by tourists and naval personnel on leave after the district emerged in 1897. The city's leaders had studied the legalized red light districts in the European ports of Amsterdam and Hamburg to understand how to monitor and regulate prostitution, and they did so until the federal government shut down the operation in 1917, fearing that enlistees headed overseas to fight in the First World War would lose their innocence in Storyville's dens of iniquity.

MARY BY YET ANOTHER NAME...

In 1943, American newsman Walter Winchell reported that the hot weather drink was the Firecracker, made from tomato juice and gin. But this was nothing new. In 1929, O.O. McIntyre reported on a popular new drink: tomato juice and gin, which was "reputed to frustrate next morning's parade of The Brooklyn Boys over the transom".

When Storyville closed down, many jazz musicians headed north to St Louis and Chicago. Ragtime hang-outs sprung up in Chicago's most infamous vice district, the Levee, which formed in 1893 during the World Columbian Exposition and was situated on the city's Near South Side. The Bucket of Blood Saloon was one of the most famous in the Levee. Situated at 19th and Federal Street, close to the high-class brothel, the Everleigh Club, made famous in Karen Abbott's 2007 book *Sin in the Second City: Madams, Ministers, Playboys, and the Battle for America's Soul*, the club remained a haven for jazz musicians and aficionados until, in the 1920s, the neighbourhood was slowly demolished.

Certainly Barton played at the Bucket of Blood. And it wouldn't be surprising for him to have fondly remembered a young waitress who had worked there as he sat in Paris sipping a farewell toast to his past with Petiot's creation.

In O O McIntyre's 1935 obituary to Roy Barton, we finally found our answer:

> *For 12 years he had been singing, playing the piano,*
> *and passing the hat in the stuffy windowless basement*
> *of Harry's New York Bar in rue Daunou. For a time*
> *he teamed up with Tommy Lyman. And now and again*
> *he came over to the Chicago Loop where he began. But*
> *always he went back to the tin-panny life that began at*
> *midnight and ended at sun-up. His "Montmartre Rose"*
> *was dedicated to the French girl he married.*

Despite the romance surrounding its name, a future French classic doesn't easily become an international staple without help.

One rainy afternoon in a dimly-lit downtown Chicago saloon, 11 May 1886, many customers attention was caught by an elegant ivory-handled umbrella leaned against a white maple panel at the end of the bar. Umbrellas were not cheap, and this one would have been quite a prize, even among the reasonably well-dressed clientele. At least a dozen of them tried to steal it. Whenever the bartender saw another man move toward the umbrella he placed two glasses at that spot in the bar. Each customer, not wanting to be caught in the act bought themselves and the bartender a drink. And all paid. Not one of them realized until too late, the umbrella was expertly painted on the panel by one of the other bartenders there, who was apparently a very talented realist painter.

Tommy Lyman was noted for coining the phrase "torch song", in the 1920s, when he worked in vaudeville on Broadway.

A College Inn Tomato Juice Cocktail sign is prominently displayed at Harry's New York Bar.

COLLEGE INN COCKTAIL.

3 parts tomato juice
1 part sherry
1 part Lea & Perrins worcestershire
1 dash Tabasco.
Fine pick-me-up for the morning
after the night.

RED MARY

In shaker:
Ice
3 dashes lemon juice
1 dash worcestershire sauce
salt, cayenne pepper
30 ml vodka
Fill with tomato juice, Shake well
and strain in large tumbler.

T HE ESSENTIAL Bloody Mary formula—tomato juice, Worcestershire sauce, lemon juice, horseradish, Tabasco sauce, other hot sauces, salt, and pepper—had been around since the nineteenth century, but it was a virgin birth. *The Medical Record* (New York: William Wood & Company), on 12 March 1892 printed this excerpt from London's *Hospital Gazette*:

> *A Recipe Returned from Over Sea.—It is reported that at the Manhattan Club in New York a warm beverage, called an "oyster cocktail," is largely dispensed. For the benefit of those who may be possessed of suicidal intentions, I give the recipe. Seven small oysters are dropped into a tumbler, to which must be added a pinch of salt, three drops of fiery Tobasco [sic] sauce, three drops of Mexican Chili [sic] pepper sauce, and a spoonful of lemon juice. To this mixture add a little*

*horseradish and green pepper sauce, African pepper
ketchup, black pepper, and fill up with tomato juice.
This should be stirred with a spoon, very slightly crush-
ing the oysters, which are then lifted out and eaten, the
liquid following as a cocktail.*

According to the *Milwaukee Journal,* in 1892, the
recipe was slow to catch on in Britain. Due to a misunder-
standing, perhaps from the misspelling of Tabasco above,
people thought the recipe called for tobacco sauce. Tabasco,
invented in 1868, was only 24 years old at this time.

When the French Lick Springs Hotel resort in Indiana ran out of orange juice one day, in 1917, its French
chef, Louis Perrin offered guests tomato juice. It was an
immediate hit. Within three years, a handful of companies
launched into commercial production. But canned tomato
juice did not take off in the US until Chicago hotelier Ernest
Byfield tasted his first glass of tomato juice cocktail, in 1927,
while visiting the Yellow Cab Company owner, John Hertz,
at his Miami vacation home.

Heir to a handful of luxury hotels including the Ambassador East as well as the College Inn Food Products Company, Byfield put his chefs to work on developing a "spiced"
formula that included lemon juice and celery. It sold 60,000
cases in the first few months, strictly by word of mouth promotion amongst his cast of A-list friends and patrons.

It took a few years for the Bloody Mary's main ingredients and originator to meet on American soil.

Two years after Harry McElhone took ownership
of the New York Bar, Petiot moved, in 1925, to US—in the
midst of Prohibition. During a trip to Canton, Ohio, he met
his future bride and was married.

The famed mural that serves
as a backdrop of the St Regis
Hotel's King Cole Bar had been
commissioned for $5,000 USD,
in 1905, by Mary Duke Biddle's
grandfather Nicholas Biddle. It
was a gift to the hotel's original
owner John Jacob Astor IV, who
hung it at another of his properties, the Knickerbocker Hotel.
The bar beneath it was known
in the years the hotel was open,
as the King Cole Room or King
Cole Bar.

When Astor died in 1912 in the
sinking of the *Titanic,* his son Vin-
cent and the estate's trustee, Nicholas Biddle, sold the hotel to
Benjamin Duke, Mary's father.

The ingredient label on this bottle of Red Snapper reads like a very familiar regional drink from Canada:
"HIGHLY CONCENTRATED HOT RED SNAPPER
A PRODUCT OF CLAMS & TOMATOES, SPICED
DIRECTIONS–EMPTY CONTENTS INTO A TUMBLER OR MUG–ADD HOT WATER AND SERVE–THAT'S ALL."

Some sources say that Petiot then headed to the Savoy in London. But there is little evidence of this fact at time of this publication. What is known is that when the repeal bells rang out, the owner of the St Regis Hotel in New York, Mrs Mary Duke Biddle, convinced Petiot to relocate, in 1934, and take a post under the Maxfield Parrish mural that adorned the hotel's King Cole Bar, heading up a staff of 17 barmen.

The year before all of this happened, American businessman and Ukrainian emigrant Rudolph Kunett purchased the rights for commercial production in the US from Vladimir Smirnoff. With the establishment of Ste Pierre Smirnoff Fils, Inc by Kunett—along with partners Benjamin B McAlpinJr, Donald M McAlpin, and Townsend M McAlpin—vodka was available in New York just in time for Petiot's arrival.

P ETIOT'S TOMATO CREATION went on the bar menu as the Red Snapper. According to legend, somewhere between its invention and its emigration to the New York, Worcestershire sauce was added to his mix. But the drink didn't click with customers. Tomatoes grown on French soil are sweeter than their American cousins. Petiot hyped up his original recipe with salt, lemon juice, and Tabasco sauce, possibly from the old Oyster Cocktail recipe, then reinstituted Barton's name for the drink.

The common story is that the Bloody Mary name was too risqué for conservative New Yorkers, so Petiot changed the name to Red Snapper. Red Snapper? Why? Odd name, isn't it? Think again. Oyster cocktails were enormously popular in turn-of-the-century America. They were so popular that businesses on the east, west, and south coasts (New Orleans, to be precise), began producing a concentrate of clam nectar, tomato juice, and spices. Advertisements chimed: "It's red and it's hot, and it adds the right touch to meats, soups and fish."

And the name of this hot sauce? Red Snapper Sauce. One of the major producers was Red Snapper Sauce Company of Centreville, Mississippi and Nashville, Tennessee. Another producer was Charles E Erath of New Orleans. J G Fox and Company of Seattle manufactured enough of the product that an urban archaeologist reported finding more than 30 empty bottles behind an old saloon in Montana, dating to the very early 1900s. Old bottles still turn up across the United States and Canada.

There is a vague possibility that Petiot chose the name Red Snapper at random, oblivious to a very common hot sauce by the same name. But there is a much greater possibility that Petiot's Red Snapper Cocktail was made with Red Snapper Sauce. This would also make it the missing link between the Oyster Cocktail, the Bloody Mary, and the Bloody Caesar.

Incidentally, the Red Snapper Company has not been entirely lost in time. Contract lawyers learn the name in law school and commonly cite it thus:

Oysters and clams weren't the only virgin versions of the Bloody. In 1933, it was reported that juice of the Great Bahamian pink conch with spiced tomato was catching on among New York's epicures.

BLOODY MARY

6 dashes worcestershire sauce
3 dashes Tabasco
pinch of salt
pinch of pepper
juice of half lemon
60 ml vodka
Above all, do not add celery salt.
Build or shake in a large tumbler.

Bolling v. Red Snapper Sauce Co, 53 So 394, 394-95 (Miss 1910) (recognizing that where a plaintiff failed to perform because of the defendant's breach, the plaintiff could recover damages caused by the defendant's breach).

However the name came about, it didn't last as long as Bloody Mary, who finally got the attention she well deserved. She was so loved by American celebrities that one even announced that he invented it. Performer George Jessel claimed in his 1975 memoirs, *The World I Lived In*, that in 1927 he invented the Bloody Mary in Palm Beach, Florida. Never mind that Jessel was infamous for far-flung and questionable reminiscences in his two previous memoirs. Never mind that Jessel was close friends with John Martin of G F Heublein, the man who, in 1939, bought out Kunett's failing vodka company and helped invent the Moscow Mule.

As Petiot commented to columnist Geoffrey Hellman in a 1964 *The New Yorker* interview:

I initiated the Bloody Mary of today. George Jessel said he created it, but it was really nothing but vodka and tomato juice when I took it over. I cover the bottom of the shaker with four large dashes of salt, two dashes of black pepper, two dashes of cayenne pepper, and a layer of Worcestershire sauce; I then add a dash of lemon juice and some cracked ice, put in two ounces of vodka and two ounces of thick tomato juice, shake, strain, and pour. We serve a hundred to a hundred and fifty Bloody Marys a day here in the King Cole Room and in the other restaurants and the banquet rooms."

Note: Petiot does not say he took it over from Jessel. He does not say that Jessel combined the vodka and tomato juice. However, his lack of clarity here has led many people to assume he meant both and to take this utterly inconclusive statement as proof that Jessel created the drink.

So where does Harry's New York Bar play a part in all of this beyond that first moment? The drink was called the Red Mary in a 1940s edition of McElhone's *ABC of Mixing Cocktails*. Also found in that edition is the College Inn Cocktail.

Was it that McElhone was not able to sell the vodka version to patrons after Petiot left the establishment until after the Second World War? Was the reason he renamed it the Red Mary because the initial "bloody" name offended his Scottish upbringing or his British patrons who were brought up in polite society? We may never know.

What we do know is that one's of the world's most loved morning pick-me-ups has engendered as much spicy conversation and controversy over its origins and that of its bloodline as its famed crystal-clear cousin, the Martini.

But that, friends, is another story.

We'll continue Vladimir's story in the bit. Now for another Harry.

Incidentally, the celery stalk became the Bloody Mary's garnish at the Pump Room at the Ambassador East Hotel in Chicago in the 1960s according to our research. That was one of the hotels that was owned by Mr Byfield of College Inn Tomato Juice fame.

NEW YORK'S KNICKERBOCKER HOTEL at Broadway and 42nd Street quickly became the hot spot for the rich and famous when it opened in 1906. Hotel resident Enrico Caruso and capitalist heir Harry Payne Whitney paid their respects at the lavishly-carved hotel bar that was presided by few celebrity mixologists of the day: Eddie Woelke, Adam Heiselman, and Harry Craddock.

Around 1900 a number of bars "where they want all the show with little expense" had glass cherries affixed to the bottoms of the bowls of their cocktail glasses. This, of course, left customers wondering where the cherry flavour in their drinks came from.

The Knickerbocker Hotel's ornate grill room bar resided at the Cedar Tavern on University Place in New York before it disappeared to Austin, Texas.

According to Savoy legend Peter Dorelli's findings in the UKBG newsletters from the 1930s, the young Craddock worked his way from the Hollenden Hotel in Cleveland, Ohio, in 1892, to the Palmer House in Chicago the following year, before taking his post at Manhattan cocktailian hangout, Hoffman House Hotel: all before joining the esteemed staff at the Knickerbocker.

This move might be explained by the movements of another New York bartender, James B Regan. Who? Haven't heard of him? Well, he didn't write a cocktail book, which is what gave virtually every bartender remembered today his fame. But Mr Regan should not be forgotten. As a shoeless boy on the oyster banks of New Jersey, he stood with his father gazing at Manhattan. His father said to him, "I give you all of that—to make good in."

He found a bar boy job in the old Earle's Hotel on Canal Street, squeezing lemons. He became a bartender at the Hoffman House Hotel. He became part-owner of the Pabst rathskeller, which stood on 42nd Street between Broadway and Seventh Avenue (the spot where the ball drops every New Year's Eve). He made the acquaintance of so many wealthy businessmen that when he decided to open his own bar, he simply turned to his best customers to find investors. After a few successful years as proprietor of the Woodmansten Inn in the Bronx, he received an invitation to return to Manhattan. One of his customers, John Jacob Astor was opening a new hotel and proposed that he manage it. On his way to becoming a multi-millionaire himself, Regan went a step further, taking on the Knickerbocker's lease. And he brought old colleagues like Craddock to work there, which brings us back to Harry.

Harry Craddock arrived in Great Britain on 27 April 1920 in Liverpool with his wife and 16 year-old daughter, Lulu.

When Prohibition took hold, Harry was fortunate that the world had remarkably efficient transatlantic transportation systems that allowed him to take his craft elsewhere. Harry fulfilled Jerry Thomas's dream of taking Europe by the scuff and teaching its citizens how to make and consume cocktails. (Plus, he still had the patronage of people like Jimmie Regan, who left Dry America and bought himself a mansion near the American Ambassador in London.)

It was no bed of roses for Harry. There was no fanfare when he arrived in London. An editorial comment appeared in a 1920 edition of *Catering Industry Employee*:

> *THE COCKTAIL IN LONDON. It is said that the cocktail offensive in London has failed, that the Englishman still sticks to the supping of his whisky and soda, instead of dashing off the "dum-dum" of gin and vermouth. Perhaps the advance of the cocktail has been checked in London. That great American exile among potations may not yet have broken through the phlegm of the Englishman. But the check is only temporary.*

Another items appears in the same publication:

London, Aug 31—(Special Cable)—"The English-man prefers to sip his whisky and soda, not to toss it off quickly. For that reason he does not take to cocktails." So said Harry Craddock, late of New York, now of London, who, last night, issued an official statement admitting defeat in his drive to substitute cocktails for the English drink. He had 200 cocktails on his wine list, but most of his patrons are Americans.

This didn't stop Craddock from campaigning for the cocktail's honour and, in 1923, he replaced the famed Ada Coleman at the Savoy. A 20 March 1923 notice on the *International News Service* read: "The cocktail season is about to open and Harry Craddock the 'cocktail king' has gone into training." The item went on to say that Craddock boasted of mixing at least 100,000 cocktails for the Savoy's American guests and a few thousand more for "visitors of other nationalities." Apparently, Craddock went into training at least two weeks before the season, working out at the gym for three hours in the morning and three hours in the afternoon just so he could be in peak condition.

He wasn't the only one taking exercise. The next year, it was noted that:

The new Lord Mayor of London is undergoing a tremendous ordeal. For the first eight weeks of his administration there is not a single day on which he has neither a banquet or a luncheon engagement. To offset this his physicians have ordered that he shall exercise daily . . . Although the Lord Mayor is himself a wine merchant, occasionally on his daily walk he slips into the Thames Embankment entrance of the Savoy to sample one of Harry Craddock's American cocktails.

We'll pick up the story of this Harry, as well, in the next chapter. But first, we should delve into the dark side of the cocktail's Golden Age.

CHAPTER FOURTEEN

The Great Experiment

A GOOD IDEA GOES FROM BAD TO WORSE

W E TALKED EARLIER about how the 1862 phylloxera plague devastated the French and Spanish wine industries by 1890, increasing spirits consumption throughout Europe. Absinthe was the most prevalent and popular spirit in France and Switzerland. But temperance groups and wine makers' associations spun a negative publicity campaign once the production numbers for spirits ran into the millions of litres. It started with absinthe being baselessly pilloried in the press as the cause of epilepsy and tuberculosis. It ended with a public outcry that absinthe was the sole reason for violent crime and social

The Dreyfus Affair, as it will always be remembered, was a shocking public scene of anti-semitism in 19th century France. Alfred Dreyfus. The attacks on absinthe, primarily produced by French and Swiss jews, were no less subtle.

unrest. Two incidents fuelled the fire: the anti-Semitic movement highlighted by the Dreyfus Affair and the so-called "Absinthe Murders."

Phylloxera was not the sole reason for the rise in absinthe consumption. In the same way the Royal Navy aided the popularity of rum and gin amongst the British public, French military fresh from the war with Algeria, during the 1840s, did the same for absinthe. The spirit was issued to troops as an anti-malarial. On their return, soldiers and officers brought the taste for this bitter anise-based spirit home with them. As wine supplies diminished and the call for cocktails rose, in the 1860s, absinthe consumption grew exponentially amongst the bourgeoisie, the avant-garde, and the working class. The 5 PM apéritif ritual became known as *l'heure verte* [the green hour].

A French-Jewish artillery officer was accused of treason at the height of absinthe's popularity. Alfred Dreyfus (1859-1935) was a victim of anti-Semitic sentiments from the time he entered l'École Supérieure de Guerre in 1892, until his release from prison seven years later.

Born in German-held Alsace, Dreyfus made it to the rank of captain in the 32nd Cavalry Regiment prior to his entry into officers' school, the final step to a post in the army's General Staff headquarters. Because of his Alsatian background, Dreyfus was automatically suspected of treason when highly-sensitive artillery information fell into the hands of the Germans. It did not help that Christian chauvinism and anti-Semitism were rampant amongst high-station military officials. Dreyfus was secretly court martialed, in 1895, stripped of his rank, and sentenced to life imprisonment on Devil's Island off the coast of French Guiana.

When the real traitor was discovered—a year later— the incident was covered up by officials. The chief of military intelligence, who disclosed the truth, was exiled to an outpost in the southern Tunisian desert.

The information somehow leaked to the press. Author Émile Zola revealed the incident on 13 January 1898 in the literary newspaper *L'Aurore*. His an open letter to Président de la République Félix Faure titled "J'Accuse" eventually led to Dreyfus' full pardon by then-president Émile Loubet on 19 September 1899.

But the seeds of anti-Semitism continued to be stoked by Dreyfus' detractors. *La Libre Parole* editor Edouard Drumont—having lost his side in the campaign for Dreyfus's release—pounced on the absinthe industry. He called the spirit a "tool of the Jews". Many of the larger absinthe producers—particularly Pernod Fils, which was then owned by the Veil-Picard family—were Jewish. Montmartre was aflame with effigies of Dreyfus being burnt in the streets. All Jews were blamed for turning good Christian wine drinkers into hallucinating, violent alcoholics.

Drumont happily reported the news that God smote the evil Jewish spirits maker on 11 August 1901: the Pernod distillery in Pontarlier went up in smoke. Lightning struck the distillery and the ensuing fire was fuelled by hundreds of thousands of litres of absinthe. Four days later, the flames were extinguished. It took another year before the Pernod distillery was back in operation.

Thujone, the allegedly psychoactive ingredient in absinthe (many tests have disproven this) appears in vintage bottles and classic preparations of the drink at much lower levels than previously thought. Under current European Union regulations, food products containing sage (such as sausages) may contain up to five times more thujone than distilled spirits. This makes sense as sage naturally contains much more thujone. Ironically, thujone levels may be even higher in alcohol-based bitters. Where does absinthe's effect come from? The high alcohol content. Drink it responsibly.

Anti-absinthe propaganda, such as this newspaper illustration, followed Switzerland's two absinthe murders and fuelled negative public opinion of the "Green Fairy".

Despite the anti-absinthe outcry and eventual ban, French and Swiss *Les Fées Jaunes* [Yellow Fairies] were unaffected by worldwide legislation. Amer Picon, Salers, Amer Besset, Secrestat and other gentian-based digestifs continue production unto this day.

In fact, the Cercle Européen d'Étude des Gentianacées, formed in Lausanne in 1993, continues to promote the healthful benefits of yellow gentian.

If you wonder what yellow gentian tastes like, drink a bottle of Moxie soda, a specialty soft drink manufactured in the US.

A pair of murders, in 1905, gave the anti-absinthe movement the final ammunition it needed. A French farm worker living in Switzerland named Jean Lanfray shot his pregnant wife and two children. He then attempted suicide. Authorities and the press blame the horrific incident on Lanfray's absinthe consumption.

Never mind that the man had two absinthes in the morning, a crème de menthe and cognac before work, at least six glasses of strong wine at lunch, a glass of wine at tea, coffee with brandy after work, a litre of wine at dinner, and then coffee with home-made brandy before he went off his head. The press named it the "Absinthe Murder".

The same year, a man in Geneva named Sallaz went on an absinthe binge, shot his wife and hacked her to pieces. Two murders in a single year sparked sensationalist press reports and massive public outcry.

The next year, the governments of Belgium and Brazil banned the "Green Fairy", followed by Switzerland (1907), and the Netherlands (1909). At the height of its popularity in 1910, *Pharmacotheon* reported that absinthe producers made and sold a record 36 million litres. The recovering wine growers barely vinified four figures worth.

Then the bombshell hit. The United States Congress voted to ban absinthe in 1912. Finally France renounced the spirit, just as the world entered the First World War.

Pernod moved its operations to Catalonia, Spain, where the spirit was still legal. Other absinthe producers, both public and private, reformulated their products without wormwood and lowered the alcohol content per a government law issued in 1922. Pastis became the replacement libation. But it took another ten years before it even remotely achieved the popularity that was absinthe's.

Mixologists adjusted dozens of recipes that included absinthe: some opted to omit the anise flavour altogether; others substituted anisette, Spanish absente, or French pastis.

Prohibition, American Style

EVER SINCE THE PILGRIMS landed in Massachusetts and the Jamestown Colony was established in Virginia, there was some talk about controlling the drinking habits of American colonists. Using religious or medical platitudes, most people who lobbied for moderation were turned down or fobbed off with half-hearted legislative lip service. Political infighting led to the dissolution of most American temperance societies by the 1820s.

Two decades later, religious fervour re-penetrated a portion of the American psyche. Protestant churches promoted temperance, publishing over a dozen journals denouncing alcohol. The American Temperance Society blossomed, soon boasting over a million god-fearing members amongst its local chapters nationwide. The powerful Anti-Saloon League arose, using the Lord's will as its rallying cry. As far as these groups were concerned, temperance was the sole cause of poverty, domestic violence, crime, and other social ills of their growing society. Temperance was also a ready vehicle for platform for launching a women's rights campaign.

The American Civil War (1860-1864) put a damper on the subject until 1873, when the Women's Christian Temperance Union was formed. Determined to promote the prohibition of alcohol and "kindred narcotics", National Superintendent Mary Hunt used legislation and education as her weapons. She taught the evils of alcohol in schools and colleges via the organization's Department of Scientific Temperance Instruction. Hunt managed to convince nearly every state in the union to initiate anti-alcohol education in schools by the end of the century.

Most temperance supporters took a civilized stance much like William and Catherine Booth's Salvation Army. When it was first organized as the East London Christian Mission, in 1865, converted British alcoholics, drug addicts, prostitutes, and petty criminals into clean-lived, Christian citizens, employing a quasi-military infrastructure. Because their son Bramwell objected to being called a "volunteer" and stoutly proclaimed that he was a "regular" soldier or nothing, in 1868, the Booths renamed the organisation the Salvation Army. It didn't take long for the London-based Salvationists to establish missions elsewhere. By 1880, "armies" were formed in Ireland, Australia, and the United States.

Back at home, opposition rose in the form of the Skeleton Army: a group of angered publicans who had lost considerable business since the Booth's began their mission. The Skeletonists disrupted Salvation Army meetings by throwing rocks, bones, rats, and tar at Salvationists or assaulting them on the streets.

PROHIBITION APPROACHED

Boston:
Signs in local barrooms read "We took the country from the Indians. They can have it back in July."

Chicago:
Bartender William E. Dorman on his plans, "I may sell mules; I gotta be in some business with a kick in it."

New York:
Unscrupulous dealers estimate their Champagne stocks will be worth $100 a quart before June 30.

Then there were followers of the American radical Carrie Nation (1846-1911), who was arrested more than 30 times between 1900 and 1910. What for? Nation would march into a watering hole with a team of women who sang and prayed while she smashed bottles and bar fixtures with a hatchet. The substantially built, six-foot-tall Nation once described herself as "a bulldog running along at the feet of Jesus, barking at what he doesn't like."

Divorced from Dr Charles Gloyd, a severe alcoholic, shortly before the birth of their daughter Charlien, Nation often attributed her passionate prohibitionists sentiments to her failed marriage. Her second marriage, to Dr David A Nation fared far better. Whilst preaching at a Christian church in Medicine Lodge, Kansas, Carrie operated a successful hotel and established a local branch of the Women's Christian Temperance Union.

Carrie claimed God spoke to her in a vision in June 1900. Responding to this epiphany, Nation gathered several "smashers" [rocks], headed to Dobson's Saloon and announced: "Men, I have come to save you from a drunkard's fate." She decimated the saloon's entire stock with her arsenal. She proceeded to repeat her performance at two water-

Carrie Nation, "the Saloon Breaker" led a violent opposition to saloons, smashing them while a group of women stood behind her singing hymns. After one such raid in Wichita, her husband suggested that she could do more damage if she used a hatchet. Thus, it became her symbol.

A former professional baseball player, Billy Sunday became an influential evangelical Christian. He supported Prohibition and is credited with helping to pass the 18th Ammendment.

ing holes in Kiowa, Kansas, wielding a hatchet. Then she performed "hachetations" throughout Missouri.

She collapsed during a speech, on 9 June 1911, died, and was buried in an unmarked grave in Belton, Missouri. The Women's Christian Temperance Union later erected a tombstone with her epitaph, reading: "Faithful to the Cause of Prohibition, She Hath Done What She Could."

The equally-radical second Klu Klux Klan of Georgia defended the state's absolute prohibition laws which were enacted in 1915: three decades after Atlanta imposed the prohibition that changed Pemberton's Coca Wine to Coca Cola.

Activist Billy Sunday (1862-1935) was a light-drinking, all-American professional ballplayer who found religion and transformed himself, during the 1880s, into a Bible-thumping evangelist. A charismatic speaker, Sunday's "fire and brimstone" sermons converted much of America's heartland to his fundamentalist approach. He also convinced many of his flock to support prohibition as a way to eradicate the slums, and "turn prisons into factories, and jails into storehouses".

In one of his more extravagant displays, Sunday staged a mock funeral for "John Barleycorn": the British and Scottish personification of the barley crop as well as the beer and whisky made from it. The funeral was held in Norfolk,

Virginia on the day Prohibition was enacted. Sunday gave the 20-foot coffin a proper send-off with 10,000 followers chanting: "Good-bye John. You were God's worst enemy. You were Hell's best friend."

The Bells Rang Out

ON 15 JANUARY 1919, 12:40 PM the people of Boston found out that molasses moves 60 kilometres per hour. The temperature that day had skyrocketed from 2 degrees Fahrenheit to 43 degrees Fahrenheit. At the United States Industrial Alcohol Company's yard, a 90-foot-wide cast iron tank filled with crude molasses awaiting transfer to the Purity Distilling Company on Willow Street ruptured, spilling its contents down Commercial Street. A 5-metre-tall tsunami of 9.5 million litres of molasses slammed through the elevated railway's Atlantic Avenue

Boston was flooded with molasses when a 2.5 million gallon tank waiting to be made into rum or industrial alcohol burst no an unseasonably warm January day in 1919.

station, breaking the girders and lifting a train off the track. The North End pier was shoved into the harbour by the force of the wave. North End Park became a lake of molasses. Twenty-one people and a dozen horses were asphyxiated. One hundred and fifty people were injured by the fast moving wall of ooze.

Known as the Boston Molasses Disaster or the Great Molasses Flood, the incident marked the end of the world's largest rum producing region: America's Northeastern seaboard.

The next day, church bells rang across the city not for the dead but to celebrate Nebraska's ratification of the Volstead Act, the 18th Amendment to the Constitution.

With the end of the First World War, sights turned homeward to Prohibition and women's suffrage as key issues in the United States Congress. President Woodrow Wilson opposed Prohibition. But both houses fell to the pressure of women's rights lobbyists. The following year was not only a presidential campaign year, but the ratification of the 19th Amendment by Tennessee. The bill was enacted just in time to kick Wilson out of the White House that November.

When Prohibition went into effect, on 16 January 1920, it wasn't as if Americans were oblivious to the fact popular vices were tagged for elimination. The saloons, music clubs, and brothels of San Francisco's Barbary Coast and New Orleans's Storyville were shut down in 1917 by municipal vice squads in an attempt to clean up their notorious images.

The Volstead Act didn't altogether ban alcohol or stop citizens from drinking it. The bill only prohibited the commercial importation and sale of alcoholic beverages for

In the days leading up to Prohibition, the temperance movement had a powerful tool: public image. They had successfully painted all drinkers as drunks and spouse abusers, and no politician wanted to be caught in the public eye supporting tolerance. This trickled down through the public consciousness. So, when it came to naming the Central Park Camels in New York (yes, the Central Park Zoo once had a bunch of camels), these symbols of the Temperance movement received appropriate names. One pair of camels was named Mr and Mrs. Prohibition. Another pair were Mr and Mrs. Volstead.

By the early 1920s, the shine had worn off the Great Experiment. While people continued to hide their bottles, they stopped hiding their feelings. In 1923, the Volsteads had a baby camel, and the news announced it had been named Hooch. In 1926, the Prohibitions welcomed their own baby, Bootlegger.

recreational consumption. Possessing and consuming liquor on private property was not illegal. Well-off Americans stockpiled private cellars of wines and spirits, both domestic and imported, in their homes and at their private clubs prior to enactment.

Some gentlemen savoured their libations mixed by bartenders who managed to secure employment at elite university clubs, country clubs, hunting clubs. Others enjoyed their cocktails at home, including United States President Warren G Harding, who kept a supply of booze in the White House during his administration.

For those who wanted a good night out, a drink could be procured at a local "speakeasy." The Lounge Era was born, in 1923, when speakeasies opened in nearly every American city, town, and rural village. But the term was born long before Prohibition.

People automatically associate speakeasies with Prohibition. The truth is, they were around for decades beforehand. The term "speakeasy" entered the American vocabulary in the late 1880s, in Pennsylvania:

> In Pittsburgh they call a place where liquor is sold without a license a "speak easy". (From an Ohio newspaper, in June 1889)

Why "speak easy"? As it was explained at the time:

> The term "speak easy," applied to a drinking-place without a license, has become popularized in Philadelphia. The Quaker City is such a quiet town that the habitués of such places have to speak easy to escape the notice of the police.

JAKE LEG

The saddest tale of Prohibition was the Jamacian Ginger incident. As many as 100,000 people drank Jamaican Ginger Extract contaminated with TOCP, a neurotoxin. Many of these poor, immigrant, and African American citizens suffered permanent paralysis, starting their feet. Because of the population it affected it received minimal attention except to inspire a series of blues songs.

Why was there a need to speak easy back then? Because of a term that was much more prevalent at that time: the "high license", which emerged around 1874.

At a time when Prohibition was being debated in town meetings across the nation, an alternate limit to alcohol sales was rapidly gaining ground. Liquor dealers were being pressed by new laws to find other lines of work or pay an exorbitant tax, around $500-1,000 USD (roughly $12,000-24,000 USD in today's currency). The high tax on liquor dealers was also supposed to reduce the taxes of working class families so it was easy to gain popular support among voters—at first.

However, rampant smuggling and unlicensed sales quickly defeated the high license, moving the nation inexorably toward prohibition 30 years later.

Where did the term "speakeasy" originate? A parable had run on and off in newspapers across the nation for at least 20 years about a father speaking crossly to his young son, and the son replying with a tearful entreaty, "Speak easy, Father." It went on to encourage all family members to "speak easy" to create a spirit of harmony in the household. So, the term had already been pressed into the minds of the masses for a few decades before it found a usage those masses would readily adopt.

In this parable, "speak easy" did not mean using a password. It meant keeping a civil and polite tongue. The term, used in this context appeared outside this parable as well. A number of writers, critical of Americans avoiding conflict at all costs and steering clear of any difference of opinion to keep peace, said America was in danger of turn-

According to John W. Fonner, a government chemist during Prohibition, the best moonshine came from around Peoria, Illinois. By 1922, he had already analyzed nearly 26,000 samples of "white mule" from around the nation. Fonner speculated that the high quality came from the talent pool there of out of work distillers from all the big distilleries. Unfortunately, his reports did not include tasting notes.

ing into "a giant speakeasy through the opposition of some people to conversation".

Thus, at a time when drinking was negatively associated with boisterous behaviour and crime, "speakeasy" was also a lesson in polite and responsible drinking.

Words that would be proven beyond dispute decades later, appeared in New York's *The World*, in 1895:

> *The "speak-easy" has always been the result whenever Prohibition has been attempted…If we had no intolerant crusade, we would have no "speak-easies".*

New York City alone reputedly sported over 10,000 of these hidden watering holes by the late 1920s. The city's 21 Club was one of the first.

Originally named the Red Head, the speakeasy was opened in Greenwich Village, in 1922, by cousins Jack Kreindler, a Fordham University pharmacy student, and Charlie Berns, a New York University School of Commerce student. All they wanted to do was earn enough money to pay their tuitions. Their cashier was future writer-producer Mark Hellinger.

The venue was moved three years later to a basement at 88 Washington Place and was renamed the Fronton. The building was condemned to make way for a subway. So the cousins moved the following year to West 49th Street. To confuse officials, a name change to Puncheon Club was amended with alternate names including The Puncheon Grotto, 42, 42 Club, Jack and Charlie's, plus the name they used whenever they got raided—Keyburn Club.

The building of Rockefeller Centre, in 1929, forced the venue's final move to 21 West 52nd Street: from that

The "21" Club was raided many times, but they were never caught with the goods. On a signal from the doorman, the bartender could pull a series of levers that tilted the bar shelves, sending the liquor down chutes and into the sewer.

When David Embury wrote *The Fine Art of Mixing Drinks* in 1948, he created arguably one of the most opinionated, radical and important cocktail books ever written. He was so happy with his new work he brought a copy into his favorite bar, the 21 Club, and showed it off to the bartenders. This set one of them, an old union bartender, grumbling behind the scenes that if some lawyer could write a book on cocktails he could write a much better one. Thus, a couple years later, Jack Townsend came out with his distinctly more opinionated tome, *The Bartenders Book*, which sadly saw a single printing before fading away. This story would have been lost as well if not for a young bartender at the '21', Brian Rea, who related it to us a few years ago.

WHISKEY PRESCRIPTION

Prescriptions such as this were only valid for seven days by federal law. Thus, millions of them were issued to treat every imaginable illness, from indigestion to nervous tension to catarrh and the vapours. Not all prescriptions were for whiskey either. One collector even found a prescription for Champagne.

point the place was known as Jack and Charlie's "21". One raid on the speakeasy turned up the cream of the city's political, social, and business elite. City officials were forced to reconsider who, how, and where they launched their raids. Not just there either. Everywhere in the five boroughs. You never could tell who would be sipping a few in Harlem and listening to Billie Holiday at Jerry's Log Cabin, Louis Armstrong at the Savoy Ballroom or the Cat's Corner. Who knew which City Hall bigwig was hiding out at Chumley's on Bedford Street?

Less well-heeled imbibers obtained federally-controlled prescriptions. A shot of whiskey (frequently prescribed as "*spiritus frumenti*") once or twice or thrice a day was what most physicians ordered for their patients. The booze was purchased at the local pharmacy: over a million gallons were sold that way.

The United States government also permitted individuals to produce small amounts of wine and hard cider for home consumption. A few former breweries sold malt extract syrup for baking and "beverage" purposes in malt-and-hop stores. The "wet" religions (Roman Catholic, Eastern Orthodox, and Episcopalian) purchased communion wine from government warehouses.

When private stocks depleted—and repeal was still not in sight—some intrepid souls smuggled whiskey from Canada and rum from the Caribbean by boat. Organised crime quickly capitalised on this venture. The trade in bootleg booze made Al Capone, Bugsy Moran, and their colleagues rich within a decade.

More daring types distilled grain alcohol in jerry-rigged stills crafted from copper pots, automobile radiators, and any other piece of metal that held steam long enough to cool it back into liquid. To say the least, the results of these experiments were well below par in quality. Amateur distillers didn't care if the lethal methanol was removed from the ethanol. They cared less if feints commingled with alcohol. They blended their base spirit in the bathtub, adding rum, brandy, whiskey, or gin "cake flavourings" found in the baking goods section at the local grocery store. Hence, the phrase "bathtub gin" was born.

Did customers care? Nope. A guy with a homemade still was an unsung hero in rural areas, just like his colonial ancestors who rebelled against the 1791 Whiskey Tax. Customers and mixologists in private employ resorted to covering up any off tastes in their liquor with additional sweeteners, pungent garnishes, syrups, and fruit juices. They gave the new concoctions cute names like Fluffy Ruffles and Between the Sheets.

BETWEEN THE SHEETS
2 parts brandy
2 parts light rum
2 parts Cointreau
1 part lemon juice
Shake with ice. Strain into a cocktail glass. Garnish with a lemon twist.

With post-war peace came a boom economy bloated by a bullish stock market. Investors played the options game, paying only a small percentage of a share price and praying the stock would rise in value before the balance was due. Those who played the game immediately after the First World War had money to blow on a good time. Some even invested on the future. A handful of forward-thinking American and Canadian businessmen formed a securities trust in 1925: They sunk their money into foreign distilleries, betting that share prices would skyrocket with Prohibition's repeal.

Home bars became part of the standard living ensemble. Sideboards, book-fronted cabinets, end tables with secret compartments, bars that rose out of coffee tables,

The
SALOON IN THE HOME
or
A GARLAND of RUMBLOSSOMS

COMPILED BY
RIDGELY HUNT & GEORGE S. CHAPPELL
WITH MANY LAVISH ENGRAVINGS
BY JOHN HELD JR.

hollow clocks, and other discreet liquor cabinets answered public demand. A bumper crop of cocktail books for home bartenders were disguised as song books, poetry, fables, anything non-alcohol-oriented.

The cocktail party was as fashionable an outing as a night at a speakeasy. British novelist Alec Waugh claimed to have invented the cocktail party in London, in 1924, when he invited guests to tea and instead served them a rum punch mixed by a visiting friend from New York.

However, in May 1917, the *St Paul Pioneer Press* reported that Mrs Julius S Walsh Jr of St Louis, Missouri— wife of the president of the Terminal Railway Company and the Mississippi Valley Trust Company—hosted a "cocktail party". Her drinks menu for serving 50 guests included Clover Leafs, Highballs, Gin Fizzes, Bronxes, Martinis, and Manhattans. By August 1917, cocktail parties on the beach were reported as an emerging trend thanks in part to another recent innovation: paper cups.

A cocktail party may or may not have taken place in the town of Piedmont near San Francisco, in a fire house kitchen in 1915. Facing dereliction of duty accusations, the firemen had every reason do deny the charge leaving us to conjecture as to whether the earliest known cocktail party took place there or not.

The invention of the cocktail dress is usually credited to Chanel. In 1926, *Vogue* magazine featured a short, simple black dress designed by Gabrielle "Coco" Chanel. Called "Chanel's Ford" the frock was calf-length, straight, and decorated with a few diagonal lines of stitching. Modern "drinking women" took to the look, adding a match-

Throughout Prohibition, a few products were not banned. Bitters, such as Campari and Fernet Branca, were considered medicinals and could be brought into the States by tourists returning from Europe. They were also imported for sale in pharmacies.

Opposite:
Cocktail books for home bartenders were published in the United States disguised as songbooks or fables to the delight of the a public who refused to go dry.

ing hat, shoes, and gloves to the ensemble to wear at early evening soirées.

Chanel's inspiration likely came from a French cocktail hot spot, Deauville, where in 1921 the "cocktail dress" was worn by society flappers "during the noon eye-opening hour". It was reported at the time that the Parisian dressmakers picked up on this Deauville trend.

Only fabulously wealthy American women could afford French couture. That didn't stop American and British designers from copying the trend, creating frocks for department store shoppers who gravitated to longer sleeves, modest necklines, and sparse ornamentation for cocktail wear: in black, of course, with gloves. French *haute couturier* Christian Dior is frequently credited with giving the cocktail dress its name in the late 1940s. The term was obviously in use long before then, but there is no question that he popularized it around the world.

There was another cocktail accompaniment that developed during the period: music made for a young generation who marched to the beat of a different drummer.

PG Wodehouse, the great British author who created Jeeves and Wooster wrote about his personal struggle in his essay, *My Battle with Drink*. In it, he detailed his first experiences, his plunge into the depths, and the good woman who finally rescued him from evil ice cream sodas and hot fudge by introducing him to Champagne.

"...he tottered blindly towards the bar like a camel making for an oasis after a hard day at the office."
—Wodehouse, *Plum Pie*, 1966.

"He said that in a situation of that sort he usually prescribed a 'lightning whizzer', an invention of his own. He said this was what rabbits trained on when they were matched against grizzly bears, and there was only one instance on record of the bear having lasted three rounds."
—Wodehouse, *Extricating Young Gussie*, 1915.

"All he can recall is waking next morning on the floor of his bedroom and shooting up to the ceiling when a sparrow on the window-sill chirped unexpectedly."
—Wodehouse, *The World of Mr Mulliner*, 1972.

The Bright Young Things

BEFORE THE BARS AND CLUBS in New Orleans' notorious Storyville district were shut down to safeguard the innocence of American military personnel, they gave birth to a music style that blended traditional African, African-American, and Western roots with two new treatments: syncopation and improvisation. Storyville jazz greats Buddy Bolden, Kid Ory, and Papa Jack Laine mentored young successors named Duke Ellington, King Oliver, Fats Waller, and Eubie Blake. Jazz soothed the souls of young Americans and Europeans who "lived for today" and eschewed traditional beliefs.

Prohibition was, in truth, the least of most Americans' concerns. The Scopes trial brought to light the rift between two types of Americans: those who embraced Victorian morals and ethics; and those who condoned radical concepts such as evolution. The division was exacerbated by the government's post-war, isolationist policy.

Strong prejudice against immigrants and minorities emerged during the First World War and got worse during Prohibition—especially in the southern states. Communism was a new word associated with Russian intellectuals who crushed their imperial government. The term "anarchy" was paired with Italian and French radical militants, who instigated labour strikes, bombed government buildings, and distributed anti-war propaganda.

American writers, artists, and musicians headed to Europe in hopes of finding intellectual freedom. Europe called on American mixologists, too. Someone had to make cocktails for Britain's devil-may-care Bright Young Things and their chroniclers Noël Coward, Evelyn Waugh, and P G Wodehouse, who frequented London's Café Royal, Ciro's Club, and the Savoy.

Someone had to serve the likes of Josephine Baker, George Gershwin, Ernest Hemingway, F Scott Fitzgerald, Gertrude Stein, Oscar Levant, and Man Ray at Paris's New York Bar. American mixologists' and Cuban cantineros' influence was felt from Barcelona to Berlin, giving Kurt Weill

"As he drained his first glass, it seemed to him that a torchlight procession, of whose existence he had hitherto not been aware, had begun to march down his throat and explore the recesses of his stomach. The second glass, though slightly too heavily charged with molten lava, was extremely palatable."
—Wodehouse, *The World of Mr Mulliner*, 1972.

"Insidious things [Mint Juleps]. They creep up on you like a baby sister and slide their little hands into yours and the next thing you know the Judge is telling you to pay the clerk of the court 50 dollars."
—Wodehouse, *Fish Preferred: A Novel*, 1929.

and Bertold Brecht, Jorge Luis Borges and Luis Bruñel places to flex their intellectual muscles.

Anthropophagia

FRUSTRATION and a desire for change were not limited to European and American shores. During this tumultuous time Brazilian nationalism was born amid two divergent social classes. Brazilian art had been a faint replica of imported European classical styles since the 1800s: a trend repeated in many post-colonial countries ruled by European-born upper classes and populated by indigenous and non-European peasantry.

Four nonconformist European imports—Expressionism, Futurism, Surrealism, and Cubism—ignited the hearts and minds of young Brazilian avant-gardes and inspired a wholly unique art form that integrated indigenous with populist subjects.

The Anthropophagy Movement embraced its own manifesto, in May 1928, written by poet-novelist-journalist Oswaldo de Andrade (1890-1954): *Anthropophagite Manifesto*. Andrade applied the metaphor of indigenous anthropophagy or "ritual cannibalism" as a way to explain how foreign influences such as the European avant-gardes' attack on cultural tradition could be consumed and transformed into unique articulations that maintained the "primitiveness" of indigenous, pre-colonial Brazil. He proclaimed that:

> *We were never catechized. What we really did was Carnaval. The Indian dressed as a Senator of the Empire. Pretending to be Pitt. Or featuring in Alencar's operas full of good Portuguese feelings.*

The movement's champions included artists Emiliano Di Cavalcanti, Anita Malfatti, and Tarsila Amaral, writer Mario de Andrade who published *Pauliceia Desvairada*, and composer Heitor Villa-Lobos. Just as in the 1800s, when cachaça was seen as a symbol of rebellion against the European-born ruling and middle classes, cachaça was consumed amongst adherents of the Anthropophagy Movement.

The return to Brazilian cultural roots and the concept of cultural anthropophagy was not only felt among the avant-garde. In the final days of the First World War, a Portuguese-imported, pre-Lent festival called "Carnaval" was consumed and transformed by impoverished *favela* (slum) residents who lived in the hills surrounding Rio de Janeiro and Salvador de Bahia. Its origins lay in ancient Greek Saturnalia festivities. The Roman Catholic Church modified the event into a religious feast that preceded Ash Wednesday and Lent. *Carne Vale* [Farewell to the Flesh] was the last opportunity to play music, eat heartily, drink, and dance before enduring 40 days of penance for past sins via abstinence, fasting, and personal reflection.

In Portugal, this Christian feast had developed into *entrudo* [a free-for-all]. Revellers threw mud, water, and food at each other in the streets. Well-heeled folk attended masquerade balls, danced polkas and waltzes—just like their Parisian neighbours. The first *entrudo* took place, in 1840, in Rio de Janeiro.

Through the decades, Brazilian *entrudos* became more elaborate as costumed revellers paraded in horse-drawn floats accompanied by military bands. Then, more and more elements of indigenous and African-Brazilian culture were adopted. The *cordões* [strings]—parading groups

In 1943, Disney cartoon hero Donald Duck tried cachaça. In the same feature, the animation company introduced their latest cartoon character, a Brazilian parrot named Joe Carioca.

of costumed musicians and dancers—appeared in *favelas* [slums] such as Mangueira Hill. (The groups were later called *blocos* [blocks].)

Rio's high society shunned the *cordões* as vulgar manifestations of the nation's non-European roots, especially their musical accompaniment: samba. Some historians believe that the word "samba" is derived from the Angolan term *semba* [invitation to dance]. Samba was also the common name for the dance parties held by slaves and former slaves living in Rio's *favelas* after slavery was abolished in 1889. The dances had roots in Congolese and Angolan circle dances, involving *umbigada* [gyrating hip movements].

Over time samba adopted influences from Brazilian *maxixe* and *marcha*, Cuban *habanera*, and German polka. Pixinguinha (AKA: Alfredo da Rocha Vianna Jr) was one of the earliest samba pioneers. But samba's most famous populariser was Carlos Cachaça. Born Carlos Moreira de Castro (1902-1995), Cachaça's story epitomizes samba's heart and soul as well as its associations with cachaça.

The first samba composer from Rio de Janeiro's Mangueira Hill *favela*, Cachaça was one of the founders of Bloco dos Arengueiro—precursor to today's world-famous Estação Primeira de Mangueira. Born of mixed African-Brazilian and Portuguese blood, Carlos was the second son of five siblings raised in the *favela* Mangueira, where his father worked as a railway employee at the Estação da Mangueira. Abandoned by his father as a child, Carlos went to live with his godfather on Mangueira Hill. By the age of ten, he paraded in Cordão Guerreiros da Montanha and other *cordões*.

Six years later, three events changed the course of Carlos' life. His mother died. Then, the person who became his life-long friend and collaborator Carlota (AKA: Angenor de Oliveira) moved to Mangueira. Then Carlos began playing *pandeiro* in a group led by Mano Elói, one of the recording pioneers of *pontos de macumba*. By the time he was eighteen, Carlos was a regular at *pagodes* [jam sessions] in Mangueira and Madureira. Although most musicians drank beer at these gatherings, Carlos ordered cachaça because he hated the taste of beer. His cohorts stared calling him Carlos Cachaça.

Also known as "O Poeta de Mangueira" [Poet of Mangueira], Carlos wrote his first samba "*Não me Deixaste Ir ao Samba em Mangueira*" [You Did Not Let Me Go to the Samba in Socks] in the early 1920s. His fame grew as samba hit the radio waves in subsequent years. But Cachaça never made royalties from the several hundred songs he wrote and performed. He earned his living just like his father, working for the railways. He continued to live in Mangueira Hill with his wife Menininha until the day he died. Carlos Cachaça saw the samba and Carnaval rise from the *favelas* to the Brazilian mainstream when he was publicly honoured in 1995 for his role as originator of samba and pioneer of the modern Carnaval. He was paraded in the annual competition atop a Mangueira float. His *bloco* won top honours that year.

Repatriation & Expatriation

PASSENGER NEGRONI

We only found one record of a Count Camillo Negroni. The passenger list from the *Fulda*, dated 16 May 1892, showed that a Count Camillo Negroni boarded in Genoa bound for New York. His age was listed as 29, and his residence was Milano. He took a cabin (430 feet long, the ship had accommodation for 120 first, 130 second, and 1,000 third-class passengers). We found only one other North American reference to a Count Negroni. In 1897, he left a job at the Imperial Bank in Winnipeg, "transferred east". Was it the same Negroni?

NEGRONI

1 part London dry gin
1 part Campari
1 part sweet vermouth
Shake with ice. Strain into a cocktail glass, or over ice in a tumbler. Garnish with an orange twist.

THE COCKTAILS that came out of the era between the world wars demonstrated the mixologist's improvisational skills: working with limited and variable ingredients; developing a sixth sense for the customer's mood; conducting a symphony of tone and atmosphere within less-formal surroundings; and adapting new ideas acquired from customers who had seen the world.

Take for example, Count Camillo Negroni, who returned, in 1920, from America to his native Italy. The young count had been a cowboy in the American west and a gambler in New York in the previous decade. When Prohibition was enacted, Negroni returned home to Firenze [Florence]. He frequented Caffee Casoni at Hotel Baglioni, where Fosco "Gloomy" Scarselli was famed for his Torino-Milanos (then called Americanos). One day Negroni asked for his Americano to be made without soda water and with gin. The Negroni was born. Or was it?

Recently, a member of the Negroni family, Noel Negroni, whose brother Héctor has traced their lineage back to 1092, questioned this oft-told tale of Count Negroni as there is scant evidence of his existence. Also, their cousin Francois Marquis de Negroni recalls his grandfather showing him a French newspaper article from the 1920s crediting a more traceable name on their family tree with inventing the drink: Pascale Olivier Count de Negroni. They are still searching for this article. Until it is found, there seem to be two competing tales of the birth of this great apéritif, but it seems wither way, it's all in the family.

While the economy was on the rise and travel was easy and cheap, Americans exerted their influence on drinks around the world. Take for example the Torino-Milano. It was renamed "Americano" because locals noticed it was a favourite among American tourists. Negroni's Americano has the added kick of gin: a palate preference more in tune with American tastes.

London bartenders concerned about serving demanding American hotel guests and the city's Bright Young Things banded together, around 1923, establishing guidelines for service and standardising recipes. The association became known as the United Kingdom Bartenders Guild, the parent of the International Bartenders Association.

SIDECAR

4 parts Cognac
2 parts Cointreau
1 part fresh lemon juice
Shake with ice. Strain into a cocktail glass. Garnish with a lemon twist.

Around the same time, Patrick MacGarry, the celebrated bartender at London's Buck's Club introduced the Sidecar. Early on, the drink appeared in two landmark cocktail books: Harry McElhone's 1919 *Harry's ABC of Cocktails* and Robert Vermiere's 1922 *Cocktails: How to Mix Them*.

According to McElhone, an American serviceman fighting on the western front came up with the Sidecar while visiting with "John", a barman at Henry's in Paris. This cognac version of a Margarita or Daiquiri was an immediate hit with both ex-pats and locals. MacGarry, however, deserves to be remembered as the man who popularised it. The name (according to 1923 news reports that also announced the Monkey Gland to the world) came from the fact the drink was potent enough to "take you for a ride".

The signature drink at Bucks' Club, however, was a MacGarry original. According to Buck's Club secretary

Captain Peter Murison, the club founder Captain Herbert John Buckmaster divorced actress Gladys Cooper, in 1921, and whiled away many an hour entertaining theatre and film folk as well as walking the links with club members. The young Buckmaster frequently brought his personal bartender Patrick MacGarry with him on his sojourns. On one such occasion, a member of the party requested a peach-and-Champagne cocktail that he tasted on the Continent (possibly made by Giuseppe Cipriani at the Hotel Europa in Venice). There wasn't any fresh peach juice, so MacGarry made the drink with fresh orange juice, champagne, and a couple of secret ingredients. (A splash of London dry gin and a dash of cherry brandy was what we discovered in a 1950s recipe for a Champagne Buck. But we never managed to convince Murison to divulge the club's best-kept secret.) Today, Buck's Fizz is still a favourite British brunch beverage. Even supermarkets carry a bottled version for imbibers who can't manage pouring the two ingredients on their own.

BUCK'S FIZZ

60 ml fresh orange juice
90 ml champagne
1 splash London dry gin
1 dash cherry brandy
Built in a champagne flute and stir.
Serve with an orange slice.

A similar refreshment was also a hit when it was created in the 1925 at the Ritz Hotel in Paris. The Ritz's Mimosa differentiated itself from Buck's Fizz with the addition of Grand Marnier and had little in common with McElhone's gin, curaçao, and dry vermouth drink by the same name.

Film director Alfred Hitchcock favoured the Mimosa as a hangover cure. The story goes that Hitchcock was having dinner at Louis Lurie's table at Jack's in San Francisco. For 52 years, real-estate magnate and theatre owner Lurie held court at the city's second oldest restaurant, hosting film stars, power brokers, and celebrities. The night Hitchcock sat at table a few attendees including Lurie suffered from the previous night's revelry. Hitchcock poured champagne into Lurie's glass of orange juice as a palliative. When asked what it was, Hitchcock said it was a Mimosa. The drink in this fashion caught on throughout the United States after the 1940s. It got a new twist in the 1990s in the hands of TV presenter Martha Stewart, who preferred hers made with sanguinello juice (AKA: blood orange juice).

The Havana Connection

UNTIL THE 1959 REVOLUTION, Havana was many Americans' local bar. A quick flight from Miami to Cuba or a fishing trip on the Gulf or the Caribbean brought a thirsty traveller to a haven of Mojitos, Daiquirís, El Presidentes, and Cubanos. It was a particularly welcome sight for parched patrons during Prohibition. Stateside publications fanned the flames of desire. *Travel* Magazine, in 1922, mentioned a rum-based cocktail that took off 30 years later, albeit in a different form: the Piña Colada.

The Daiquirí, the Mojito, and Cuba Libre were the royal court of the Havana bar circuit. Let's digress about the Daiquirí for a bit.

CUBAN-STYLE PIÑA COLADA
1 part Cuban rum
1 barspoon simple syrup
juice of 2 lime wedges
2 parts fresh pineapple juice
Shake with ice. Strain into a tall glass. Garnish with a wedge of lime.

The Daiquirí

THE DAIQUIRÍ has very close associations with Cuba's fight for independence, from its birth through its evolution into the world's most beloved Cuban cocktail. The first cry for independence, in 1868, was sounded at

Yara, near Santiago de Cuba and echoed through the nearby mining village of Daiquirí.

In their bid for freedom, the Mambises, led by Antonio Maceo, fortified themselves with the Daiquirí's parent, Canchánchara. It was simple blend of rum, lime juice and "honey": a term frequently used in Cuba in describe molasses. The drink was made in batches and poured into bottles. Strapped to their saddles, the bottled Canchánchara was not only a welcome thirst-quencher for the freedom fighters during the long, arduous campaigns against the Spanish colonial army. It was also an excellent painkiller for the wounded.

But even this was not the original. A 1754 French-Spanish dictionary defines *"ponche"* as the combination of *aguardiente de caña* (rum), lime, sugar, and water. That same dictionary called it a *"Bebida Inglesa"* [English drink]. Introduced to western Europe by English sailors who encountered it in India with the addition of tea, Punch was its esteemed ancestor and first arrived, in the 1660s, when the British fleet captured Santiago de Cuba.

The Canchánchara was certainly present 220 years later—at the height of the Spanish-American War [1895-1898]— when the town of Daiquirí became the focal point of an offensive that saw Spanish troops attacked from the land by General Calixto García's Cuban Liberation Army and from the sea by Admiral William T Sampson's American naval forces led by General William Shafter, who landed 17,000 troops on the shipping docks owned by the Spanish-American Iron Company on Daiquirí Bay.

Some Daiquirí legends say that when the 300-pound, 63-year-old Shafter first tasted the Canchánchara, he declared that "the only missing ingredient is ice."

The story of the Daiquirí's birth has been reiterated in dozens of fashions. And we're going to do it for you here—with a few adjustments.

New York mining engineer Jennings S Cox Jr (as opposed to senior who was a an American stockbroker) was the general manager of the Spanish-American Iron Company, starting in 1896, and a member of the American Institute of Mining Engineers. So was colleague F D Pagliuchi, who besides being an engineer, was a war correspondent for *Harper's Monthly* and a commander in the Liberating Army of Cuba. (He wrote a detailed account of the US Navy landing that was published in the 1898 *Harper's Pictorial History of the War with Spain*.)

When bartender Emilio "Margato" González—famous for popularising the Daiquirí in Havana—passed away a number of years later, it was F D Pagliuchi who documented the incident of the drink's invention.

Apparently, the editor of *El Pais* newspaper made a mistake in writing Maragato's obituary, crediting the bartender with the Daiquirí's origination. Pagliuchi sent the following correction, which was also publishing in the 1948 book *El Arte del Cantinero*, the official handbook of the Cuban bartenders' association:

> *Dear Sir:*
> *In today's edition of your appreciable periodical "El Pais" I have read an article titled, "There died yesterday evening 'Maragato', the inventor of " Daiquirí." Allow me to clarify that the delicious 'Daiquirí' was*

DAIQUIRÍ NO. 1

4 parts Cuban rum
1 part Fresh squeezed lime juice
1 tsp granulated sugar
Shake the ingredients on a combination of crushed and rock ice and strain into a pre-chilled coupe glass. Garnish with a wedge of lime. If blending, double the amount of sugar and blend with approximately 300 ml of crushed ice.

DAIQUIRÍ NO. 2 (VERSION A)

12 parts Cuban rum
3 parts fresh squeezed lime juice
1 tsp granulated sugar
2 parts fresh orange juice
1 part curaçao
Shake the ingredients on a combination of crushed and rock ice and strain into a pre-chilled coupe glass. Garnish with a twist of orange. If blending, double the amount of curaçao and blend with approximately 300 ml of crushed ice.

DAIQUIRÍ NO. 2 (VERSION B)

6 parts Cuban rum
2 parts fresh squeezed Seville orange juice
2 tsp granulated sugar
1 part curaçao
Shake the ingredients on a combination of crushed and rock ice and strain into a pre-chilled coupe glass. Garnish with a twist of orange. If blending, double the amount of curaçao and blend with approximately 300 ml of crushed ice.

not invented in Havana, but in the mines of Daiquirí, by the Engineer [Jennings] Cox [Jr], the director of these mines.

At the conclusion of the war of independence of Cuba [in 1898], in which I had very active part, I obtained American capital to reactivate the old El Cobre copper mines situated near Santiago de Cuba, of which I was the director. While occupied in this work, I had occasion to go to Daiquirí to speak with mister Cox. Concluding the matter that I took to Daiquirí, I asked mister Cox if he was going to invite me for a cocktail.

In the sideboard of the mine's dining room, there was not gin nor vermouth; there was only Bacardí, lemons, sugar, and ice. With these elements we did a very well shaken and very cold cocktail that I liked much. Then I asked Cox: — and this: how is it called? He answered: "'Rum Sour'. In the United States there is a drink that is called a 'Whisky Sour', which is made with whisky, sugar, lemon juice and ice". But I said to him: "This name is very long, why not call it Daiquirí?"

Later, we went to Santiago de Cuba; to the bar of the American Club, where there were already a few acquaintances asking for a Daiquirí. The bar attendant answered that he did not know what it was. At that time Cox explained to him how it was made, recommending to shake it up and serve it very cold. Some of the friends who were in the bar also asked for a Daiquirí. We all liked it and very soon this cocktail made itself popular in Santiago, where from it went on to Havana and today it has a worldwide reputation. The above description is the real version of how the famous 'Daiquirí' was invented.

(In *The Gentleman's Companion*, Charles H. Baker added a friend of his to this cast of characters: Harry E Stout, whom he said was another mining engineer based with Cox and present for the drink's creation.)

After independence was won, the Daiquirí became a fashionable drink especially appreciated by mining engineers who frequented the Venus Hotel in Santiago de Cuba just to partake in this refreshment. It then made an appearance in Havana at the Plaza Hotel, introduced by its famed bartender Emilio "Maragato" González.

It was in the hands of Constantino Ribalaigua Vert, who took over La Florida, in 1918, that the Daiquirí's children—the Hemingway Special and the Floridita Daiquirí—were born and thrived. Inspired by this simple sour concoction, Constante tested six versions.

Constante's frappéed Daiquirí No. 4 became best known as the Floridita Daiquirí. United Press journalist Jack Cuddy noted in the 1937 book *Cocktails: Bar la Florida* that early on Constante blended his concoction with ice in an electric mixer ("one of those malted milk stirrers in American drug stores"). That was before he ordered a Flak Mak ice-crushing machine from the United States. And when the Waring blender was launched, in 1938, El Floridita was one of the first establishments to adopt its use.

Cuddy also documented Constante's method, tossing two ounces of rum into a cocktail shaker and then:

Add one teaspoon of finely granulated sugar. Do not use powdered sugar which Constantino insists has starch in it. Then add one teaspoon of Maraschino—a cordial which is made from wild cherries grown in Dalmatia. Squeeze the juice of half a lime. Next toss in finely shaved ice until the shaker is nearly full. This ice must be shaved so fine that it's almost snow. Do not use cracked ice. Then place the shaker under an electric mixer: one of those malted milk stirrers in American Drug stores. Let it stir for about three minutes. If you

DAIQUIRÍ NO. 3 (B. ORBON)

12 parts Cuban rum
2 parts fresh squeezed lime juice
1 part fresh grapefruit juice
1 part maraschino liqueur
1 tsp granulated sugar
Shake the ingredients on a combination of crushed and rock ice and strain into a pre-chilled coupe glass. Garnish with a wedge of lime and a cocktail cherry. If blending, double the amount of sugar and maraschino liqueur before blending with approximately 300 ml of crushed ice.

DAIQUIRÍ NO. 4 (FLORIDITA DAIQUIRÍ)

12 parts Cuban rum
3 parts fresh squeezed lime juice
1 part maraschino liqueur
1 tsp granulated sugar
Shake the ingredients on a combination of crushed and rock ice and strain into a pre-chilled coupe glass. Garnish with a wedge of lime and a cocktail cherry. If blending, double the amount of sugar and maraschino before blending with approximately 300 ml of crushed ice.

DAIQUIRÍ NO. 5

12 parts Cuban rum
3 parts fresh squeezed lime juice
1 part homemade grenadine
(1 part fresh pomegranate juice to 2 parts sugar)
1 part maraschino liqueur
Shake the ingredients on a combination of crushed and rock ice and strain into a pre-chilled coupe glass. Garnish with a wedge of lime and a cocktail cherry. If blending, double the amount of grenadine and maraschino liqueur before blending with approximately 300 ml of crushed ice.

*haven't an electric mixer, shake it rapidly in a regular
cocktail shaker for about four minutes. Meanwhile
chill your glasses by pouring in cracked ice and a bit of
water. Now toss the cracked ice and water and strain
your Daiquirí from the shaker into the glasses through
a half-strainer—one that is not too fine.*

What was achieved with new labour-saving devices such as the electric mixer and the blender was best described by Ernest Hemingway in his posthumously published 1970 novel *Islands in the Stream*:

*He was drinking another frozen Daiquirí with no
sugar in it and as he lifted it, heavy and the glass frost-
rimmed, he looked at the clear part below the frappéed
top and it reminded him of the sea. The frappéed part
of the drink was like the wake of a ship and the clear
part was the way the water looked when the bow cut
it when you were in shallow water over marl bottom.
That was almost the exact colour.*

Hemingway's Special

RETURNING FROM THE HORRORS of the Spanish Civil War in 1938, Ernest Hemingway settled into room 511 at the Hotel Ambos Mundos on 153 Calle Obispo and began to write his novel For Whom the Bell Tolls. The story goes that Hemingway took a break one day and stopped into El Floridita at the other end of the street near Parque Central, where he ordered a Daiquirí from Constante.

In spite of the opinions of his doctor friends, Hemingway was convinced that he had diabetes. Consequently, he excluded all sugar from his diet, though he was never concerned about his alcohol consumption. Constante offered him a sugar-free Daiquirí with a double dose of Cuban rum. This Daiquirí Del Salvaje, soon became the Daiquirí a la Papa, then Daiquirí Como Papa.

Enamoured with his new discovery, Hemingway returned every day at 11 AM dressed in Bermudas, short-sleeved shirt and espadrilles. He always sat on the same bar stool and downed a couple of his special Daiquirís. Sometimes he would return at 5 PM to consume a dozen more.

Later, cantinero Antonio Meilan modified the recipe by adding grapefruit juice and immortalized it under the appellation "Hemingway Special" or "Papa Doble".

After Hemingway moved out of the hotel and into his home La Finca Vigía, he continued his frequent visits. Floridita's Daiquirís became such a source of inspiration for him that sometimes he brought in a thermos bottle to have it carefully filled with his favourite refreshment. Hemingway called this his *viaticum* [Latin for "provisions for a journey"], his *trago del camino* [gulp for the road], which helped him continue the happy reverie begun in the Floridita during the ride back to La Finca Vigía in San Francisco de Paula.

HEMINGWAY SPECIAL (PAPA DOBLE)

12 parts Cuban rum
3 parts fresh grapefruit juice
2 parts maraschino liqueur
1 part fresh lime juice
Shake the ingredients on a combination of crushed and rock ice and strain into a pre-chilled coupe glass. Garnish with a wedge of lime. If blending, double the amount of maraschino liqueur before blending with approximately 300 ml of crushed ice.

Cuba Libre

I T WAS THE BATTLE CRY of freedom-fighting Cubans from the days when the Mambises, led by Antonio Maceo, stormed the countryside during the Ten-Year War (1868-1878): "Cuba Libre!" It resounded when the Cuban Liberation Army boldly fought the War of Independence

(1895-1898) from Cienfuegos to Santiago, from Dos-Rios to Manzanillo.

No one is absolutely certain who invented this simple, refreshing concoction made with two of the world's most popular ingredients: Cuban rum and cola. Some people say it was invented in 1902 at La Florida to commemorate the island's independence.

A few facts substantiate part of this claim. According to the company's historical records, Coca-Cola was first exported in 1900 to Cuba, right after the very first bottle of syrup left the United States bound for Great Britain that very same year (Coca Cola had been invented only 14 years earlier, in 1886 in Atlanta, Georgia). It is quite possible that glasses of rum and cola were served up icy cold to the celebrating politicians and diplomats who worked at the nearby Capitol Building.

The list of original Cuban cocktails is far lengthier than the Cuba Libre, Daiquirí, and Mojito. In the Cantineros Association's 1948 handbook *El Arte del Cantinero* we found: A Pie, Almendares, Aperital, Arcoiris, Auto, Bacardi, Beloo Monte, Berry, Bowman, Bowman-Rum, Café, Caffery, Caledonia, Callito, Canchancharra, Casiano, Casino, Chaparra, Chaparra, Chocolate, Cocktail Comodoro, Colonial, Country Club, Cuban Coronation, Cuba Bella, Cuba Libre, Cuban Blossom, Cuban Bronx, Cuban Manahttan, Cuban Rose, Cubanito, Daiquirí, Daiquirí Floridta, Delio Núñez, Dorothy Gish, El Mundo, El Presidente, Elixir, Florida, Florida Special, Flying Tiger, Forestier, Golden Glove, Graham Special, Granadine, Greta Garbo, Guggenheim, Habana Beach, Habana Special, Habana Yacht Club, Havana Opera, Hemingway Special, Ideal, Isle of Pines, Jai Alay, Jaimanitas, Largo,

Llerandi, Lobo del Mar, Longines, Maragato, Mary Pickford, Méndez, Méndez Vigo, Menieta, Miramar, Mofuco, Mojito, Monjita, Mulata, Nacional, Niña Bonita, Obispo, Ojen, Panchito, Pancho Arango, Paraíso, Perfecto, Pineapple Fizz, Playa, Plaza, Plus Café, Rainbow, Remero Special, René Morales, Robin, Ron Collins, Ron Punch, Rum Alexander, Rum Cocktail, Rum Daisy, Rum Julep, Rum Old-Fashioned, Rum-Dubonnet, Rum-Vermouth (dulce), Rum-Vermouth (seco), Santa Marta, Seillana, Sloppy Joe's, Sweet Lady, Tango, Tequila, Urruela, Vermouth Batido, and Yacht Club.

In addition to this vast contribution to the bartending world, one Cuban venue birthed cocktail culture in another country. Opened in 1820 as La Piña de Plata, the watering hole near Parque Central was renamed Bar Ristorante La Florida when Don Narciso Sala Parera took it over in 1898. Regulars fondly called it by the diminutive "La Floridita". Although most Havana cantineros made their cocktails icy cold by shaking them in a two-part or three-part shaker set, Parera trained his staff to mix their drinks the old fashioned way, pouring or "throwing" the liquid from one mixing glass to another while stabilizing the ice with a julep strainer held over one of the glasses.

One of Parera's cousins Miguel Boadas was a master at mixing in this remarkably theatrical style. By 1925, Boadas was ready to spread his wings, and emigrating to Barcelona. Wherever he worked, he attracted the attention of the city's most brilliant artists, philosophers, and writers. He opened his own place in October 1932. Las Boadas on Calle Tallers, off the city's busiest thoroughfare La Ramblas, was Spain's first cocktail bar. Boadas's first original offering was eponymously named and served at the opening. He

BOADAS

1 part curaçao
1 part Dubonnet
1 part light rum
Shake ingredients over ice. Strain into a cocktail glass. Garnish with a morello cherry.

CANALETAS

1 part Campari
1 part Dubonnet
1 part gin
dash of Cointreau
Shake ingredients over ice. Strain into a cocktail glass. Garnish with a morello cherry.

went on to create a perfect Manhattan made with Canadian whiskey, a Negroni variation called Canaletas, and dozens of other delights.

His daughter Maria Dolores was born the year after. Playing with bar glasses as a child, she learnt her craft early in life. After her father's death, in 1967, she continued his tradition of mixing drinks in the Parera fashion and welcoming Barcelona's intellectual elite along with her husband Jose Luis Maruenda ("Josep"), who had also been trained by Don Miguel.

One of Two Harrys Returns and Another Arrives

AS HEAD BARMAN AT THE SAVOY armed with a repertoire of hundreds of mixed drinks, Harry Craddock had become the toast of London by the late 1920s. A particularly surprising offering was the insidious White Cargo which Craddock invented to commemorate the success of the West End production of Leon Gordon's play *White Cargo* based on Ida Vera Simonton's novel by the same name.

THE WHITE CARGO

1 part French vanilla ice cream
1 part gin
No ice is necessary; just shake until thoroughly mixed, and add cold water or white wine, if the concoction is too thick.

Craddock published his inventive collection and his drinks wisdom in his 1930 *The Savoy Cocktail Book*, which is considered to be one of the staple classics of twentieth-century written cocktailiana.

The United Kingdom Bartenders Guild had seen two presidents, William Tarling and Harry Craddock. One had published a plethora of recipes under his own venue's name. The other was not going to let the UKBG live under that shadow. Tarling, then UKBG President, published *The Café Royal Cocktail Book*, a compendium of recipes that best demonstrated the broad scope of British bartending knowledge. Inside this 1937 volume there are some remarkable surprises: More than a dozen tequila drinks such as the Toreador and the Picador—a precursor to the Margarita—plus a handful of vodka drinks were documented. (We'll talk about the tequila drinks from this book later.) Only 1,000 copies were printed by the guild, making it one of the rarest volumes to obtain to this day.

Bellisima, Harry!

YET ANOTHER AMERICAN named Harry got involved in the business in 1929 in a most unusual way. Giuseppe Cipriani was tending bar at Venice's Hotel Europa, where a young trust-fund dilettante named Harry Pickering was a regular patron. One day, Harry came into the bar in a very melancholic mood. He'd been cut off from his pocket money by his aunt, who had sent him to Europe to dry out after his notorious escapades in America's speakeasies and cocktail parties. Apparently, she had discovered that he was getting into just as much trouble in Europe.

Harry asked Cipriani to lend him enough money to pay his hotel bill, his bar tab, and his ticket home: about 10,000 lire ($5,000 USD). Cipriani was not a rich man. But out of sympathy, he asked his wife if he could loan their entire life savings to this desperate American. Believe or not, she agreed. Pickering went home to face his aunt.

For 146 years, this iconic establishment drew in the world's rich and famous. (Well, at least for the last 130 years of its life.) It all started in 1864 when Daniel Nicols escaped a trip to debtors prison in France by running away to London with his wife. They didn't have a cent, but managed to scrape enough together from odd jobs to open a tiny place, the Café Restaurant on Glasshouse Street near Piccadilly Circus. It was successful enough, as a rendezvous for Frenchmen fleeing the Franco-Prussian War and the Communes, for Nicols to pay off his French creditors and expand over the entire block.

In the 1880s, his son-in-law suggested a better name, and Café Royal was born. A staunch chauvanist, he also selected Napoleon's crowned initial for the café's logo, though Nicol presumed it was his own.

Closed in December 2008, Café Royal will live on in its namesake cocktail book penned by bartender William Tarling.

Not certain he would ever see his money again, Cipriani was relieved to see Harry walk into the Europa two years later. He ordered a drink and handed Cipriani 10,000 lire, adding: "To show my appreciation, here's 40,000 more—enough to open your own bar." Cipriani exclaimed, "We'll call it Harry's Bar!"

Open for business on 13 May 1931, Harry's Bar became a regular International Bar Fly pit stop for visitors to northeastern Italy. Shortly after the opening, Cipriani introduced a seasonal sparkling cocktail, combining white peach purée, a touch of grenadine for colour, a dash of lemon juice for freshness, and bubbly Prosecco. Cipriani really didn't bother to name the special house apéritif until 1948, when a retrospective of Renaissance artist Giovanni Bellini was exhibited in Venice.

For centuries, artists may have been influenced by the consumption of drinks. And obviously artists inspired mixologists in the naming of some cocktails. But there is one spirit whose invention was directly inspired by a young, aspiring artist.

BELLINI

4 ripe white peaches
1 bottle chilled Prosecco
Cut the peaches into eighths, peel, and place in a blender or food processor. Blend to a purée. If the peaches are a little firm, add 2 tbs water and 2 tbs sugar before blending. Press the purée through a sieve. Half-fill six champagne flutes with the purée. Top with Prosecco and serve.

The True Pastis of Marseilles

DESPITE THE INTERNATIONAL COCKTAIL BOOM, pastis was still the preferred French apéritif, especially in the summertime and especially in southern France. After absinthe was banned in France, substitutes were made at home. People purchased wine-based spirit from local wineries or the pharmacy and rectified it with anise seeds. No two pastis tasted the same. Sure, there were government limits on the alcohol content, the addition of sweetening, and the distillate's clarity when diluted with water. Officials were still pressured by wine growers to eradicate distilled spirits in France. They still subscribed to the feeling anise-flavoured spirits were dangerous and caused drunkenness.

Yet, the bars and cafés that made the finest pastis were always busier than the ones that made didn't, especially when served with a splash of water and a side of anchovies and olives.

Pastis time was the moment in every day when people gathered to discuss work, politics, current events, literature, art, and just about anything that could expand into deep-seated debate and discussion. This was the observation of young Paul Ricard (1909-1997), who worked in his father's wine business in Marseilles while studying art. After release from mandatory military service, Ricard attempted to set up his own line of table wine, then brandy: designing and illustrating his own packaging and posters. While selling his brandy to local bars, he came to an epiphany:

> *The popularity of pastis made its mark on me. I wondered quite seriously whether it would be a good idea to develop a product which would satisfy the taste of all those pastis lovers, to take over the whole market, a market which did not even have to be created, since it was already there.*

Government restrictions on the manufacture of all anise liquor were relaxed on 7 April 1932. This allowed Ricard and his brother to produce and market his personal creation: Ricard, real Marseilles pastis. The recipe distilled

RICARD

Serve 1 part Ricard in a glass. Add 10 parts cool water. Then a cube of ice. Too much spirit or adding ice before the water made the drink look and taste incorrect.

WHISKEY SOUR

2 parts fresh lemon juice
1/2 tsp sugar
3 parts rye or bourbon whiskey
Shake ingredients over ice. Strain
into a sour glass. Garnish with a
lemon wedge and a maraschino
cherry.

ALEXANDER

2 parts London dry gin
1 part crème de cacao
1 part sweet cream
Shake well and strain into a cocktail
glass.

BACARDI

5 parts Bacardi light rum
3 parts fresh lemon or lime
juice
2 parts simple syrup
1 part grenadine syrup
Shake with ice. Strain into a cocktail glass.

BRONX

12 parts gin
6 parts orange juice
1 part sweet vermouth
1 part dry vermouth
Shake with ice. Strain into a cocktail glass.

CLOVER CLUB

9 parts gin
3 parts raspberry syrup or grenadine
3 parts simple syrup
4 parts fresh lemon juice
1 egg white
Shake very well with ice. Strain into
a wine glass.

DRY MARTINI

3 parts London dry gin
1 part dry vermouth
1 dash orange bitters
Stir with ice. Strain into a chilled
cocktail glass. Garnish with a lemon
twist or green olive.

from anise seeds, star anise, liquorice, and herbs harvested in Provençe, was less sweet than competitors. Ricard was very exacting in the serving of his pastis.

The brothers Ricard started their company with a loan of 600 litres of alcohol and money to purchase a second-hand still, a stock of bottles, and three vats of alcohol from former absinthe-producer Pernod. As with his other ventures, Ricard designed the label and poster himself.

The overwhelming reception the product received throughout southern France and Catalonia in its first year was beyond the dreams of the young aspiring artist. Although the Vichy government prohibited the production of pastis in 1940 because they believed the pre-war pastis craze was responsible for France's defeat against German occupation. It didn't last long. After the Second World War, Ricard became one of world's most influential liquor producers.

The Art of the Barware

ART SOMETIMES OVERTAKES DESIGN with its demand for form following function. Such is the case in the design of silver jewellery and silverware. In 1920, James Napier took over the E A Bliss Company located in Meridien, Connecticut. The firm specialized in making silver products, but shifted its interest to making modern jewellery. The Jazz Age's free-flowing money had triggered an increased demand for trend-right baubles: Egyptian- and Aztec-influenced Art Deco wrist cuffs, earrings, barrettes, brooches, and necklaces: must-have trinkets for a cocktail

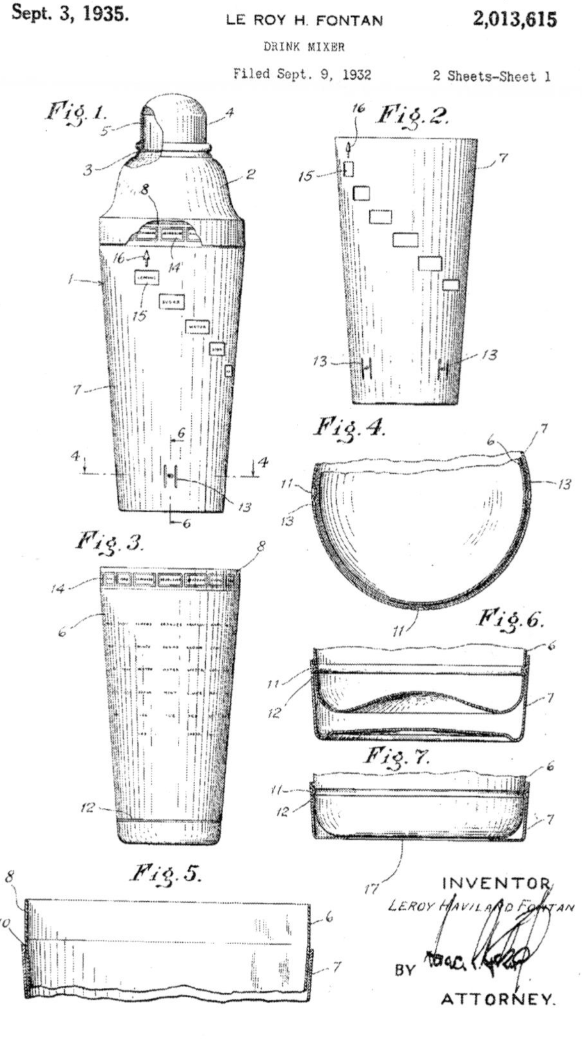

LE ROY H. FONTAN

2,013,615

DRINK MIXER

Filed Sept. 9, 1932   2 Sheets-Sheet 1

Fig. 1.

Fig. 2.

Fig. 4.

Fig. 3.

Fig. 6.

Fig. 7.

Fig. 5.

INVENTOR

LEROY HAVILAND FONTAN

BY

ATTORNEY.

DUBONNET

1 part Dubonnet
1 part gin
Shake with ice. Strain into a cocktail glass.

GIN RICKEY

60 ml gin
juice of 1/2 lemon
Built in a small tumbler. Add 1 lump of ice and a twist. Stir and fill with soda.

OLD FASHIONED

1 sugar cube (1 tsp)
1 tsp water
2 dashes Angostura bitters
60 ml rye (or bourbon) whiskey
Muddle sugar, water, and bitters together until the sugar is mostly dissolved. Fill glass with ice, then add the whiskey. Garnish with a twist of lemon peel, or orange slice and cherry. Serve with a swizzle stick and/or straw.

ORANGE BLOSSOM

1 part gin
1 part fresh orange juice
Shake ingredients over ice. Strain into a cocktail glass.

PALM BEACH

7 parts London dry gin
2 parts fresh grapefruit juice
1 part sweet vermouth
Shake ingredients over ice. Strain into a cocktail glass.

frock. Napier changed the firm's name to Napier Company two years later.

A forward-thinking gentleman, Napier could see the end of frivolity (and his largest market) as the economy headed into a tailspin. But he could also see that repeal of the

Patented just before the repeal of Prohibition, the Napier "Tells-You-How-Mixer" presented the formulas for 15 cocktails right on the shaker.

Volstead Act was imminent. Franklin Delano Roosevelt won the 1932 presidential election on a repeal platform.

Napier commissioned designer LeRoy H Fontan to develop a silver barware piece. The result: Fontan patented the "Tells-You-How Mixer" (9 September 1932, Patent No. #2,013,615) which featured recipes for the Sidecar, Tom Collins, Whiskey Sour, Alexander, Bacardí, Between the Sheets, Bronx, Clover Club, Dry Martini, Dubonnet, Gin Rickey, Manhattan, Old Fashioned, Orange Blossom, and Palm Beach. At first, it was exclusively sold at Saks Fifth Avenue in New York. Within the next decade, Napier Company produced some of the most daring and now collectible cocktail shaker designs in the nation.

AFTER REPEAL

"The bars feature freak drinks now--concoctions like one-half cherry soda and one-half gin, one half tomato catsup and one-half bourbon; beer with an egg in it...Think I'll stay on the wagon."
— James Aswell, 1934

Happy Days

WHEN UNITED STATES PRESIDENT Franklin Delano Roosevelt rang in repeal of Prohibition on 5 December 1933, he did it by shaking a Martini in the White House. Humorist H Allen Smith at one time claimed to have the nation's real first legal sip by bribing an operator to send an advance warning—three clicks on the telegraph—just before the announcement of repeal went over the national wire.

Remember, we mentioned earlier that women were instrumental in forcing national prohibition legislation into Congress packaged along with women's suffrage. Why? They hoped to gain voting rights while fighting crime, poverty, domestic violence, and moral decrepitude. But mostly, they wanted to gain equal rights by exerting political power.

And women voters realized by the end of the Roaring Twenties that Prohibition had failed. It was obvious at the time: the Volstead Act contributed to the rise of organized crime, political corruption, violent crime in urban areas, violent crime in rural areas (a first), and increased mortality from the ingestion of frequently-toxic, illegally-made booze. Prohibition made criminals out of the majority of American citizens, as they continued to drink.

Many of the women who had marched in favour of Prohibition, now campaigned against it and against the politicians they had put into office. The Women's Organization for National Prohibition Reform grew to a membership of 1.5 million in 1931, ready and willing to influence the structure of the 1932 Democratic Party platform. Although the repeal bill amended the Constitution and raised toasts of "happy days are here again" across the country, many state-level prohibition laws were not repealed until 1966. In fact, Prohibition in the United States has never been completely repealed. The state of Texas has 46 dry counties out of 254. In 2006, the town of Rockport, Massachusetts voted to repeal its alcohol ban. Ocean City, New Jersey (population over 15,000 as of 2005) is still dry today. "Dry" was a term that continued to apply to the liquor industry after repeal as the 1930s progressed.

SUCKER-PUNCHING AMERICAN WHISKEY

When Prohibition was repealed, stocks of Scotch were poised outside the three-mile limit on ships waiting to swoop in. Canadian distilleries were ready to boost their capacity. American whiskey makers? They had no staff, no stock, and would require from three to seven years just to age their new whiskies. By the time they were up and running, the American palate had moved onto imported goods. It would be years before they fully recovered.

CHAPTER FIFTEEN

How Dry We Were

THE RECONFIGURATION OF THE LIQUOR INDUSTRY

R EPEAL DAY CELEBRATIONS left bleary-eyed Americans awaking the next morning to the reality that they were still in the midst of the Great Depression. Triggered by the stock market crash of 24 to 29 October 1929, money for fun dried up. The ensuing domino effect caused mounting consumer debt, reduced demand for new products, wage cutbacks of as much as 50 percent for the precious few who still had jobs. Defaulted loans brought about bank failures. Neighbouring Canada and countries not yet recovered from the First World War were the next to fall. Britain, France, Germany and Italy were hardest hit, leading to further political unrest across the continent.

The American liquor and brewing industries already suffered enough from Prohibition. Many of those who

The advent of modern agricultural techniques, cutting down windbreaks so tractors could plow endless uninterrupted fields, proved disastrous when the American west was stricken by prolongued drought.

tried to relaunch their businesses were then sucker-punched by both lack of capital and credit. The handful that did open their doors and stayed open did what any self-respecting business would do in a bad economy. They slashed the quality to reduce overall production costs.

The demand for liquor was high. But the economy mandated a cheap retail price. The cheaper price meant that the end product resembled the sort of spirits a bartender would have been shot for serving in a nineteenth-century Wild West saloon.

One more blow dashed the hopes of many American liquor producers against the rocks of reality.

Black Sunday

THE FALTERING AMERICAN farming industry had been over-stimulated during the First World War by massive military orders for grain. As stock prices crashed on Wall Street, farmers got slammed with the biggest reality hit of all. The arable prairies of both the United States and Canada were less than fertile after Henry Ford's mass-produced, gas-powered tractor was introduced, in 1917, in response to market demand. Once the tractors replaced horses and ploughs, the ground was decimated. Rather than employing ecologically sound practices such as crop rotation, the planting of cover crops, and allowing fields to go fallow for a season to encourage retention and regeneration of topsoil, farmers leached valuable nutrients by ploughing deeper with the new invention and immediately planting like-kind crops season after season. Wet lands were drained to make room for more crops. Marginal lands surrounding the Great Plains zone were similarly overdeveloped and stripped of natural vegetation. Windbreaks and other natural obstacles could be dragged away with these machines, which could till fields by the unbroken mile. Then the rains stopped.

Three years of drought triggered an environmental nightmare. Starting on 11 November 1933, a series of dust storms stripped what little precious topsoil remained on the ravaged land. On 11 May 1934, a "black blizzard" cleared most of the Great Plains, blowing micro-fine silt into massive drifts that covered Chicago, Buffalo, Boston, New York, and

Washington DC. The remaining topsoil swept out over the Atlantic, forever lost.

The "Black Sunday" storm of 14 April 1935 turned day into night. Extensive damage in the Midwest was coupled with reports that visibility was less than five feet in some areas. What was once a verdant home to millions of buffalo, elk, and deer as well as a proverbial land of milk and honey for thousands of hopeful settlers was reduced to millions of acres of pitiful desert.

With nothing left of what little they had, over 500,000 homeless sharecroppers, tenant farmers, and their families made an exodus westward, from 1934 to 1939, in search of work as meagerly-paid itinerant fruit and vegetable pickers in California. The new Agricultural Adjustment Administration programme to limit crop production and raise consumer prices did not aid these second-tier farmers, only the landowners.

Although the Resettlement Administration (RA), the Farm Security Administration (FSA), the Rural Electrification Administration (REA), the Tennessee Valley Authority (TVA) and other welfare projects attempted to relieve the plight of the rural poor, the schemes did not last long enough to have the desired effect. The Supreme Court ruled, in 1936, that President Roosevelt's New Deal programs were unconstitutional. The Great Depression took another dip into the economy, in 1937, as a disgruntled world saw massive labour strikes and political upheavals churn the waters of discontent within the social sphere.

The rains returned in 1940 and the next economic stimulus arose as the United States entered the Second World War, 8 December 1941, with the attack on Pearl Har-

bour, Hawaii. The ravaged dust and sand of the Great Plains were again recruited to produce for the wartime efforts.

Dust storms stripped the fertile topsoil from midwestern fields, blanketing the eastern seaboard and carrying it as far as the Atlantic Ocean.

Both American and Canadian liquor industries were hard hit by this one-two-punch of economic and environmental catastrophe. American whiskey distillers secretly sent agents to the Pacific Northwest to purchase potatoes for making Bourbon and rye. Without the necessary expertise to properly ferment and distil potatoes, the results were less than impressive. Most liquor required doctoring with artificial aromas and caramel colouring. North America was not the only continent to suffer a downturn in liquor quality.

GREAT BRITAIN was barely back on its knees from the economic hit of the First World War when the Great Depression saw massive unemployment and rampant poverty put the country in a stranglehold for much of the early 1930s. Economic apprehension took an even greater bite with the country's withdrawal from the gold standard and the overall devaluation of the pound sterling. Global exports were down. Consequently, there was little incentive for British liquor producers to distil quality spirits. By the mid-1930s there were only eight functioning licensed distilleries in Scotland and only two in Ireland. British spirits production came to a grinding halt when the government called for military rearmament, in 1936, with the rise of Nazi Germany and the eventual onset of the Second World War three years later.

Two ironic twists of fate befell the crippled industry. The first was obvious. Bartenders had become used to doctoring poorly-produced booze, adding syrups and liqueurs to drinks. Patrons were used to the taste and called for those drinks even in places where the booze was better made.

COSMOPOLITAN

60 ml London dry gin
2 dashes Cointreau
Juice of one lemon
1 tsp raspberry syrup
Shake and strain into a stemmed cocktail glass.

Answering the demand created by consumers' interest, a glut of cocktail books landed in the market. Boston distiller Ben Burk, in an effort to stimulate interest in his Old Mr Boston products, published *Old Mr Boston Official Bartenders Guide* in 1932, which was fashioned after Harry Craddock's *The Savoy Cocktail Book*. (Craddock's book was a major hit in the United States after repeal.)

Burk wasn't the only one. Every minor publisher and every high-end publishing house capable of producing a list of recipes offered a paperback or hardcover cocktail book. Not caring about the quality of the recipes listed, they dumped in as many as they could find, just to get a toehold.

However, there was one recipe that caught our eye as we scanned the recipes in a humble 1934 volume entitled *Pioneers of Mixing Gin at Elite Bars: 1903-1933*.

The accumulated knowledge of "American Travelling Mixologists" Charles C Mueller, Al Hoppe, A V Guzman, and James Cunningham contained a recipe for a Cosmopolitan that might contained a twinge of familiarity to those of you who have walked into a bar or club or cocktail party in the past two decades.

That same year, the staff at *Esquire* magazine lampooned the "Ten Worst Cocktails of the Previous Decade," listing the Bronx, Alexander, Pousse-Café, Sweetheart, Orange Blossom, Pink Lady, Clover Club, Fluffy Ruffles, Pom Pom, and the Cream Fizz.

In the midst of all this mayhem, the second twist of fate saw an old ethnic spirit re-enter the cocktail arena as a major player.

A Little Kick to It

ADESPONDENT Vladimir Smirnoff was still living in Paris when he befriended a naturalized Ukrainian-American visitor named Rudolph Kunett. In wine- and pastis-centric France, Smirnoff failed miserably at convincing the locals to drink an tasteless, colourless, ethnic spirit such as vodka, despite Pete Petiot's efforts to introduce a simple drink like the Bloody Mary at the New York Bar. The French had no desire to associate, even on a social level, with a spirit that reminded them about political issues such as communism. "Pastis time" debates were enough for them. The only people who bought vodka were homesick Russian exiles and other East European ex-pats. Kunett missed vodka, horribly. This spirit was the liquor of

PINK LADY

1 egg white
1 tb grenadine
15 ml gin
Shake ingredients over ice. Strain into a cocktail glass.

FLUFFY RUFFLES

1 part light rum
1 part sweet vermouth
Stir in a mixing glass over ice. Strain into a cocktail glass. Garnish with a lemon twist.

POM POM

2 parts dry vermouth
1 part London dry gin
2 dashes orange bitters
Stir in a mixing glass over ice. Strain into a cocktail glass.

CREAM FIZZ

2 parts fresh lemon juice
1 tsp sugar
4 parts gin
1 part cream
Shake ingredients over ice. Strain into a collins glass. Add ice and soda.

MOSCOW MULE

60 ml vodka
30 ml fresh lime juice
3 dashes Angostura Bitters
Built in a collins glass filled with
cracked ice. Top with ginger beer.
Garnish with a lime slice.

his childhood. He was willing to bet on the success of vodka in the American market based on his own homesickness and the re-emergence of the cocktail trade.

He purchased the United States rights to both Smirnoff's recipe and brand name. That same year, Kunett opened the American Smirnoff Distillery in Bethel, Connecticut. But he forgot something. Isolationist America still didn't welcome foreigners. They still feared the "commies" and didn't readily accept anything that wasn't clearly American. His vodka was an ethnic spirit. Just like ouzo, pastis, and kirschwasser, vodka was not something the average American drank. Only one person was willing to usher vodka into American bars: Pete Petiot, whom we talked about earlier.

Let's consider another vodka adherent, John G Martin, for a bit. Martin was president of G F Heublein Company, of Hartford, Connecticut. Heublein was a producer of foods, wines, and bottled cocktails (they had bottled Manhattans, Martinis, and other drinks starting in 1892, and trend analysts quickly forecast that Heublein's bottled products would be the end of the bartending profession). Martin saw the potential, but the lack of current success was also obvious. Sadly, one drink does not establish a brand, much less a new liquor category, as Rudolph Kunett had quickly discovered. Petiot's success with the Bloody Mary was not enough to sustain a full production line.

LEAVES YOU BREATHLESS?

Not long after Heublein bought Smirnoff, they ran out of corks on the bottling line and used corks marked "whiskey" to finish a bottling run. A dealer in South Carolina received 25 cases, but wasn't sure how to sell this unfamiliar spirit. He opened a bottle, smelled it and tasted it. Then he read the cork.

He advertised it as "White Whiskey--which has no color, no smell, no taste!"

Intrigued customers snapped up this novelty product, and mixed it with everything from milk to Coca Cola.

So in 1939, he sold his interests in Smirnoff vodka to G F Heublein Company for $14,000 USD. But he still had faith, taking on a management position with the brand.

Around that time, Los Angeles restaurant owner John A Morgan (Jack, to his friends) returned from a trip to Britain. Falling in love with ginger beer, he set himself up with the task of introducing it to the United States. Packaged in crockery bottles emblazoned with the restaurant's name—Cock 'n' Bull—Morgan produced his first load of the spicy brew. Morgan arrived in New York where he met his friends Martin and Kunett at the Chatham Hotel's bar in 1941.

As Morgan told it to Clementine Paddleford, who put it in a 1948 *New York Herald Tribune* article:

> We three were quaffing a slug, nibbling an hors d'oeuvre and shoving toward inventive genius." The three of them played around with their respective ingredients until they settled on a hefty shot of vodka, a few ounces of ginger, beer and a squeeze of lime in a mug filled with ice. Morgan continued, "It was good. It lifted the spirit to adventure. Four or five later, the mixture was christened the Moscow Mule—and for a number of obvious reasons.

The three friends chipped in to purchase 500 copper mugs embossed with "Little Moscow" and awaited the delivery of the first carload of ginger beer. When it arrived, the 21 Club, the Waldorf-Astoria Hotel, and the Sherry Netherlands Hotel all gave the drink an enthusiastic reception.

When the United States entered the Second World War, Morgan's ginger beer project went on hiatus while he served in the military. It never really gained a second wind when he returned.

But Kunett's and Martin's vodka continued its entry into the cocktail lexicon, picking up momentum immediately after the war. We'll explain later.

MARY PICKFORD

3 parts light rum
2 parts unsweetened pineapple juice
1 tsp maraschino liqueur
1 tsp grenadine
Shake ingredients over ice. Strain into a cocktail glass. Garnish with a cherry.

STAR COCKTAIL

1 part London dry gin
1 part calvados
1 dash French vermouth
1 dash Italian vermouth
1 tsp grapefruit juice
Shake ingredients over ice. Strain into a cocktail glass.

SUMATRA KULA

adapted from "Beachbum Berry's Sippin Safari"

1 part fresh lime juice
1 part grapefruit juice
1 part orange juice
1 part honey-mix (equal parts honey and water, warm up to mix, let cool and bottle, keeps in the fridge for about a week)
3 parts light rum
6 parts crushed ice

Put everything in blender, saving ice for last, blend at high speed for no more than 5 seconds. Pour into a pilsner glass, add crushed ice to fill. Garnish with a mint sprig

ZOMBIE

2 parts white rum
2 parts light rum
2 parts dark rum
2 parts apricot brandy
2 parts pineapple juice
2 parts papaya juice
1 part 151-proof rum
Dash of grenadine

Shake all ingredients other than the 151-proof rum with ice. Pour drink and ice into a tall glass and top with the high-proof rum.

The Birth of Tiki

THE INFANT American motion picture industry moved from New York and New Jersey to Hollywood just after the First World War. Producers realized the reliable weather, warm temperatures, varied natural scenery, and very cheap land made it easier to crank out movies by the score each and every week of the year. Within two decades, movies were a major industry, making and breaking the careers of screen idols such as Mary Pickford, Charlie Chaplin, Fatty Arbuckle, Rudolph Valentino, Theda Bara, and Greta Garbo. Some of New York's top playwrights and composers moved to Hollywood to supply scripts and scores when sound was added to the magic: Dashiell Hammett, George S Kaufman, George Gershwin, and others followed the call.

The public jammed movie theatres around the world to watch their new on-screen heroes and heroines. The movie theatre was an oasis of cheap, mindless entertainment that helped them forget their own mundane lives for an hour or so.

Movie magazines told readers what the stars were wearing, eating, drinking, and where they were travelling. Drinks were named after these celebrities and marketed as the star's favourite sip. The Mary Pickford was created in the 1920s for "America's Sweetheart" by a Havana bartender while she was filming in Cuba. The Star Cocktail was created for early film flame Ivor Novello as part of a promotion sponsored by Booth's Gin in Britain. Those are only two of dozens of examples invented in the first few decades of Hollywood's Golden Age.

Two men who epitomised the era's bartending profession were favourites of the 1930s California celebrity circuit. Charismatic and more than a little bohemian, both men applied all the flair, flourish, and showmanship that hadn't been seen since the days of Jerry Thomas and Harry Johnson. Their repertoires, however, exemplify how the cocktail evolved. Just like their predecessors who had nicknames like "Panama Joe", "The Professor", "The Dean," and the "Doctor", Victor Bergeron and Ernest Gantt are commonly remembered by their bar monickers "Trader Vic" and "Don the Beachcomber".

For Hollywood folk, Havana was too far to travel for a tropical weekend getaway. But Hawaii was a relative hop, skip, and a jump. The stars got a taste for Polynesian. In 1933, Ernest Raymond Gantt (1907-1989) served it to them when he opened the minuscule Don's Beachcomber Bar on McCadden Place in Hollywood. Decked out with his personal collection of South Seas trinkets and stuff he picked up on California beaches, Gantt offered patrons strong rum potions with names like Sumatra Kula and Zombie.

Gantt acquired his repertoire when he left his native Louisiana, in 1926, and bummed around Jamaica, Tahiti, Australia, and the South Pacific. A complete departure from other celebrity watering holes such as the Brown Derby and Chasen's, Gantt's casual place was a hit with Hollywood trendsetters. He quickly opened a restaurant across the street—Don the Beachcomber—where the menu featured Polynesian-style Cantonese dishes and *pu pu* platter starters along with his growing list of tiki drinks. But the tiki concept

TRADER VIC MAI TAI

8 parts 17-year old J. Wray & Nephew Rum over shaved ice
Add juice from one fresh lime
2 parts curacao
1 part rock candy syrup
2 parts orgeat
Shake vigorously.
Add a sprig of fresh mint

DON THE BEACHCOMBER MAI TAI

6 parts Myer's Plantation rum
4 parts Cuban rum
3 parts fresh lime juice
4 parts grapefruit juice
1 part Falernum
2 parts Cointreau
2 dashes Angostura bitters
1 dash Pernod
Shell of squeezed lime
1 cup of cracked ice (size of a dime)
Shake for 1 minute. Serve in a double old-fashioned glass. Garnish with four sprigs of mint. Add a spear of pineapple. Sip slowly through mint sprigs until desired effect results.

was not solely the provenance of Gantt, who changed his named to Donn Beach.

Up in the San Francisco Bay area, Victor Jules Bergeron Jr (1902-1984) also had ambitions. With $500 to $800 USD borrowed from his aunt, Bergeron hired a carpenter to build him a shack, and opened a bar across the street from his parents' grocery store on San Pablo Avenue in Oakland. He called it Hinky Dink's and served up a retinue of strong rum drinks accompanied by slightly exotic fare. Three years later came a moment of inspiration, and a trip to Los Angeles.

"I got the idea" Vic recalled, "from a couple of guys who said Don the Beachcomber was selling a lot of food and booze in Los Angeles. I looked over his place and decided I could build a better mousetrap."

Bergeron changed name to Trader Vic's, a nickname given to him by his first wife Esther, referring to his habit of trading meals and drinks for services and supplies. As for his food, Vic said, "I had never been out of the country, but I ate in Chinese restaurants every night."

As Bergeron's place took on even more tropical flair, it attracted sophisticated San Franciscans who were willing to pop over the Oakland Bridge including city literati Lucius Beebe and Herb Caen. It was Caen who put Trader Vic's on the map, commenting in 1936 that the "best restaurant in San Francisco is in Oakland."

Of course, in a trend-driven state such as California, one would naturally assume the tiki-bar concept went the same direction as Sixties go-go clubs. Instead, the Second World War added to tiki's appeal, especially when veterans returned home from Guam, Samoa, Hawaii, Tahiti, and New

TRADER VIC'S HOLLOW LEG

Son of a French Canadian waiter who worked at the Fairmont Hotel in San Francisco, Victor Bergeron was diagnosed with bone tuberculosis from tainted milk, and his left leg was amputated at age 6. He would later dare unsuspecting customers to stab him in the leg with an ice pick. Once, when he noticed legendary San Francisco journalist Herb Caen watching him adjust his leg he commented, "Let me tell you something kid. Don't get one of these things unless you really need it."

Guinea. Beach and Bergeron became friendly competitors as they opened branches throughout the United States, Europe, and Asia well into the 1960s.

The two tiki titans did tangle on one point. Both men claimed to have invented the Mai Tai. Bergeron said he created it in 1944 for some visiting Tahitian friends. His goal was to create a rum equivalent to the Manhattan, Martini, and Margarita. Upon tasting the simple concoction of Jamaican and Martinique rums, orgeat syrup, curaçao, and lime juice garnished with a mint sprig, one of the guests cried out: "*Maita'i roa ae!*" [Out of this world!].

Donn Beach claimed he invented it in 1933. Truth is, Beach's recipe was completely different from Bergeron's. His included fresh lime and grapefruit juices with the rums plus Angostura, Pernod, Falernum, and no orgeat. So like the Derby, Piña Colada, and a handful of other cocktails that share a name, the two originators of the two Mai Tais deserve equal credit for their completely different inventions.

HURRICANE

4 parts vodka
1 part grenadine syrup
4 parts London dry gin
4 parts light rum
2 parts 151 rum
4 parts amaretto
4 parts triple sec
grapefruit juice
pineapple juice

In the order listed, pour all but the juices into a hurricane glass three-quarters filled with ice. Fill with equal parts of grapefruit and pineapple juice, and serve.

RUM WAS THE MAIN INGREDIENT in another wartime concoction, the Hurricane. When America went to war, whiskey was hard to come by since most grain went to the war effort. Distributors in New Orleans and elsewhere made bars place 50-case orders of rum just to get one case of whiskey.

Pat O'Brien's in New Orleans' French Quarter was no exception. Faced with a load of rum, in 1942, his bartenders were asked to come up with a recipe that would quickly use up the supply. Following the sweet, fruity drink standard of the day, they came up with a gigantic dark rum, passion fruit syrup concoction served in a hurricane-lamp shaped glass.

Despite lowered consumer expectations in the United States, by the 1930s, the cocktail had quite noticeably become a part of civilized and even uncivilized life—by western standards—throughout the world.

In 1931, American journalist Charles H Baker Jr took an odyssey, searching for the finest food and drink in such obscure corners as Cairo, Mindinao, Calcutta, Mexico City, Buenos Aires, Borneo, Jaipur, and Yokohama. Everywhere he went, everywhere he looked there was a bar, a bartender, and some unique, carefully prepared variation on the words "cocktail" and "mixed drink."

Even in the wilds of Siberia, Baker discovered a vodka concoction whose descendant became a resounding 1970s hit: The Vladivostok Virgin.

While in Buenos Aires, wandering journalist met "two young gentlemen from the Argentine . . .and who own polo ponies, ranches, and things." He tried the gentlemen's Mi Amante during a local heat wave "with results entirely at odds with the first reaction to its written formula."

Eight years later, when he published his notes in his 1939 book *The Gentlemen's Companion: Being an Exotic Drinking Book or, Around the World with Jigger, Beaker, and Flask*, he documented how deeply the cocktail had become engrained in the world's minds and hearts. Even cocktails with familiar names had personal twists that made the drink the particular bartender's own. The global industry had reached a point in which customised classic were the norm,

THE VLADIVOSTOK VIRGIN

3 parts vodka
3 parts London dry gin
2 parts unsweetened grapefruit juice
dash of Angostura bitters
Shake with big ice and serve in a large saucer champagne glass with a paper-thin slice of cucumber floating on top.

MI AMANTE

60 ml London dry gin
240 ml coffee ice cream
Put into a chilled shaker and shake well, or better still, in The Blender. Pour into larger saucer type champagne glasses.

locally-sourced ingredients replaced hard-to-get originals, and proportions were adjusted to suit local tastes. The true creativity of cuisine had reached its zenith, albeit hidden from public scrutiny because celebrity names weren't attached to their consumption or creation.

In this same volume, Baker also brought to light a technological advancement that changed the face of bartending for the next 40 years—The Blender.

The Philadelphian's Drinks

UNBRIDLED, UNABASHED promotion is not always an enviable trait. But in the harsh light of life and business, no one is going to tirelessly promote an idea as well as the person who thought of it. Although celebrité is frequently a self-promotion vehicle, Fred Waring (1900-1984) and his friend Rudy Vallee (1901-1986) used their cache of fame to promote a household appliance, and changed the way drinks were made.

We told you earlier how the Ramos Gin Fizz required a row of strong bartenders to shake it to its signature creamy consistency. Before the Twentieth Century, frappéed drinks were merely shaken vigorously and poured over crushed ice, never achieving the smooth as snow consistency of modern frozen drinks.

Surrounded by the technological advances of the Industrial and Modern Ages, esteemed cocktail connoisseurs such as journalist Charles H Baker Jr believed progress could only make a cocktail better. "Of course most

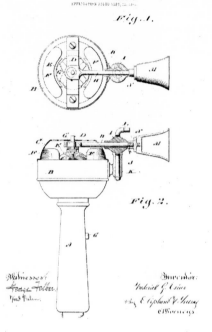

Fig. 1.

Fig. 2.

Frederick Osius's design for an electric hand-held vibrating massager inspired the invention of the blender.

cold drinks may be mixed, or shaken, by hand. Of course underground tunnels may also be dug by hand," he commented in *The Gentlemen's Companion*. "But modern machinery saves hours of wasted time and effort."

Enter Fred Waring.

He was best known in his lifetime as "the man who taught America to sing." A big-band band leader, Mr Waring toured the United States with his orchestra, the Pennsylvanians. After more than 40 years and scores of hit records, he was travelling up to 40,000 miles a year, mostly by bus to perform across the country.

But it was not Mr Waring's music that prompted Charles H Baker Jr to show his gratitude to him:

> *"For cooling Daiquiris, gin fizzes, making grenadine juice from pomegranates, for a dozen and one unexpected uses, we find this deft gadget indispensable. If this slight paean of appreciation and gratitude to Mr Waring for his aid to the mixing profession should make even one person beat a trail toward him seeking his mousetrap, that result is amply deserved—just as correctly as the Frenchman who thought up the drip coffee biggin, the chap who fabricated the first double boiler, the first deep fat kettle for the preparation of food."*

Opposite:
Poplawski's electric mixer was originally intended to blend Horlicks Malted Milk at soda fountains.

However, Mr Waring did not invent the blender. That credit goes to Stephen Poplawski of Racine, Wisconsin, a town that is also the birthplace of the hair dryer, electric

Jan. 15 , 1924.

S. J. POPLAWSKI

BEVERAGE MIXER

Filed Feb. 18 , 1922

1,480,914

2 Sheets—Sheet 1

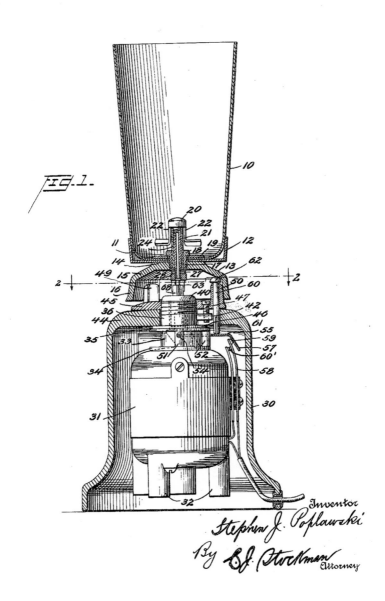

FIG.1.

Inventor
Stephen J. Poplawski

By C. J. Stockman
Attorney

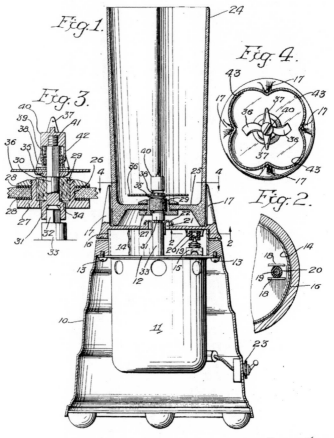

Fig. 1.

Fig. 4.

Fig. 3.

Fig. 2.

Inventor:
Frederick J. Osius
by his Attorneys
Hanson & Hanson

hair clippers, the lawn mower, floor polish, and the vacuum cleaner. Yet Poplawski's 1922 invention, the Beverage Mixer might never have been born if not for the work of two engineers, Chester Beach and Frederick Osius, and a marketing expert, Louis Hamilton, who founded the Hamilton Beach Company in 1910 with an electric hand-held vibrating massager (Patent #847,360).

Poplawski saw an opportunity in Beach and Osius' small electric motor and began building electric mixers for soda fountains to mix Horlicks Malted Milk (yet another recent Racine invention—one that an appreciative explorer, Admiral Byrd named the Horlicks Antarctic mountain range after). Poplawski received Patent #1,480,914 on 15 January 1924. However, his invention was far from perfect. It frequently broke down, and it desperately needed a good marketing person behind it.

A few details are lost in history at this point. But by 1938, Frederick Osius purchased Poplawski's patent and registered an improved version: Patent #2,109,501. (Poplawski had second thoughts later on, prompting him to design yet another blender and patent it in 1942.) Aware that Fred Waring was passionate about gadgets in addition to being wealthy and famous, Osius approached Mr Waring backstage at the Vanderbilt Hotel in New York.

Unaware that Waring suffered from a stomach ulcer, Osius was surprised by Waring's keen interest. Mr Waring immediately saw the device's potential as a must-have for every kitchen, especially his own. He put $25,000 USD into additional research. A teetotaller, he did not think of its practicality behind the bar. Instead, after he and Osius worked out a seal around the blades that would stop them

FROZEN STRAWBERRY DAIQUIRI

45 ml light rum
30 ml fresh lemon juice
1 teaspoon sugar
6 large strawberries (fresh or frozen)
240 ml cracked ice

Blend all ingredients and pour into a stemmed cocktail glass. Garnish with a fresh strawberry.

Opposite:
Combining Poplawski's electric mixer with his own knowledge of small electric motors, Frederick Osius's finished electric mixer design created a worldwide trend for blended frozen drinks.

from leaking, he is reputed to have made endless purées of sauerkraut, cucumbers, and other vegetables for himself and others. He did this so often that members of the orchestra considered mutiny at one point. (It is interesting to note that Waring had studied Architectural Engineering at Pennsylvania State University before he entered the music profession.)

Then, one fateful evening, Mr Waring received a backstage visit from a good friend, the crooner Rudy Vallee. He offered to make Rudy his favourite drink, a Frozen Strawberry Daiquirí, which took nearly as long to make conventionally as the Ramos Gin Fizz. Vallee apologized that he didn't have that much time. Waring tossed the ingredients into the blender and made him a drink in 30 seconds. This was the birth of the blended version of the drink.

Vallee was so impressed he asked to be Waring's sales representative. He took a few blenders with him as he performed across the United States. At each bar he visited, he asked for a Frozen Strawberry Daiquirí. A blender demonstration inevitably ensued. And another blender was sold. Vallee sold thousands of blenders this way.

The most notable bar to adopt the blender in those early days was El Floridita, where the signature drink—the Daiquirí Floridita—required both a Flak Mark ice-crushing machine and a Waring blender to be executed to frosty perfection.

But it was not until after the Second World War that blender sales sky rocketed. It was the dawn of the Jet Age. People embraced new technological advances. Behind the bar, frozen orange juice concentrate allowed bartenders in northern climates to serve Screwdrivers. In Puerto Rico, the modern Piña Colada was born thanks to tinned Coco Lopez and the Waring blender.

So why does Fred Waring receive such credit for the blender when someone else invented it, someone else improved it, and someone else discovered the target market and tirelessly promoted it? He was the financial backer. He changed the name of the company from Miracle Mixer Corporation to the Waring Corporation. He believed in the blender. And he was said to be a very charming person.

However, fame of this sort is fleeting. Charles H Baker may not have been aware that the following would apply not just within the early pages of his book, but also in the world at large: "Future reference to this mechanical unit will refer to it plainly as The Blender."

VESPER
6 parts London dry gin
2 part vodka
1 part Lillet Blanc
Shake vigorously until frosty cold.
Strain into a champagne goblet.
Garnish with a large thin slice of lemon peel.

V Of My Own Invention

ODKA HAD TWO CHAMPION DRINKS in the years immediately following the Second World War: the Bloody Mary and the Moscow Mule. But neither drink had the genetic élan of the Manhattan, the Martini, the Daiquirí, or the Rob Roy. That is, until a British novelist published a concoction that demonstrated the spirit's versatility as a flavour enhancer.

Creator of the James Bond spy novels, Ian Fleming (1908-1964) was a well-heeled, black sheep of an aristocratic family. After failing his foreign service exams he tried to follow in his illustrious brother Peter's footsteps writing for Reuters News Service. No fortune to be made there. So he dabbled in banking before landing a post with naval intelligence just as Britain declared war on Germany. The seeds of his inspiration were sown during those war-torn years.

Fellow Etonian and part-owner of the North American Newspaper Alliance, Ivar Bryce invited Fleming to Jamaica to attend a naval conference on Nazi U boat warfare in the Caribbean and to visit his own estate. The serenity of the tropical landscape was a stark contrast to the war-ravaged urban rubble of London: Lush fruits and bountiful fish instead of ration books and food shortages. Spirits that flowed like water. It was too much for an uncompromising, hard drinking, heavy smoking aristocrat to resist. He built Goldeneye, an unpretentious winter escape from London life and his work as a reporter for Kemsley Newspapers Limited. There, from January through March, he basked in the island's beauty when he wasn't womanising or gambling.

All of that changed when Fleming found himself waiting at Goldeneye for his pregnant, long-time mistress Lady Anne Rothemere to finalise her divorce. On 17 February 1952, he sat at his desk and began first draft of his novel *Casino Royale*, which introduced the super-spy character James Bond.

Published in 1953, Fleming described the contents and execution of his perfect "violet hour" libation:

> *"A dry martini," he said. "One. In a deep champagne goblet."*
>
> *"Oui, monsieur."*
>
> *"Just a moment. Three measures of Gordon's, one of vodka, half a measure of Kina Lillet. Shake it very well until it's ice-cold, then add a large thin slice of lemon-peel. Got it?"*

Through the guise of James Bond, Fleming justified this recipe by adding: "I never have more than one drink before dinner. But I do like that one to be large and very strong and very cold and very well-made. I hate small portions of anything, particularly when they taste bad. This drink's my own invention. I'm going to patent it when I can think of a good name."

Though drink historians generally credit the Vesper to Gilberto Preti at London's Duke's Hotel (truly, one of the world's greatest bartenders and one of the greatest Martini bars), Preti would have been around fifteen years old when the drink was invented. So who really invented the Vesper?

In his 1975 memoirs *You Only Live Once,* Bryce explained how his close friend conjured up the name of the drink and *Casino Royale*'s heroine. While in Jamaica, Fleming came upon the house of an elderly couple and was invited in for evening drinks. Their butler offered him a frozen rum concoction, commenting that "vespers are served." Vespers or evensong is the sixth of the seven canonical hours of the divine office that fall at sunset, the "violet hour".

The drink itself? Bryce and Fleming created the gin-and-vodka cocktail and named it. Fleming inscribed Bryce's presentation copy of *Casino Royale*: "To Ivar, who mixed the first Vesper, and said the good word."

It was the first and only time the drink occurred in the fourteen-novel Bond pantheon. According to the statistics calculated by The Minister of Martinis on the Atomic Martinis web site, Bond ordered 19 vodka and 16 gin Martinis—not quite as impressive as the 37 orders for straight bourbon or the 30 calls for Champagne. Maybe it was the

JAMES BOND'S TOP TEN DRINKS

More obsessive than we are, The Minsiter of Martinis at www.atomicmartinis.com painstakingly researched both the James Bond novels and films to determine what the superspy drank. here's what he found:

In Ian Fleming's novels, James Bond's Top Ten favourite drinks were:
1. Bourbon
2. Sake
3. Champagne
4. Scotch and soda
5. Vodka Martini
6. Straight Scotch
7. Gin Martini
8. Beer
9. Long drink (Cognac and soda)
10. Red wine

In the films, his call list only slightly differs:
1. Champagne
2. Vodka Martini
3. Red wine
4. Straight vodka
5. Scotch whisky
6. Bourbon
7. Brandy
8. Vesper
9. Rum
10. Sake

visual allure of the sleek Silver Bullet in its stemmed cocktail glass that grab the public's attention.

Fleming's works did not receive international notoriety until US President John F Kennedy listed *From Russia with Love* as one of his favourite books. That was quickly followed by movie deals for *Dr No* (1962), *From Russia with Love* (1963), and the blockbuster *Goldfinger* (1964). In the first film, the villainous doctor serves Bond a Vodka Martini shaken not stirred. Not quite a Vesper, the Vodka Martini became the iconic libation for every male—young, old, and in between—who dreamt of living the life of an international super spy, a playboy.

Playboy Magazine was founded by Hugh Hefner in the same year that *Casino Royale* was published, featuring Marilyn Monroe as the cover girl and centrefold. The publication and its chain of nightclubs, espoused a lifestyle of sophisticated libertarianism. The quintessential playboy was well-read and well-versed in food, fashion, film, fine wines, fine spirits, fast cars, and feminine pulchritude. He was James Bond's American counterpart. Throughout the 1960s, he was the ideal man, icy-cold Vodka Martini in hand, that every woman wanted and every man wanted to be.

Underneath the Coconut Tree

JAMES BOND never ordered one of the following drinks in Fleming's novels. It is hard to picture Ernest Hemingway setting a frosty one down next to his typewriter. Yet the Piña Colada is the drink of choice for countless cruise ship passengers, sunburnt tourists sporting loud Hawaiian shirts, infrequent imbibers, and, in truth, the one of the most broadly influential cocktails ever created.

Of course, like many great flavour combinations, before the drink's history began, the Piña Colada had an extensive pre-history. Literally translated, Piña Colada means "strained pineapple". Minus the coconut, the combination of rum and pineapple dates back centuries.

In his 1824 *An Essay on the Inventions and Customs of both Ancients and Moderns in the Use of Inebriating Liquors*, Samuel Morewood wrote, "Time adds much to the mildness and value of rum, which the planters, it is said, often improve by the addition of pineapple juice."

By this time, rum infused with pineapple was also very popular in parts of Europe, where fresh pineapple was far too costly for all but the wealthy. In Charles Dickens' 1838 book *The Posthumous Papers of the Pickwick Club*: "Mr Stiggins was easily prevailed on to take another glass of the hot pineapple rum and water, and a second, and a third, and then to refresh himself with a slight supper previous to beginning again."

The recipe was simple, as given in Elizabeth Hammond's circa 1817 book *Modern Domestic Cookery, and Useful Receipt Book*:

> *An excellent flavour may be given to it by putting into the cask some pineapple rinds. The longer rum is kept, the more valuable it becomes. If your rum wants a head, whisk some clarified honey with a little of the liquor, and pour the whole into the cask. Three pounds of honey is sufficient for 60 gallons.*

The first record of Europeans encountering a pineapple points to the island of Guadeloupe in November 1493. Sailors on Columbus' second voyage named the curious fruit *piña* as it resembled a giant pine cone. The native Taínos were already drinking pineapple juice—which they called *yayamaby*—for refreshment and as a digestive aid, especially after consuming meat. Taíno women were known to use it as an exfoliant and skin whitener. It was Christopher Columbus who brought the first pineapples to Spain. And this exotic fruit enchanted Europe.

It was not long before the pineapple became a symbol of wealth and hospitality throughout Europe and the colonies. Ship captains would mark a triumphant return from the tropics by placing a pineapple at their front gate: a gesture adopted from Caribbean tribes. Plus, the pineapple became the crowning glory on many upper-class European tables.

In the Caribbean, *jugo de piña* became *piña fria* during the early 1800s, after Cuban officials issued a plea for ice that was answered with shipments both from Spain and New England. By the turn of the twentieth century, advances in transportation meant flocks of tourists could join the Caribbean planters in the enjoyment of frosty rum-and-pineapple libations.

No doubt people in cold climates were by now taking advantage of pineapple shipments from Jim Dole's newly founded Hawaiian Pineapple Company which strove to put the fruit in every American grocery store.

In the American territory of Puerto Rico, the ingredients even played a pivotal role in local politics when, in 1917, Prohibition was voted on by local referendum. The ballots—designed to be easily understood by a rural populace with a low literacy rate—were printed with a bottle of rum on one side and a pineapple on the other. Surprisingly, the pineapple was the overwhelming favourite, and Puerto Rico became officially "dry" until 1933.

Cuba never succumbed to this "Noble Experiment". A *National Geographic* writer in 1933 reminisced: "I have sat at a side walk café table, surrounded by well-dressed, well-fed people, sipping a Piña Colada, and listening to an orchestra . . ." But what was he sipping at the time?

Harry La Tourette Foster, in his 1928 travel book *The Caribbean Cruise*, wrote: "For the teetotaller, there are plenty of non-alcoholic drinks obtainable in most places. In Havana, for instance, a favourite iced drink is *jugo de piña* or Piña Colada . . ."

A *Hartford Courant* article published on 20 August 1922, reflects this ambiguity: "Down in Havana, Cuba, there is a soft drink that is very caressing to the oesophagus, known in Spanish as either *piña fria colada* or *piña fria sin colada*, which might be copied in the United States where soft drinks are now legion."

A 16 April 1950 article in *The New York Times* titled "At The Bar" boldly stated that: "Drinks in the West Indies range from Martinique's famous rum punch to Cuba's *piña colada* (rum, pineapple and coconut milk)." Yet, the official 1948 book of Cuba's bartending guild, *El Arte del Cantinero*, contained only a non-alcoholic recipe for chilled and sweetened pineapple juice under the tag "Piña Colada". It is likely that drink had been served for more than a century in at least one legendary Havana location. A bodega called Piña de Plata [The Silver Pineapple] opened, in 1820, in Havana. It is said they sold fresh juices, and their beverage sales were

PUERTO RICAN PIÑA COLADA

1 part white rum
1 part sweetened coconut cream
3 parts fresh pineapple juice

Combine ingredients in an ice-filled blender. Blend. Pour into a goblet or hurricane glass. Garnish with a pineapple slice.

so successful that, in 1867, they became a bar, changing the name to La Florida, later to become El Floridita.

Far more important than the first collision amongst rum, pineapple, and coconut in a blender is the drink's transition from ignominy to ubiquitous cabana libation. Who standardised the Piña Colada into the drink we all know today? The mass media and the Commonwealth of Puerto Rico claim that the modern Piña Colada was introduced in San Juan, on 15 August 1954, at the Caribe Hilton's Beachcomber Bar.

Opened in 1949, with a prime beach front location and modern amenities it drew an affluent, international clientele: John Wayne, Elizabeth Taylor, Jose Ferrar, Gloria Swanson and a host of others. Joan Crawford declared the Caribe Hilton's Piña Colada was "better than slapping Bette Davis in the face." These were the celebrities who made the drink glamorous and, for a short time, far more sophisticated than any frozen drink has a right to be.

One claim frequently ignored by most cocktail authorities is that Coco Lopez launched the Piña Colada out of obscurity. This appears to be true. Certainly, the modern Piña Colada would not exist—much less become widely adopted—if not for pre-made cream of coconut.

A common cooking ingredient throughout the tropics, but very labour intensive to prepare, cream of coconut was first packaged as Coco Lopez, in 1954, by Ramon Lopez Irizarry, an agricultural professor from the University of Puerto Rico who automated this arduous task. Irizarry personally approached bartenders and chefs around San Juan, encouraging them to experiment with his new creation. The Coco Lopez company then continued to spotlight the Piña

Colada in its promotional literature for over 30 years, spreading the drink around the world. It finally found its way into the *Old Mr Boston Deluxe Official Bartenders Guide* sometime between 1970 and 1972.

The Further Drying of the Martini

DEMAND FOR VODKA MARTINIS soared from the Fifties through the Sixties, while the Martini (as opposed to the Dry Martini) became known as a Gin and It or Gin and French in Great Britain. A lot had happened to the Dry Martini between the two world wars. Who knows if it was a depressed economy, unavailability of ingredients, or bartenders streamlining their formulas that dropped the orange bitters from many cocktail recipe books. But the saddest evolution in the Martini's life was when the vermouth, French or Italian, dried up as vodka replaced gin in the glass.

Post-war mixologists (both the First and Second World Wars) did not have the luxury of a proper bar education like their predecessors. Bartending knowledge was always transferred from master to apprentice. Many masters were lost in the wars and their knowledge died with them. The wisdom of using fresh vermouth seemed to disappear in the post-war years.

It is important to understand that vermouth is an aromatised wine, and consequently it is subject to the same pitfalls as wine if left open in a warm room for days, weeks, and months. Vermouth sours to a scary point. Why ruin the perfect Silver Bullet with more than a whisper of sour vermouth?

The quality of some mass-market gin production had deteriorated since the 1930s because of economic and political abominations. Couple that with the lack of trained personnel (it seems as if bartenders who knew how to handle vermouth had all but disappeared during the Second World War) and you have a lousy drink.

Not that vermouth was easy to get at the time. The French weren't about to give up their stores of aromatised wine to the Germans during the occupation. Hence, Ernest Hemingway documented the 15:1 super-dry Montgomery is his 1950 *Across the River and Into the Trees*:

> *"Two very dry Martinis," [Colonel Cantwell] said.*
> *"Montgomerys. Fifteen to one."*
> *The waiter [at Harry's bar in Venice] who had been in the desert, smiled and was gone . . .*

Hemingway named the variation after Second World War Field Marshal Bernard Law Montgomery, leader of the British Eighth Army, who campaigned in North Africa. The tale was that "Monty" would only attack Nazi General Ernst Rommel's forces if he outnumbered his formidable foe by a 15:1 ratio.

Matters got worse at the close of the Korean War and the dawn of the Cold War. In a 30 January 1952 *Los Angeles Times* article Timothy G Turner lamented that the 3:1 Gin Martini was quickly being replaced by the 10:1 formula. What horrified the writer was that vodka was replacing gin, commenting that:

Joe Stalin must be laughing his head off. They've got
us American drinking vodka. And what is worse the
vodka is not drunk straight as those nefarious Musco-
vites drink it, with a nibble of caviar, but it is used in
place of gin to make Martini cocktails.

Characterless vodka mixed 15:1 with past-its-sell-
by-date vermouth apparently struck a chord in California.
It did on the east coast, too. Men in grey-flannel suits subscribed to three-Martini lunches, swigging down rudimen-
tary classics even though they were not the same drinks that
their fathers had consumed in decades gone by.

SCREWDRIVER
45 ml vodka
orange juice
Build in a highball or collins glass
over ice.

Another technological wonder further challenged
the industry after it was created in a Florida laboratory (and
now accounts for 80 percent of Florida's orange crop): frozen
concentrated orange juice.

Never So Dreadful

A COCKTAIL GENERATION GAP was evident. In a
1952 *Los Angeles Times* article, Art Ryon commented: "While concurring with Tim Turner's lament on
these pages about the recent practice of substituting vodka
for gin in Martinis, we regret that he didn't go further. Do
you realize, Tim, that the latest craze in the amateur set is
vodka and orange juice?"

What was the provenance of this phenomenon?
A 1959 article in *The Washington Post* offered up the story
that:

It was in Ankara [Turkey] during World War II that
a group of American fliers invented a drink called the
'Screwdriver'—orange juice and vodka—because they

TEQUILA SUNRISE NO 1

45 ml tequila
1 tsp grenadine syrup
1/3 tsp crème de cassis
juice of half a lime
Build tequila and lime juice in a highball glass filled with ice. Pour grenadine and cassis so they drop to the bottom of the glass. Do not float and do not stir. Top with sparkling water and garnish with a lime slice.

TEQUILA

1 part fresh lime or lemon juice
1 tsp grenadine
2 parts tequila
Shake.

TEQUILA SUNRISE NO 2

3 parts tequila
1 part or more grenadine
orange juice
Build in a tall glass filled with ice. Add tequila and orange juice. Pour grenadine to the bottom of the glass. Do not stir.

JALISCO

1 part orange juice
1/4 tsp grenadine syrup
2 parts tequila
Shake.

couldn't stand Turkish vodka. This was a slur on Ankara's estimable cuisine which at its worst is never so dreadful as the Screwdriver.

It all started when powdered citrus juice was developed for the military during the Second World War. The Florida Citrus Commission turned its attention, around 1943, to concentrating orange juice via vacuum evaporation. To this concentrate, lime juice was added to retain the flavour and appearance. Then the mixture was frozen. Introduced to the public, in 1946, frozen orange juice concentrate put frozen foods on the proverbial map. The restaurant industry welcomed a labour-free, non-seasonal option to fresh-squeezed juice. The modern housewife saw it as an economical and labour saving solution to squeezing oranges.

A seemingly obvious progression occurred when a new, hip spirit trend met this new, hip convenience drink.

Another drink made a radical transformation in the hands of frozen orange juice concentrate: the Tequila Sunrise. First exported to the United States, in 1873 by Don Cenobio Sauza, tequila took its time entering the cocktail repertoire.

South of the Border

TEQUILA MADE prolific early appearances as a feature ingredient in a 1937 British cocktail book, *The Café Royal Cocktail Book*, edited by William J Tarling, not in an American one. Fifteen recipes using the agave spirit were documented: Bullfighter, Jalisco, Matador, Metexa, Mexican Eagle, Mexico, Picador, Pinequila, Rio Grande,

Senorita, Sombrero, Tequardo, Tequila, Tia Juano, and Toreador along with a glossary note that mentioned tequila "is used with success in cocktails." It was the truth. Success came quickly to tequila, not so much in London as it did way out west in southern California and Arizona.

Three formulas are of particular note: Jalisco, Picador, and Tequila. Why? Because each hearkens to two drinks that were popularised during the 1940s in the US. An unusual drink was mentioned an untitled story that appeared in a September 1940 edition of *The Los Angeles Times* that read:

> *"He ordered a Tequila Sunrise and she said she'd*
> *have the same because she'd never tried one."*

Many historians point to the Arizona Biltmore Hotel in Phoenix as the originator of the Tequila Sunrise. The original 1930s recipe does not remotely resemble what 1960s barmen conjured up. This libation bears a close resemblance to the *Café Royal Cocktail Book*'s Tequila cocktail:

Grenadine syrup was one of those ingredients that experienced a sad reinvention during the years between the world wars. Originally produced from pomegranate seeds, grenadine was transformed into a candy-coloured sugar syrup by modern technology. It had more in common with the liquid found in a jar of commercially produced, vibrant red cocktail cherries than it did with its flavourful ancestor. But then, the same was true for post-war cocktail cherries and their relationship to preserved Marasca (or maraschino) cherries, a particular variety of Morello cherry with limited availability outside of Italy.

The desire to use ready-made, pre-mixed juices in the Cold War era altered the blushing Tequila Sunrise. Fro-

MARGARITA

2 parts tequila
1 part Cointreau or triple sec
1 part fresh lime juice
Rim a cocktail glass with a lime slice and coarse salt. Shake ingredients over ice, then carefully pour into the glass. Garnish with a fresh lime slice.

PICADOR

1 part fresh lime or lemon juice
1 part Cointreau
2 parts tequila
Shake, strain, and serve.

zen orange juice concentrate overtook hand-squeezed, fresh lime juice. Crème de cassis was dropped in favour of speed and economics. The result was a drink that more closely resembled the *Café Royal Cocktail Book*'s Jalisco.

Like the other classic "M" cocktails, there are numerous tales and debates over the Margarita's origins. The list is impressive:

1934:

Willie: at the Los Dos Republicos in Matamoros created it for Marguerite Hemery

1936:

Danny Negrete at the Garci Crispo Hotel made it as a wedding present for his sister-in-law Margarita.

1938:

Danny Herrera at the Riviera del Pacifico Hotel and Casino in Ensenada, Mexico crafted it for actress Majorie King.

Circa early 1940s:

Enrique Bstate Gutierrez of Tijuana, Mexico divined it as a homage to actress Rita Hayworth, whose birth name was Margarita Cansino.

1942:

Francisco "Pancho" Morales at Tommy's Place in Juarez, Mexico improvised the drink for a woman who asked for a Magnolia.

1948: Margaret Sames, an Alcapulco bar owner.

Once again, the drink closely resembles the *Café Royal*'s Picador.

It makes no difference who originated the trend. And what a trend it was. In the hands of bartenders who catered to the Hollywood elite, it was no wonder tequila drinks made neck-and-neck headway with vodka in the public eye.

The Duke

HOLLYWOOD was the birthplace of a few more drinks that formed the standard cocktail menu during the last half of the twentieth century. Donato "Duke" Antone, owner of Duke's Blackwatch Bar on Sunset Boulevard, claimed to be the inventor of a number of familiar libations. The two with the great staying power were the Harvey Wallbanger and the White Russian. Legend has it that Antone crafted the Harvey Wallbanger for a Manhattan Beach surfer who was a regular patron. Vodka and frozen orange juice concentrate had another champion!

Antone's variation the Freddy Fudpucker catered to the growing number of tequila aficionados looking for an alternative to the "standard" Tequila Sunrise.

There was another flavour that 1950s imbibers embraced: coffee. You could it started with the Irish Coffee. The story goes that Joe Sheridan, chef at Foynes Air Terminal in County Clare, Ireland, made this welcome drink for weary American passengers as they debarked transatlantic flights on board the Pan Am Clipper flying boat.

The tale continues that *San Francisco Chronicle* travel writer Stanton Delaplane brought the concoction home with him and convinced the Buena Vista Café to serve it, in 1952, as winter set in over the Bay Area.

HARVEY WALLBANGER

3 parts vodka
1 part Galliano
6 parts orange juice
Build vodka and juice in a highball glass filled with ice. Float the Galliano on top. Garnish with an orange slice.

IRISH COFFEE

1 part Irish whiskey
1 part strong black coffee
2 tsp granulated sugar
2 tbs whipped cream

Heat a glass mug. Add the whiskey, sugar, and hot coffee. Stir and float the cream on top. Do not stir.

BLACK RUSSIAN

1 part vodka
1 part Kahlúa
Build in a rocks glass filled with ice. Serve with a pair of sip sticks for stirring.

WHITE RUSSIAN

5 parts vodka
2 parts Kahlúa
3 parts fresh cream
Build in a rocks glass filled with ice. Do not stir. Serve with a pair of sip sticks for stirring.

QUICK BARTENDER, GIMME FOUR DOZEN IRISH COFFEES

To meet the inevitable crush when a plane arrived, the bartenders at Foynes Air Terminal would set up the glass mugs with Irish whiskey and simple syrup. They would brew the coffee and keep the cream at hand so they could quickly assemble dozens of fresh hot drinks in a matter of minutes.

Two years earlier, in Brussels, the American Ambassador to Luxembourg Perle Mesta was treated to a cold coffee concoction created by Hotel Metropole barman Gustav Tops. Called the Black Russian, the drink featured a dark coffee liqueur that was launched, in 1936, by Pedro Domecq: Kahlúa.

What do these drinks have to do with the "Duke"? Everything. Antone placed a White Russian on his drinks menu that blended the spirit of the Black Russian with the creaminess of Irish Coffee.

T HE ERA OF FAST, FROZEN, instant meals, instant puddings, instant breakfast, and instant drinks shifted the public palate for libations to anything that was fast and/or sweet. Building and blending overtook shaking and stirring behind mainstream bars. Fast turn-around had Jet Age appeal. A new generation of bartenders joined the ranks simply to pay their rent whilst waiting for that big break in acting or writing.

There were lights within the tunnel. Hotel bars and some fine-dining establishments continued to hire and train bar staff who practised the old mantra of service and quality. Adherents were also found in the occasional pub or neighbourhood bar.

Classic cocktails, such as they were, still played well amongst war veterans and conservatives: they were the backbone of solidity and reliability with their suburban homes and family values. They drank after-work cocktails in respectable establishments. They made cocktails at home, even Daiquirís with honey! They went to cocktail parties that were far tamer than those thrown by their sophisticated parents. But their children were not about to subscribe to this whitewashed routine.

Taking a cue from the 1920s Lost Generation, the disillusioned 1950s Beat Generation pushed the envelope of poetic, literary, musical, and artistic boundaries. Inspired by Beat legends such as William S Burroughs, Allen Ginsberg, Jack Kerouac, Lawrence Ferlinghetti, and Gregory Corso, rebellious college kids eschewed anything that was associated with the "establishment". That included Manhattans, Martinis, Mai Tais, and Mojitos.

Economics played its hand, partnered with generation rebellion. The people who could afford to go to hotel bars and fine restaurants lived on another planet from the people who disagreed with post-war isolationist policies whether they were political, religious, educational, financial, or legal. Another factor also divided social factions: recessions.

The twentieth century was fraught with post-war recoveries, depressions, and recessions. The late 1950s and early 1960s economic downturns tore at the deepening generation rift just as much as parent-child disagreement over nuclear power and foreign affairs. The widening gaps ripped apart when a new invention that pandered to soft-drink swigging youth changed the face of mainstream bars.

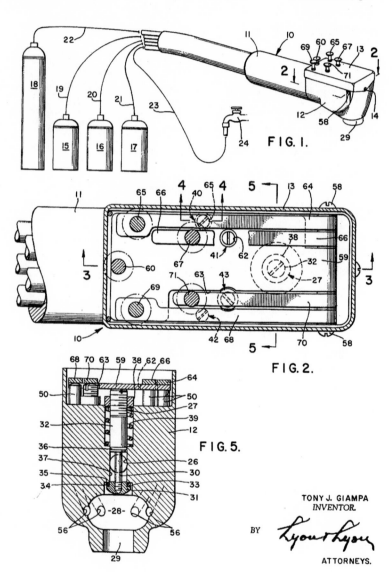

FIG. I.

FIG. 2.

FIG. 5.

TONY J. GIAMPA
INVENTOR.

BY

ATTORNEYS.

The Fast Lane & a Quick Buck

O N 3 OCTOBER 1961, Tony J Giampa of Los Angeles, filed a patent application for a beverage dispenser that was capable of mixing and housing more than one type of liquid. Unlike the counter-mounted models found in soda fountains, Giampa's device left the bar top free of obstructions. As the demand for fast and cheap drinks accelerated, so did interest in this invention. Giampa was issued US Patent 3,168, 967 on 3 February 1965. The soda gun replaced the shaker as mainstream patrons yelled out calls for Jack and Coke, Rum and Coke, Cape Cod, Madras, Screwdriver, Vodka Tonic, Gin & Tonic. Anything that could be purchased in bulk syrup or juice concentrate and blended in the gun with soda or tap water and mixed with spirits was acceptable. Young club-goers thought: "Why spend hardearned cash on a "fancy drink" when you could get a fast, cheap drink?"

The late 1960s recession opened a new fissure in the social fabric. This time it was between the white-collar and the working classes. The "fat cats" in the brokerage houses, ad agencies, and banks could afford sophistication. But what was left for the working stiff? The 1973 oil crisis bored further holes in concept idea of affordable leisure.

The 1977 film *Saturday Night Fever* worked its superficial magic on disenfranchised youth, who dreamt of fame, fortune, glitz, glitter, sex, music, and sophistication, even if it was only lived out on the weekends at the local

Opposite:
Able to dispense anything cold and wet that mixes with spirits, the soda gun changed the face of bartending by offering fast, cheap drinks instead of "fancy" ones.

disco. Aside from a lack of expendable income, were they no different from the 1920s Bright Young Things whose motto was "live for today"? They were not alone. Punks followed the darker route paved by the 1920s Lost Generation and the 1950s Beat Generation. The one thing these social groups had in common was alcohol: just as long as it wasn't the stuff their dismayed parents drank.

Civilisation, on a global level, morphed into a complex zygote. Each "cell" had its own trappings: fashion, music, colloquialisms, food, and drink were all dictated by one's choice of lifestyle. When the early 1980s ushered in a perceived reprise from economic woes (backed by easy, lucrative credit), the zygote was poised for inquisitiveness as to what the true "better things in life" were which led to better quality liquor and a cocktail revival that continues to this day.

Epilogue

HERE'S WHERE WE END our story—at least for a few months—whilst we catch our breath. After all, history is best assessed after the dust settles and a younger generation of researchers armed with global accessibility to information have time to collect, question, and analyse the facts surrounding the latest Cocktail Renaissance. We look forward to reading the tales of their spirituous journeys. Until then, join us in celebrating the cocktail Renaissance that is sweeping around the globe by seeking out and enjoying the newest and the latest (in moderation of course). Cheers!

Index

About the Authors

THE INSEPARABLE COCKTAIL COUPLE, Anistatia Miller and Jared Brown, are directors of Mixellany, Limited, publishers of *Mixologist: The Journal of the American Cocktail* and other books on spirits and drink history. They are also the authors of over 30 books including *Shaken Not Stirred: A Celebration of the Martini®* and *Spirituous Journey: A History of Drink, Book One*, which won the 2009 Gourmand World Cook Book award for Best Drink History in the UK.

Miller and Brown's writing has also appeared in *Mixology* (GER), *Imbibe* (UK), *Theme, Class, Diffords Guide, Wine Spectator, Cigar Aficionado*, and *Food Arts*. During their years as contributing editors for *Gotham, Hamptons, Aspen Peak*, and *LA Confidential*, they wrote a variety of cocktail, food, and travel columns.

Not content to simply write about the subject, Miller and Brown are both veteran bartenders, and have earned numerous awards for their work in distilleries in the US and Europe. Lately they were proud to be on the tasting panels for Beefeater 24 and No. 3.

Jared Brown is also the master distiller of Sipsmith Gin and Vodka, the first new distillery to be licenced in London in nearly 200 years.

Together they were co-founders of the Museum of the American Cocktail and directors of Exposition Universelle des Vins et Spiritueux, overseeing the restoration of one of the world's largest collections of wine and spirits.